RISK MANAGEMENT OF EXTREME EVENTS IN BANKING

A Case For A Dedicated Tail Risk Governance In The Banking Industry

Pascal vander Straeten

Value4Risk

Risk Management

Of Extreme Events

In Banking

Risk Management Of Extreme Events in Banking

A Case For A Dedicated Tail Risk Governance In The Banking Industry

Value4Risk

First published 2020

by Value4Risk LLC

ISBN: 978-1-7341841-2-9

ISBN-13: 978-1-7341841-2-9 (Value4Risk LLC)

Library of Congress Control Number: 2021900193

Value4Risk LLC, Dallas Fort Worth, Texas

To the love of my life, Barbara, who always gives me all the energy and support to help reach my goals.

Table of Contents

Other Publications By Pascal vander Straeten

Author

Tail Risk Management: Building A Resilient Financial Business In A Volatile World, 07/2017, 226pp.

Overture to Geofinance: Global Finance, Geopolitics, & Wielding of Power: Theory & Praxis, 04/ 2018, 354pp.

Principles of Supply Chain Risk Management and Banks: How Supply Chain Resilience in a Digital Age Helps Banks Navigate Through Extreme Events, 10/2019, 722pp.

Treatise on China's Clandestine Financial Warfare: China's Intelligence Community and the Communist Party As Key Players in Geofinance in the 21st Century, 08/ 2020, 591pp.

Prologue

"You cannot separate extreme risk taking from risk management. And extreme risk management isn't something passive."

Because of the world's quickly becoming a global village with interconnectedness in every field possible (and its increasing social and economic interdependency) coupled with a growing population and larger concentration of assets in high-risk areas, volatility as a consequence is bound to increase and hence also the likelihood of extreme risks.

This is an important issue for investors because greater integration among world markets implies stronger co-movements between markets, therefore nullify much of the gain out of diversification across borders, besides being vulnerable to the caprices of global capital. In essence, I am referring here to volatility spillovers or in other words the financial contagion link between market integration/ linkages and volatility.

Now, to go back to extreme risk (or aka tail risk), economic as well as behavioral analysis (i.e., behavioral economics studies the psychological perspectives of human decision making, risk assessment, and consumer behavior) helps determine how people will respond to this more dangerous world. But the traditional economic view suggests that human actions can be predicted as if people were always completely informed, perfectly responsive to economic fluctuations, and rational, in the sense of having stable, orderly preferences that always maximize their individual economic well-being. In fact, disasters seriously challenge this view. The recent global financial crisis in the Western world highlights three critical elements where behavioral scientists have found the rational predictions of many economists and financiers to be flawed (Michel-Kerjan and Slovic, 2010):

First, people don't think extreme risks will happen to them. This is partly because the human mind is not very good at understanding a low probability of occurrence. To illustrate this: what does it mean to you to live in a flood plain or an earthquake zone if you learn that there is a one-in-100 chance of experiencing a disaster next year? Or, what are the chances that the international (western) order as we have known it since the end of World War Two will eventually be metamorphosed? Or, what are the chances that the European Union will disappear? For many it is hard to translate this number into concrete action. As a result, people typically just ignore these dangers. This explains why so few countries have implemented risk-reduction measures that have proved to be cost--effective. Betting against the odds—or animal spirits—people continue to build in high-risk areas, and do not prepare. Then economic/ political/ natural disasters hit with catastrophic consequences.

Second, we fail to learn from others' misfortunes. After the strong emotion people typically feel during a crisis (driven in part by live media coverage), their attention fades. This is true in developing and developed countries alike. Not even seven years after the GFC, one of the most devastating financial crises in Western history, the new president elect in the US was thinking about chopping off some parts of the Dodd-Frank legislation. Those who have not suffered from the GFC personally view the possibility of a financial disaster hitting their markets again as so improbable it could simply be disregarded. But as we speak, financial institutions in the West are still overleveraged and off-balance sheet activities remain as important as ever.

Third, research shows that humans cannot grasp the full significance of disaster statistics. If you heard that the Federal Deposit Insurance Corporation (FDIC) closed 455 failed banks in the U.S. from 2008 to 2012, and later learned it was 465, would your brain appreciate the difference? Probably not. But the difference is huge; in contrast, in the five years prior to 2008, only 10 banks failed. Moreover, people are more likely to relate to an individual bank they used to work with than to a larger group of banks in crisis. Insensitivity to the prospect of large financial losses violates the traditional view of economic rationality, according to which we should care more about two firms suffering than one, and even more about thousands of casualties. Often we do not.

What lessons should decision makers draw from these observations? We know that human reason often fails when it is most needed. People have intuitive and analytic thinking skills that work beautifully most of the time to help them navigate life. But those skills often fail when the potential losses are catastrophic or their probability appears to be low enough that the risks can be ignored. Understanding such behavioral quirks is critically important to those in charge of developing long-term strategies to make their countries and firms more resilient. Overcoming these obstacles to rationality requires that the knowledge developed by decades of research on human behavior in the face of risk be translated more systematically into actionable decisions. This constitutes the very foundation of a new and more effective response to tail risk. It is essential mitigating all the financial disasters still to come.

Now, granted, time and again I hear that tail risk management is seen as something that is required by the regulators, perhaps by the board or top management, but is not seen as something that helps individual managers succeed. And, how many times do you hear that boards are not receiving the information they need to know whether the tail risks to the organization's strategies are managed appropriately. Or, that practitioners are failing to obtain the support and resources necessary for effective, mature tail risk management.

This is all due, in my opinion, to a misunderstanding of extreme risk and the controls necessary to manage tail risk at acceptable levels. The misunderstanding is due to the inappropriate focus on "tail risk" instead of "resiliency" or "sustainability". How do you get the attention of managers, executives, and board members — by talking about how to increase the likelihood of their and the organization's success, and the likelihood of greater levels of success.

You don't manage extreme risk for tail risk's sake. You manage extreme risk to achieve and optimize the resiliency of the company. And that is what risk and controls is all about. It is all about increasing the level of confidence in achieving or surpassing objectives to acceptable levels or better. Another obstacle for tail risk practitioners is the language they use. They use the babble of risk, audit, and controls instead of the language of the business. If you are trying to persuade a manager to embrace new ideas, do you talk to him in the terms he uses or in some strange language he doesn't understand?

Let's consider a situation where an executive is considering the investment program for a new product that the company plans to introduce in country XYZ in a few months. The goal of the investment program is to help drive sales and gain larger market share as well as prevent rival companies from passing the entry barrier, but of course without impairing sales of other existing products. To be successful, the management and business teams have to address a number of uncertainties and understand how they impact the business model of the firm. These need to be understood, assessed, and where appropriate actions have to be taken. Various tools exist to that respect such as risk mapping, early warning, supply chain risk management, reverse stress testing, financial continuity planning, etc.

In essence actions are needed to ensure that these uncertainties and the effect they might have on achievement of objectives are: (i) identified/ mapped; (ii) understood/ measured/ assessed. This includes assessing whether the measures taken to date (such as completion of market research) and that continue to be taken (such as monitoring feedback as the product is being rolled out for testing) provide an acceptable level of confidence in the success of the investment program. In other words, they provide reasonable assurance that the uncertainty and its potential effects are at acceptable levels. By the way, these measures can be considered risk treatments or controls. and, (iii) where the level of uncertainty (likelihood and effect) is unacceptable, additional actions need to be taken.

Another way of putting the situation is this: management needs to have an acceptable level of confidence that the investment program will be successful. This requires that certain things necessary for success happen and that other things that might impair success do not. Actions need to be taken in both cases: to increase the likelihood that positive things happen (and the size of any beneficial effect) and decrease the likelihood that negative things happen (and the size of any adverse effect).

What I have been talking about is the consideration of tail risk (low probability of uncertainty but high severity if taking place) in every decision that is made, from the setting of strategy to the daily management and operation of the business. Granted, they tend to be slower to arrive and while monitoring them should be frequent, addressing them is typically not an everyday activity.

The "extreme risk" is that by keeping our eyes away from that horizon, we fail to understand and address uncertainties that may lead us to make poor decisions and fail to take necessary actions in running the business. With our eyes away from that horizon, we can lose track of our navigation route and end up where did not intent to end up.

In a nutshell: unless we stop talking about the management of extreme risk events in a defensive way using the babble of the extreme risk practitioner and start talking about the optimization of resiliency and sustainability in a positive way in the language of the business, we are unlikely to succeed. And building more resilient and sustainable business models is what it is all about, right?

Acknowledgements

I have been working intensively on the contents of this book for over five years. I wrote a somewhat similar book in 2017 that was addressing the topic of extreme risk management from a business model perspective. This time I wanted to update the book with a deeper focus on the risk management of extreme events as it applies to the banking industry. This topic of extreme risk management has always interested me to such a point that I am even completing a PhD about it with a British university.

I have a passion for financial risk management and geopolitics, and over the years I have specialized in the risk management of extreme events, institutional banking, and capital markets activities as well as corporate finance, with a particular focus on initiating and enhancing efficiencies in relation to risk processes that focus on proactive risk management and economic capital savings. I have more than twenty-five years of professional experience, with assignments in Australia, Belgium, France, Germany, Italy, Luxembourg, Spain, the United Kingdom, and the United States. Most recently, I ran the credit-risk management of the financial markets activities of a large global commercial bank.

Currently managing my own financial- and political-risk advisory and research firm (Value4Risk), I aim to assist businesses and financial organizations in weathering extreme (tail) risk events as well as in creating a risk-aware corporate culture with business resiliency. I have a proven track record of setting up, building, and expanding risk-management frameworks and processes. My expertise includes day-to-day management of large credit-risk and underwriting departments, designing and executing risk policies, regulatory-change management, developing and implementing training modules in relation to enterprise risk management as well as financial and political tail-risk management, and developing risk-mapping, early-warning, and reverse stress-testing tools.

Finally, I want to thank my wife, Barbara, for tolerating my incessant disappearances into my man cave/ library/ office. A lifelong partner makes both the journey and the destination worthwhile.

A Word From The Author

Particularly in the aftermath of the GFC, one of the lingering queries in financial risk management literature has been whether banking crises can be predicted in any real sense. This has also been a major concern of mine ever since I started my own company (Value4Risk). Now, the idea with me has never been to really predict the future (because no one really can), but instead to focus on two areas that would lead to mitigate the path leading to as well as the effects of a nasty future.

The first area of focus is to construct a dash board of key risk parameters with the underlying idea being to compel risk managers to get down their ivory towers and step into the real world, and try to understand its trends and challenges, and translate them into quantitative easy-to-read parameters that they can monitor and update on daily or weekly basis. In other words, the purpose is to instill a discipline that current risk managers lack: reach out to the business developers, and translate their key market concerns is parametric indicators. It will help the risk manager to better understand the environment in which the business model of the firm is operating.

The second area of focus is by building stronger risk management processes with a focus on thinking and planning for extreme events, or what I call extreme risk management. Obviously you cannot avoid extreme risks, but you could mitigate their effects, either by conducting 'pre-mortems' thereby reducing the likelihood of an extreme event occurring (through better strategic risk management), or by having in place post-factum tools that would limit the effects of an extreme event (through financial contingency planning for example).

The challenge for risk managers is to find those indicators that can provide senior executives with reliable early warnings of trouble. It's a very complicated task, if not impossible. Because when you think about it: do you really think we can construct measures of asset bubbles or define illiquidity criteria? That based on interest rate curves or volatility indices we could project future market behaviors with certainty?

However, what we can do is devise ways to identify "too big to fail" or "too interconnected to fail" institutions. We can also identify the architectural features of financial networks that make them prone to cascades of distress. We could strike the right balance between the transparency needed to make risks evident, and the privacy required for markets to function.

Now, it is worth to remind you that I am primarily a practitioner of risk —not an analyst but as a decision-maker, an eyewitness of the poor, even disastrous translation of risk research & theories into practice & procedures (Jones, 2014). I spent more than two decades as an international risk manager before becoming a full-time scholar and consultant in the areas of extreme risk and probability, so I travelled the road between theory and practice in the opposite direction of what is commonly done.

Built upon my international risk management experience I now specialize in errors linked to current risk management practices and the blindness from the models of risk management, and propose risk management models (not mathematical, but organizational) to better understand extreme risks. Now, I will be upfront and in no uncertain terms about predictive risk analytics: this measure, if I read it well, aims at the creation of an omniscient Soviet-style central risk manager.

As a reminder, predictive risk analytics is meant as the use of data, statistical algorithms and machine-learning techniques to identify the likelihood of future risk outcomes based on historical data. The goal is deemed to go beyond descriptive statistics and reporting on what has happened to providing a best risk assessment on what will happen in the future. The end result is to streamline decision making and produce new risk insights that lead to better actions. To my opinion, predictive risk analytics makes us fall into the naive illusion of risk management that got us here —the same illusion has led in the past to the blind accumulation of Black Swan risks.

Black Swans are these large, consequential, but unpredicted deviations in the eyes of a given observer —the observer does not see them coming, but, by some mental mechanism, thinks that he/she predicted them. Simply, there are limitations to our ability to measure the risks of extreme events and throwing government money on it will carry negative spill-over effects. Financial risks, particularly those known as Black Swan events cannot be measured in any possible quantitative and predictive manner; they can only be dealt with nonpredictive ways. The system needs to be made robust organically through resiliency, not through centralized risk management.

I will keep hammering that predicting financial risks has only worked on computers so far (not in the real world) and there is no compelling reason for that to change—as a matter of fact such class of risks is becoming more unpredictable. In essence, risks need to be handled by the entities themselves, in an organic way, paying for their mistakes as they go. It is far more effective to make bankers accountable for their mistakes than try the central risk manager version of Soviet-style central planner, putting hope ahead of empirical reality.

Fat-tailed risks are intrinsically hard to evaluate. Already, in 2008, despite manifest proof to the contrary, leading financial institutions often applied risk models based on the idea that outcomes followed a normal or Gaussian probability distribution. It's easy to show that this is not the case for daily stock and other returns. The characteristic distributions exhibit excess kurtosis, and are hard to pin down in terms of specific distributions. The defining events that might tip the identification one way or another are rare. So, mistakes are easy to make, and possibly have big effects.

I believe that "less is more" in complex systems—that simple heuristics and protocols are necessary for complex problems as elaborate rules often lead to "multiplicative branching" of side effects that cumulatively may have first order effects.

So instead of relying on thousands of meandering pages of regulation, I recommend we should enforce a basic principle of "skin in the game" when it comes to financial oversight: "The captain goes down with the ship; every captain and every ship." In other words, nobody should be in a position to have the upside without sharing the downside, particularly when others may be harmed. While this principle seems simple, we have moved away from it in the finance world, particularly when it comes to financial organizations that have been deemed "too big to fail."

And you what, the best risk-management rule was formulated nearly 4,000 years ago. Hammurabi's building code specifies: "If a builder builds a house for a man and does not make its construction firm, and the house which he has built collapses and causes the death of the owner of the house, that builder shall be put to death." Clearly, the Babylonians understood that the builder will always know more about the risks than the client, and can hide fragilities and improve his profitability by cutting corners—in, say, the foundation. The builder can also fool the inspector (or the regulator). The person hiding risk has a large informational advantage over the one looking for it.

Introduction

The risks posed by epidemics, stock market crashes, and massive avalanches are characterized by losses of huge magnitude but infrequent occurrence (Cox, 2012). Analyzing and managing such extreme risks are inherently difficult. The limited data we collect on these rare events is unlikely to be representative (Franklin et al., 2008). This lack of data often results in a tendency for policymakers to under-invest in protecting against these risks. When these disastrous events finally eventuate, people are likely to over-invest in response due to their lack of experience and cognitive errors (Noll, 1996). Extreme risks pose challenges for conventional models of risk analysis and risk management, and they invite development of new approaches to complement existing methods (Buchholz and Schymura, 2012). Historically, these risks have usually been managed on a piecemeal and ad hoc basis (Scott, 1996).

This study investigates whether existing risk management tools for addressing extreme events in the banking industry are associated with lasting resilience of banks. Although banks have in place sets of risk tools to address extreme risks, it remains unclear whether the existing risk management fit contributes to lasting resilience within the banking industry. To illustrate the validity and dynamics of the fit-resilience association, I perform a retrospective case study of an exemplary relationship between the existing extreme risk management tools and the banks, and see how the latter have become more resilient since the application of these risk measures.

Case findings show that the existing risk framework to address extreme events is associated with poor resilience of banks. This misfit is only temporal, however, as banks can borrow from the corporate world a set of qualitative risk concepts to alter the poor relationship in terms of resilience between existing risk tools and banks and regain resilience. Furthermore, the case demonstrates the importance of a set of qualitative extreme risk management tools that should be embedded in the strategic planning and organizational design of the bank, as existing (quantitative) risk controls appeared unable to overcome difficulties in achieving better resilience. In this respect, the case also shows the bank management's active role in establishing an organizational governance and business process that is better tailored to address extreme risk environments by borrowing from the corporate world qualitative risk concepts such as HRO, supply chain risk management, and business model reverse stress testing.

The resulting leap of resilience indicates that the degree of resilience is commensurate with the degree of adaptability of the organizations. Finally, the case reveals that relying on qualitative risk framework built upon organizational design and strategic planning requires the management of the bank (as well as all of its employees) to be well aware of its use. Otherwise, the importance of qualitative risk tools will be underestimated when extreme risk events do take place, and valuable competitive advantage will be lost.

Merits Of Case Study Analysis As Research Method

A case study analysis requires the researcher to investigate a business problem, examine the alternative solutions, and propose the most effective solution using supporting evidence. Case studies portray real life situations involving decision making by a set of organizations (Soy, 1997). It improves analytical thinking developing openness for different views on the same subject. Case studies relate directly to the common reader's everyday experience and promote an understanding of complex real-life situations. Its detailed and in-depth results are not taken out of context and help create new theories as well as add strength to previous research (Krusenvik, 2016).

A case study includes background information on the specific topic, an analysis of the case under study showing problems or effective strategies, as well as recommendations. This case study will focus on an entire industry, namely the banking industry. I will use the method to build upon theory, to produce new theory, to challenge the existing theory that consists to think that risk management should be decided using exclusively excel sheets, while I advocate to also embrace a set of qualitative risk management methods that I would borrow from corporate sectors that equally experience an extreme environment.

I intent to enrich this case study with semi structured interviews that I will conduct with a couple of banks. Indeed, I will use the case study for both descriptive and empirical research. On the one hand, I will use in descriptive research the case study describes a situation about how extreme events are being managed in the banking industry. On the other hand, I will the case study empirically to gain understanding and describe the of senior banking executives when facing extreme events. It will describe what course of action the senior banking executive will take when addressing an extreme event.

Hence, Flyvbjerg (2006) states that: "The advantage of the case study is that it can "close in" on real-life situations and test views directly in relation to phenomena as they unfold in practice" (p.235). Lindvall (2007) agrees and states that the most obvious advantage is that the case study provides a detailed analysis in the individual case.

Another feature of conducting a case study analysis is, as Eisenhardt (1989) and Merriam (1994) indicate, its unique strength: its ability to handle and combine multiple kinds of data collection methods (documents, interviews, questionnaires, objects and observations). Murphy (2014) explains this strength by saying that case studies as a research method is non-prejudicial. Focus groups are just as valued as questionnaires and participant observation.

Chapter 1. Extreme Risk Taxonomy

Extreme or tail risk is not a new risk, but hard evidence suggests that this risk is significant and may be growing as a result of a combination of increased globalization, deepening interconnectedness and financialization of the economy. Moreover, it does not affect only banks but also large corporates. Virtually every catastrophic financial institution loss that has taken place during the past 20 years, including, amongst others, Barings Bank, Long Term Capital Management, Allied Irish Bank-All First, Northern Rock, SocGen, Bear Stearns, Lehman Brothers, Dexia, Fortis/ABN-AMRO, and American Insurance Group (AIG) has been caused or exacerbated by operational failure. As a result, extreme risks (aka extreme risks) are gaining greater visibility within the insurance industry as well as many other industries.

Designing a practical approach for addressing operational risk is proving to be an intimidating task, however. At present, there is little industry consensus regarding what constitutes a comprehensive risk management framework for addressing extreme risks or how to implement a viable risk management program focused on extreme risks. Many pundits will associate extreme risks with operational risks. As a reference, the banking industry has been focused on the operational risk problem for over ten years. It is not clear whether this approach is prudent, however; at present, very few banks are willing to claim that their operational risk management programs have met original expectations or have added tangible value. Many risk professionals look at operational risk management to address extreme risk issues, and so the question is whether the existing governance and framework for operational risk management would be a good fit to manage extreme risk events. As a reminder, the objective of the Ph.D. research is to address this issue, and so it is essential to review some of the fundamental assumptions upon which most existing risk management frameworks are based and to determine whether these assumptions are appropriate.

1.1. Literature Review On Tail Risk And Extreme Risk

Academic and relevant practitioner and policy literature were reviewed using keyword searches for four approaches suggested by Parties (risk reduction, risk retention, risk transfer, and measures to address slow onset climatic processes). The literature reviewed includes: (i) Peer-reviewed journals in English using keywords; (ii) Review of practitioner and policy literature using keyword searches;

The literature review sought references and keywords used included (but were not limited to): extreme risk, tail risk, enterprise risk, emerging risk, event risk, systemic risk, black swans, catastrophic risk, loss and damage, risk, risk management, disaster risk, and natural hazard. In the world of statistics, "tails" refer to the end portions of distribution curves, the bell-shaped diagrams that show statistical probabilities for a variety of outcomes. Tail events can be defined as "low-probability, high-severity events that can dominate the impacts and "societal concerns for many issues, of which climate change is a signal example. This is the problem known as 'fat tails." (Nordhaus, 2011). To depict the point at issue about fat tails, it is helpful to first portray a probability distribution such as the normal distribution or familiar 'bell curve'. The normal distribution shows most observations clustering around the center, with few revealing highly divergent results.

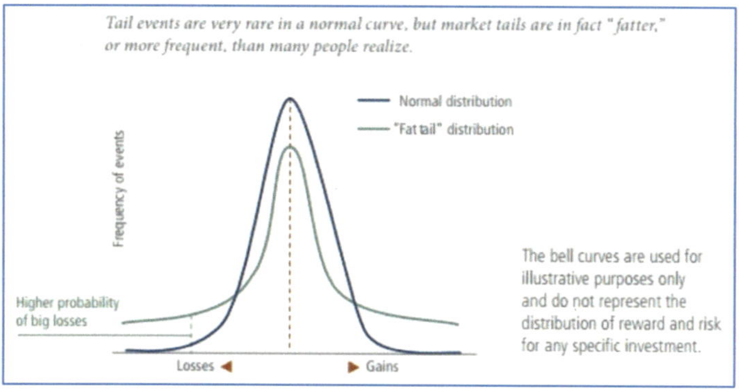

Source: From the *Financial Times* Lexicon

Applying this statistical concept of tail risk to the realm of investment portfolio management, extreme risk can be defined as a type of portfolio risk that emanates when the possibility that the return on an investment will change by more than three times the standard deviations from the mean than what is disclosed by a Gaussian normal distribution. Extreme risks encompass events that reveal a small likelihood of occurring and take place at both ends of a normal distribution curve. Conventional portfolio strategies traditionally follow the notion that market returns follow a normal distribution. However, the concept of tail risk indicates that the distribution of returns does not behave in a normal way; instead, the distribution is skewed and displays fatter tails. The fat tails indicate that there is a possibility, which may be marginal, that the return on an investment could move beyond three standard deviations. Hedge fund returns display a distribution pattern that is often with fat tails.

When a portfolio manager builds a portfolio of investments, it is assumed that the distribution of returns will exhibit a normal distribution. Under this hypothesis, the likelihood that returns will oscillate between the mean and three standard deviations, either positive or negative, is around 99.7%. In other words, the probability of returns moving more than three standard deviations beyond the average is 0.3%. The hypothesis that market returns exhibit a Gaussian normal distribution is crucial to many financial models, such as the Black-Scholes Merton option-pricing model and Harry Markowitz's modern portfolio theory (MPT). However, this assumption does not correctly mirror real market returns, and extreme events are known to have a significant impact on market returns.

As such, most asset managers are only interested in the downside risk (i.e., shifting more than three standard deviations below its actual price; see Akoundi 2012; Bhansali 2008; Newhouse 1982). The traditional method that consists of embracing a reasonable approximation of market returns to predict the distribution of changes in price will underestimate the actual value for extreme risk due to the occurrence of fat tails in financial data.

From a literary perspective, the concept of extreme risk has been long debated ever since the early 1960s. Also, scholars, such as Mandelbrot (1963) with his fractal theory, disputed the conventional wisdom revolving around Gaussian market return distributions by applying the power law to depict the unconditional tail distributions of market returns. The same year, Fama (1963), in line with Mandelbrot, postulated that prices in certain markets exhibit sudden, massive shifts that one would not foresee under a model of Gaussian normally distributed market returns. A decade later, the academicians Blattberg from Carnegie and Gonedes from the University of Chicago together recommended (1974) using the Student (or t) distribution to explain the fat tails of market return distributions observed in previous research studies. Over the next fifteen years, scholars such as Akgiray & Booth (1988), Hols & de Vries (1991), and Jansen & de Vries (1991) deepened the research studies on the shape of fat tails, proving that the tail behavior of market returns is substantially different from the remainder of the distribution of market returns.

When transposing the discussion of the concept of extreme risk to a more holistic approach to risk management, and particularly in a behavioral context, it has made the debate about extreme risks even more salient. For a proper comprehension of extreme risk, it is crucial to start with the academic distinction between objective and subjective risk. The former is characterized by statistical estimates of the negative impact of an extreme event while the latter is driven by the understanding of the probability of an adverse outcome (Boholm, 1996). Thus, it is an opposition between a positivistic view, using mathematics and statistics tools to make assessments about risks, and an ontological perspective that embraces an interpretivist perception of risk.

There is also a concept of risk involving time, probability and decision-making (Luhmann, 2005) whereby risk is a way to address potential future problems, nothing else than a time management tool. Based on these conceptual delimitations, we can further consider daily used confused meanings that are extreme, catastrophic and unexpected events. As such, risk event has been a vague concept being the subject of a multitude of definitions based on specific cases and contexts (Aven, 2012).

Indeed, many definitions of risk exist in common usage; however, the following definition was established by an international committee sponsored by over 30 countries and is based on the contribution of numerous subject risk professionals. Indeed, according to the guideline ISO 31000 promulgated by International Organization for Standardization (ISO, 2002), risk is defined as the "effect of uncertainty on objectives" (Lyon and Popov, 2020). In this definition, uncertainties encompass events (which may or may not take place) and uncertainties triggered by ambiguity or absence of information. It also includes both positive and negative impacts on objectives. OHSAS (Occupational Health & Safety Advisory Services) claims (BSI, 2007) that risk is "the combination of the probability of a hazard resulting in an adverse event, and the severity of the event"[1]. In other words, the term risk describes a type of future condition, incident or event that is unpleasant, and if it occurs will lead to an undesirable outcome, such as a system failure, a fraud or a lack of shortage of resources.

Bier et al. (1999) define extreme risk as an indication that the attributes inherent in such an extreme event have simultaneously very low frequencies and very high impact severity. As such, extreme risk is sometimes defined less strictly, as merely the risk (or probability) of rare events (Akoundi, 2012). So, indeed, occasionally, some event occurs that no one expected. An extreme event is a product that, from the perspective of the regularity of historical events or perhaps only from perception, should happen only once in a thousand, million, or billion years. Significant extreme events include the discharge of the first nuclear bombs over Nagasaki and Hiroshima in 1945; the Korean War in 1950–1953; the Six-Day War in 1967; the sharp rise in oil prices in 1973; the Iranian Revolution in 1979; the 23 percent fall in stock prices on October 19, 1987; the destruction of the Twin Towers on September 11, 2001; the global financial crisis in 2007–2008; and the Greek debt crisis in 2009–2010.

Last but not least, over the last decade, the concept of extreme events has also been vulgarized in the literature with the term 'black swan'. Indeed, the black swan theory is a metaphor describing an event that comes as a revelation, has an important impact, and is usually inappropriately rationalized in hindsight. The term *black swan* has recently been popularized through the book written by Nassim Nicholas Taleb (2007), *The Black*

---

1 "Risk is a combination of the likelihood of an occurrence of a hazardous event or exposure(s) and the severity of injury or ill health that can be caused by the event or exposure(s)" (OHSAS 18001:2007, but replaced by ISO 45001:2018).

Swan. Taleb's definition of a black swan is neat, as it rests on three main attributes: the event (1) should be an outlier, (2) should have an extreme impact, and (3) could, in hindsight, be rationalized. A black swan is precisely that; it is a tail or extreme risk event that no one expected, but as it took place, it had a disastrous impact on its environment.

As already mentioned, Taleb (2007) developed the theory to explain:

- "The disproportionate roles of high-profile hard-to-predict rare events that are beyond the realm of normal expectations in history, science, finance, and technology."
- "The non-computability of the probability of the rare consequential events using scientific methods (owing to the very nature of small probabilities)."
- "The psychological biases that blind people, both individually and collectively, to uncertainty and the massive role of rare events in historical affairs."

Taleb was not the first to popularize the term *black swan*. In the eighteenth century, David Hume (1777), through his theory of inductive reasoning, questioned whether giving credence to the properties of a particular class of objects based on some limited number of observations of particular instances of that class (e.g., the inference that "all swans we have seen are white; therefore, all swans are white," before the discovery of black swans) would necessarily lead to the ultimate truth, or in other words whether one could extrapolate a general observation from a limited sample of observations. An additional example is presupposing that a sequence of events in the future will occur as it always has in the past (e.g., that the laws of physics will hold, as they have always been observed to hold). Hume called this the principle of uniformity of nature. Way before Hume, there was Sextus Empiricus (AD 160), who questioned the validity of inductive reasoning, claiming that a law-like rule could not be developed from an incomplete set of instances. In more contemporary times, Karl Popper (1950) also wrestled with the idea of *black swan* by trying to address the problem of induction.

Popper held that seeking theories with a high probability of being true is a false goal that conflicts with the search for knowledge. Science should seek theories that, on the one hand, are probably false (which is the same as saying they are highly falsifiable, and so there are many ways they could turn out to be wrong), but that, on the other hand, have had all actual attempts to falsify them fail so far (they are highly corroborated).

1.1.1. Ancillary Concepts On Extreme Risk: Risk Vs. Uncertainty

Risk and uncertainty are really two ends of a single spectrum (Conerly, 2013); that is, either you know the probability, or you do not know the probability.

Source: Prpic (2016), "Project Risk Management Incorporating."

As such, risk is different from uncertainty, according to the great economist Frank Knight (1921). He used risk to describe cases of known probability, while uncertainty, according to Knight, is when one faces unknown probabilities.

It is beneficial to comprehend the distinction between uncertainty and risk, and to relate this to business applications (Leitch, 2016):

- Risk: we do not know what will happen next; however, we do know what the distribution looks like.
- Uncertainty: we do not know what will happen next, and we do not know what the possible distribution looks like.

The future is always unknown, but that does not make it "uncertain." John Maynard Keynes (Bradley, 2011) used the example of a corporation contemplating a capital investment in a copper smelter, which could last for a long time. The company has no accurate idea regarding what the price of copper will be in twenty to thirty years, nor is it sure what will be the probability of different possible prices.

When you apply this concept, for instance, to existing supply chains in the corporate world, enterprises know that having a supply chain almost always involves a certain amount of risk; however, (Noyes, 2015a) few do enough to shield against the one-off, extreme random episodes that can rattle them. Such events sometimes referred to as *black swans*, include unanticipated catastrophes, such as Hurricane Katrina, the BP *Deepwater Horizon* oil rig explosion, the 9/11 terrorist attack, the tsunami that hit Japan in 2011, and even the Volkswagen emissions scandal (Noyes, 2015b).

While most risk planning processes focus on events that happen relatively often, such as routine weather emergencies, they often ignore the extreme cases considered too unlikely to worry about. Although such events are unlikely, the probability they will take place is not zero, as history has repeatedly proved. Black swans are never expected. There are numerous cases of low-probability, high-impact disturbances. People do not believe they can happen, but they do—and there will be more. However, it is not easy to see the full picture. A large company can have several hundreds of suppliers and contractors, for instance, and each of those third parties may have sub-suppliers of their own. With all those moving parts, managing all the locations disruption can hit is a delicate matter.

1.1.2. Crash vs. Volatility vs. Extreme Events

Given the recent financial turmoil in 2008, the study of extreme events has become a central preoccupation for academics, investors, and policymakers alike. However, what differentiates a crash from an extreme event?

A study by Sofiane Aboura (2012) highlights that it is easy to become confused about crash and extreme events. She used an augmented extreme value theory approach. The extreme value theory has widely documented ways in which extreme events can be quantified. According to Aboura, in order to be labeled as a crash, it has to have three attributes: (1) a sudden event causing (2) a significant decline on (3) a one-day horizon.

With the latter in mind, she argues that it is almost impossible to hedge a portfolio against a crash within one day or less. An extreme event is not the result of a sudden event, as a crash would be, but instead the fruit of a long period of volatility. In other words, if a business is in a period of high volatility, the occurrence of extreme risk is much higher than if the same firm is in a low volatility environment. Volatility represents the degree of ambiguity about the financial markets or the economic scenery of which the markets are a part.

This correlation between volatility and extreme risk has been explicated through new statistics called conditional kurtosis and conditional skewness. In essence, kurtosis (i.e., the shape of a probability distribution) and skewness (i.e., a measure of the irregularity of the probability distribution) are statistics used to determine how far a distribution deviates from the normal distribution.

The term *conditional* here is used in the Bayesian sense of the term (Venkatesh, 2012). Namely, Bayes's theorem answers the question: "What is the probability of event A given that event B has occurred?" Here we are asking: "What is the kurtosis (or extreme risk) given that we are in a high (or low) uncertainty environment?" In high uncertainty, kurtosis is a high positive number with a high level of significance showing that the tail is much fatter than the normal distribution (Peters & Miranda, 2014). By contrast, the low-uncertainty kurtosis is also significant, but kurtosis is negative, meaning that the tails are slender than those of the Gaussian normal distribution.

1.1.3. Known Unknowns vs. Unknown Unknowns

The known unknowns and unknown unknowns in an organization differ from person to person. Getting people together to share information and make joint decisions is the best way to deal with the unknown (vander Straeten, 2017). There is a fascinating book written by Diebold (2010) that provides a clear understanding of what we know, do not know, and cannot know, which should guide any reasonable approach to managing financial risks.

These comprise the following:

- There are known knowns, meaning there are things out there we know that we know. This is what we call emerging risks.
- There are known unknowns, and these are things that we know we do not know.
- There are also unknown unknowns; there are things we do not know that we do not know. This is what we call the extreme risks.

The exciting part about this understanding is that over time the gradual recognition of previously unknown unknowns leads to the proliferation of a family of known unknowns, which can then be tackled by traditional hypothesis forming and testing, occasionally discovering another unknown unknown, and so the cycle continues. In other words, over time, unknown unknowns tend to become known unknowns and eventually even known knowns as science progresses.

1.1.4. Extreme Events And Unexpected Losses

Since the 1980s, the Basel regulation has developed an approach to calculate the economic capital needed to absorb losses caused by events for which the probability is difficult to estimate.[2] In practice, in the financial world, economic capital approaches use a model based on the value at risk (VaR). Within the prudential framework, economic capital should provide compensation for unexpected and unanticipated losses that are being accounted for when financial institutions are compelled to function outside of their normal operating environment.

To estimate economic capital, the VaR model essentially breaks the return distribution down into two segments: a likely expected loss and an unlikely unexpected loss. Unexpected loss is estimated by setting an extremely high threshold (unlikely

---

[2] The Basel regime is an international system of capital adequacy regulation designed to strengthen banks' financial health as well as the safety and soundness of the financial system (Dowd, 2011). It was incepted with the 1988 Basel Accord, colloquially known as Basel I, and was then modified. Basel II had still not been implemented in the US when the global financial crisis hit in 2008, and in the aftermath of the collapse of the banking system, banking regulators rushed out Basel III.

probability). The difference between unexpected and expected loss serves as an estimate for economic capital.

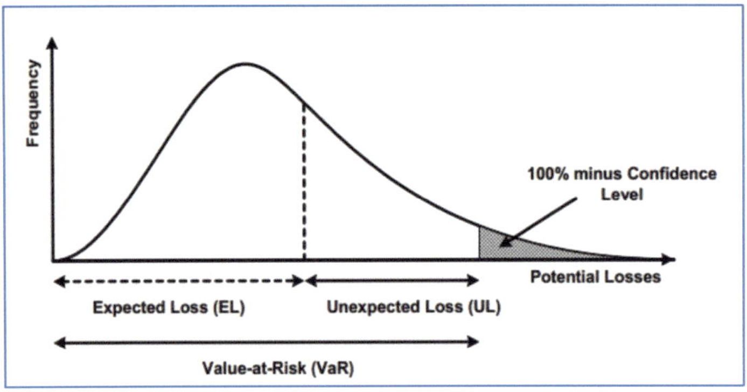

Source: From the Center for Safety Research, Department of Transport Science, KTH Royal Institute of Technology (Gorton, 2015).

The typical loss profile from financial risk includes extreme random losses among frequent incidents of low-loss severity. Firms categorize operational risk losses as expected losses, which are absorbed by net profit, and unexpected losses, which are covered by risk reserves through core capital or hedging. The expected loss corresponds to a loss that emanates from the day-to-day business, while the unexpected loss is the number of standard deviations away from the expected loss (cf. and this is the tail of the distribution) (Zaher, 2012).

Expected losses are typically covered through ratings as well as loss given default (provisions), while unexpected losses are merely covered by capital. While organizations should generate enough expected revenues to sustain a net margin after accounting for the expected component of financial risk from predictable failures and defaults, they also need to deliver adequate economic capital to make up for the unexpected component.

The unexpected loss is calibrated at, for example, the 99.95 percent confidence level, which from a rating perspective corresponds to an "AA" rating, meaning in practice this is variously expressed as a risk of defaulting once in two thousand years or, as one in two thousand AA-rated banks defaulting in any given year. This is based on statistics that are mirror-based and not forward-looking.

Therefore, financial firms calibrate their economic capital models according to management's risk appetite, which is usually in line with the firm's target rating. Where the financial institutions still get it wrong on unexpected losses is that the confidence interval is based on the assumption of a normal distribution, whereas extreme (tail risk) events are not based on a Gaussian bell shape curve.

As a result, they use that system to calibrate their business model in such a way as to reach, for example, an AA rating (still under a normal distribution with a couple of standard deviations from the average). Economic capital is set based on high-probability events, while it should also encompass low-probability, high-severity events mirrored by the recent GFC, a deflation scenario in Europe, or the collapse of China's house of cards. Under the existing rules of economic capital, unexpected losses are measured by the variability around expected losses. Moreover, as Moody's KMV states (Dvorak, 2005), "The level of economic capital implies a probability of capital exhaustion and an associated debt rating. Given the portfolio loss distribution and a target debt rating, the required economic capital may be inferred."(Dvorak, 2005).

1.2. Typology Of Extreme Risks

There are different categories of extreme risks (Hodgson & Yin, 2013):

- Financial extreme risks revolve around solvency and whether an organization can service its debts with the available treasury. In the interconnected and globalized system of financial markets, excessive leverage means insolvency for one organization can suddenly trigger a systemic problem. The main triggers for financial risks are plunging asset prices and sliding incomes, or they can be generated by an economic recession in the real economy and contaminate the financial sector through defaults on loans and other receivables. Financial extreme risk examples include an insurance crisis and (another) banking crisis.

- Economic extreme risks are less comparable, ranging from a deflationary depression to a regime of hyperinflation and a come-back gold standard (before the 1970s). These risks have their origin in imbalances, which cause instability. Imbalances are everywhere; just look at the high percentage of household debt relative to income, excessive government debt relative to GDP, falling government revenue relative to expenditures, increasing imports relative to exports, dwindling foreign reserves and, perhaps, the exuberance of the financial sector relative to the economy in certain countries (cf. aka, financialization of the economy). While the correction of imbalances can take place smoothly there is plenty of room for random, and therefore painful, jumps.
- Infrastructure extreme risk covering computer hacks causing system failure to the shut-down of an electricity grid. The widespread utilization use of computing technology means that all critical infrastructure networks, whether power plants or financial clearing systems, are exposed and highly vulnerable to cyber-attacks and security breaches[5].
- Resource scarcity as highlighted by Thomas Malthus. It could be about 'anything': arable land, water, mineral commodities or energy. The central theorem is the likely mismatch between the (linear?) evolution of the supply curves for finite resources and the (exponential?) change in demand curves given existing rates of population growth and increasing living standards.
- 'Other' extreme risks relate to (geo)political and environmental themes. If we consider the way we are mistreating the environment, and the political structures we have (or more importantly, do not have) for dealing with it, as well as with the economic, social, and financial issues, then we end up with ample scope for unpleasant surprises. A

major war, political upheaval, killer pandemic, and climate change are telling illustrations in this group.

1.3. Drivers Of Extreme Events

Evgueni Ivantsov (2013) has written an excellent book about extreme risks, and he examines how these extreme events take place. His findings show that four of the most standard causes of extreme risks are the following:

The phenomenon of unknown unknowns relatively rarely triggers extreme risk events. Many events are without precedent, undercutting the basis of this type of reasoning altogether. It can only relate to very new financial instruments (e.g., exotic derivatives) of which the behavior is less known to market participants.

Coincidence of multiple noncritical errors has triggered many extreme events in different areas of human activity. Ivantsov cites a relatively recent example in the financial world: the June 12, 2012, failure of the Royal Bank of Scotland's payment system, which led to around 750,000 bank customers being unable to use their credit and debit cards.

Reckless behavior was and remains the source of many extreme events. A deliberate human error can trigger an accident. Ivantsov illustrates this by referring to the Chernobyl disaster (April 24, 1986) caused by operators breaking the operation rules. In the financial industry, the most notorious examples of such extreme event causes are cases of "rogue" trading or large-scale frauds (e.g., Nick Leeson and Barings Bank in 1992, Bernard Madoff and the Ponzi scheme in 2008, and Jérôme Kerviel and Société Générale in 2008).

Strategic mistakes are often the primary causes of extreme risk events; yet it is difficult to spot these errors, and for many years they remain under cover until, by coincidence, these mistakes become apparent. Ivantsov showcases this by flagging the Fukushima Daiichi nuclear disaster (Ōkuma, Fukushima, Japan, in 2011), the second-largest nuclear accident after Chernobyl (also Level 7 on the International Nuclear Event Scale). Indeed, the event reveals a case in which a strategic mistake triggered a failure of crucial systems, which in turn led to an extreme disaster (on March 11, 2011, the plant was hit by a tsunami, and the subsequent failure of the emergency cooling system caused the explosion). The fundamental cause of the accident was a string of strategic mistakes in both the plant location and its design.

However, you look at it; unfortunately, strategic blunders are the most common cause of extreme events in the financial sector and, most likely, in the nonfinancial sector. What does this tell us? These extreme events are usually steered by human factors driven by greed, ego, grandeur, and so on.

There is no such thing as an invisible hand that would put a grain of sand in our complex machines. Instead, humans are the cause of all evil. As already illustrated through the abovementioned examples, many notorious failures came as a direct result of strategic mistakes made in the financial services industry by the firm's senior executive leadership teams (e.g., UBS, AIG, Northern Rock, HBOS, RBS, Dexia, Financial Assured Guarantee, and Wachovia). In the case of the nonfinancial industry, Enron, WorldCom, Swissair, Polaroid, Commodore Computers, and Pan Am resulted from wrong strategic decisions or unfortunate incidents.

This categorization of the four critical underlying causes of extreme risk events not only helps us better comprehend the nature of extreme risk but also provides us with clues on how we can prevent extreme risk events going forward. Only the first category—cases stemming from unknown unknowns—is entirely unavoidable. However, even for unknown unknowns, I honestly have my doubts. For example, in the case of exotic collateralized debt obligations (CDOs) or credit default swaps (CDSs), one must know that sooner or later this scheme of selling toxic assets through highly rated debt is bound to fall apart.

The Ponzi scheme went on because the market supporting these subprime assets remained bullish (and rating agencies were corrupted in pretending that senior tranches in these investment vehicles were safe investments), but once the trend became bearish, the whole scheme collapsed. Therefore, here too I would say that the human factor (greed, ego, and complacency) played a significant role. As for the other three categories, they are indeed preventable. Errors and failures of different elements of the system (isolated or simultaneous) are preventable. Human reckless behavior and as Ivantsov (2013) states "the violation of the existing rules and common sense can also and must be preventable via the strict governance and comprehensive control of all key activities that have extreme risk-linked exposure".

Granted, we cannot adequately protect ourselves from threats that we do not know about; however, we can instead try to protect ourselves from harm caused by, for instance, cases of bad leadership decisions. Therefore, one could state that extreme risks are not always an unavoidable evil. It is true that, when people deliberately abuse the system, it may take years before these mistakes become known. Additionally, if the leadership team leads with a bad example, quite possibly staff will mimic this wrong behavior.

For example, look at the recent scandal regarding retail banking practices at Wells Fargo in early 2017 in which aggressive sales incentives and business culture pushed employees into defrauding customers by opening accounts and buying products they had not requested. That is why, for people inside the organization, it is almost impossible to spot the strategic error well before it triggers the extreme event.

1.4. Other Risks

And, then finally, event risk, systemic risk, and emerging risk are frequently swapped with the term extreme risk:

Emerging risks are risks which may occur or which already exist that are difficult to measure and may have a high potential for loss. Moreover, emerging risks are characterized by a high degree of ambivalence; even primary data, which would help evaluate the frequency and severity of a specific risk, are often flawed. Emerging risks are known unknowns while extreme risks are unknown unknowns. Illustrations of such risks include asbestos liabilities genetic engineering climate change, and nanotechnology.

Systemic risk is the feasibility that an event at the firm level could cause severe disruption or trigger the collapse of an entire industry or economy. Systemic risk was a significant contributor to the financial crisis of 2008 and the euro debt crisis of 2010. Financial institutions considered to be a systemic risk are colloquially called "too big to fail." These organizations are large relative to their respective industries or make up a significant part of the overall economy (i.e., one of the traits of the financialization of an economy). A company highly interconnected with other organizations throughout the world is also a source of systemic risk.

Event risk is the likelihood that an unanticipated nonrepeating event will negatively affect an organization, industry or region. In comparison to extreme risk, the latter is sometimes defined less strictly, as merely the risk (or probability) of rare events.

1.5. How Extreme Risks Do Affect Businesses Models

Tail risk is usually discussed in the scope of portfolio investments and financial hedging strategies; however, the nonfinancial world is also vulnerable to extreme risk. Therefore, there is a need to help create awareness among the executive leadership of financial firms (but also among business entrepreneurs in the nonfinancial world) that extreme risk does affect their income decisions.

Extreme risks affect entrepreneurial decisions and business models as risk-averse executives, who differ in their skills and who face idiosyncratic efficiency risk, make investment and business income decisions. Depending on the development stage of the firm, entrepreneurs can diversify or not. The upside and downside risks are illustrated by the fatness of the right and left tails of the bell-shaped normal distribution curve that represents the business income risk. Global interconnectivity makes organizations more dependent on each other than ever. Information today is scattered and processed faster, leaving management with a shorter timeframe to respond to an incident.

No entrepreneur or board member wants his or her company to experience the fate of MF Global, Enron, WorldCom, AIG, Bear Stearns, or Lehman Brothers. Therefore, minimizing exposure to sudden catastrophic events—known academically as extreme (tail) risks—must be a top priority for executive boards because of their devastating financial impact. As entrepreneurs and board members seek (Karamjeet, 2014b) "to shield their businesses from these threats, they should remember that risk has two distinct dimensions: one, when managed effectively, drives the revenue engine; the other, if not managed effectively, threatens financial havoc in the event of a massive crisis". Companies have historically used conventional risk management to provide oversight for the former; however, companies also need to manage the latter dimension—low-probability extreme risk—but not as a mere extension of the traditional risk management discipline. Failure to do this can be a recipe for disaster, not only as the objectives are starkly different but also because traditional risk management tools cannot even measure these critical threats objectively.

That is why, during the GFC in 2008, well-known financial institutions such as Washington Mutual, Lehman Brothers, and Bear Stearns were caught by total surprise when their business models abruptly failed. So how can executive boards safeguard their organizations that they do not operate too close to the edge and become unwitting victims of "too much extreme risk"?

According to Paul Karamjeet (2014a), three turnarounds need to take place:

First, an executive board needs to acknowledge that an organization will blunder not because it has too much risk but because it has excessive extreme risk. This distinction is critical because, in a first step, extreme risks need to be identified and mapped. Traditional risk management is based on the theory of probability, where the cost of being wrong is the loss of profits. However, with so-called extreme risk, the cost of being wrong can be deadly for companies. Traditional risk management foresees that things will go awry and provides for solutions. With extreme risk, it is mostly assumed that there is no telling how a catastrophic event can arise, as experienced by Swissair, Polaroid, PanAm, Enron, LTCM, or BP in the *Deepwater Horizon* disaster, although extreme risks are often the result of strategic mistakes. Karamjeet (2014a) rightly points out that since the company's survival could be at stake, it is "dysfunctional to address a company's sustainability using the classic drivers of traditional risk management, such as probabilities and expected values. Obviously, a new approach is needed".

Second, extreme risk requires metrics to measure it so it can be managed effectively. Boards and organizations embrace well-defined benchmarks, such as profitability, earnings, and volatility, to run their businesses. Should there not be one for extreme risk too? Today's complexities of the banks' revenue models make it crucial that extreme risk is measured markedly, transparently, and straightforward so that effective oversight can be conducted. Many mathematical models that do exist claim that they can measure extreme risks, such as the conditional value-at-risk (CoVaR), expected shortfall (ES), and extreme value theory (EVT). The insurance industry's customarily used concept of a "probable maximum loss" (PML) model can also be an effective tool for extreme risk management. This method can capture extreme risk repeatedly at financial and industrial companies alike so that they can avoid being blindsided in crises. However, I opt for a more qualitative approach using risk mapping, reverse stress testing, supply chain risk management, scenario planning, and other methods to identify where in a firm's process and organization extreme risks are stored.

Third, companies need sound policies and procedures to manage and mitigate extreme risks diligently. This must start with the unmistakable board oversight of how much extreme risk is too much, and what limitations and governance are explicitly required for its effective management. Boards can focus on the extreme risk dilemma only if they create a company-wide culture of awareness that identifies potential sources of future extreme risks, establish specific risk monitoring processes that include nontraditional threats, and fully integrate risk not only into the business strategies and decision making but also into the finance/treasury department, as much of the information will need to be shared between these areas. These steps need to be formalized through guidelines. However, foremost, boards need a financial contingency plan that should be looked at more broadly than the well-business contingency plan.

Chapter 2. Governance Extreme Risk Management

Extreme or rare risks are perceived as catastrophic risks that are either beyond our control (such as earthquakes, floods, droughts, storms, hurricanes, volcanic eruptions, and so on), the result of our own technological developments or the consequence of our strategic mistakes.

The proliferation of new sources of risks imposes new responsibilities concerning their determination, understanding, and management. Government organizations as well as private institutions such as industrial companies, insurance companies, and banks which have to face such risks, in their role of regulators or of risk bearers, must ensure that the consequences of extreme risks are supportable without endangering the institutions in charge of bearing these risks. In the financial sector, crashes probably represent the most striking events among all possible extreme phenomena, with an impact and frequency that has been increasing in the last two decades (Malevergne and Sornette, 2006).

Consider the worldwide crash in October 1987 which evaporated more than one thousand billion dollars in a few days, the collapse of the internet bubble in the early 2000s in which more than one-third of the world capitalization of 1999 disappeared after March 2000, or what about the global financial crisis of 2007-2008 and the Eurozone debt crisis of 2010?

It is thus highly desirable to have the tools for monitoring, understanding, and limiting the extreme risks of financial markets. Fully aware of these problems, the worldwide banking organizations have promoted a series of advices and norms, known as the recommendations of the Basle committee. The Basle committee has proposed models for the internal management of risks and the imposition of minimum margin requirements commensurate with the risk exposures. However, some criticisms have found these recommendations to be ill-adapted or even destabilizing.

This controversy underlines the importance of a better understanding of extreme risks, of their consequences and ways to prevent or at least minimize them. Tackling this challenging problem requires to decompose it into two main parts. First, it is essential to be able to accurately quantify extreme risks. This calls for the development of novel statistical tools going significantly beyond the Gaussian paradigm that underpins the standard framework of classical financial theory inherited from Bachelier (1900), Markowitz (1959), and Black and Scholes (1973) among others (Malevergne & Sornette, 2006).

These tools are VaR, CoVaR, Expected Shortfall, Extreme Value Theory, etc. Second, the existence of extreme risks must be considered in the context of the practice of risk management itself, which leads to ask whether extreme risks can be diversified away similarly to standard risks according to the mean-variance approach. If the answer to this question is negative as can be surmized for numerous concrete empirical evidences, it is necessary to develop new concepts and tools for the construction of business models and processes with minimum (but unavoidable) exposition of extreme risks. These concepts are qualitative by nature and some of them could be borrowed from the corporate world (Malevergne and Sornette, 2006).

2.1. Regulatory Framework On Extreme Risk Management

2.1.1. General Prudential Environment To The Banking World

Banks (Franklin, 2008) are regulated in various ways, but from the point of view of risk, the most important target of regulation is banks' reserves against risk. The nature of a bank is to take in funds, then lend most of them out for profit, while reserving some against risks. The risks are varied: of default by creditors, of movements in exchange rates, of the disappearance or devaluation of assets, and "operational risk," a heterogeneous category that will be discussed later. A prudent bank must quantify all those risks to reasonable accuracy and reserve sufficient funds against them (or against all but the most huge and uncontrollable of them).

The purpose of regulating risk is to ensure a sound and stable financial system, i.e.,. preventing systematic collapses. A strong and resilient banking system is the foundation for sustainable economic growth, as banks are at the center of the credit intermediation process between savers and investors. Moreover, banks provide critical services to consumers, small and medium-sized enterprises, large corporate firms and governments who rely on them to conduct their daily business, both at a domestic and international level (Taskinsoy, 2013).

Proposals set out to achieve this objective include requiring financial institutions to keep adequate capital available as a cushion against negative market outcomes. Such proposals have, e.g.,. been set forward by the Basel Committee, which in 1993 first set out procedures that deal specifically with market risk.

Risk management is a critical first line of defense in the resilience of financial institutions. As highlighted in the chapter about the definition on extreme risks, the latter are a type of risks with very bad outcomes or "high consequence", but of low probability. The estimation of the probability of extreme events is difficult because of the lack of data; they are events that have not yet happened or have happened only very rarely, so relevant data are scarce. Thus, standard statistical methods are generally inapplicable.

If, however, there is some relevant data, the probability of events at or beyond the range of the data may be estimated by the statistical methods of extreme value theory, developed for such purposes as predicting 100-year floods from a limited range of data of past floods. In such cases a mathematical function may be fitted to the data and extrapolated beyond the range of the data to estimate the probability of extreme events. The results need to be treated with caution because of the possibility that the largest values in the past are unrepresentative, and the possibility that the behavior of the system has changed. But, alas, in the majority of the cases involving extreme risks the event of interest is very different from existing experience, there may be no relevant guide in the past data.

Given that the frequency and impact of totally unexpected events is generally underestimated, there is no prospect of predicting them. And, that's why embracing qualitative risk methods to manage extreme risk events may seem as a supplemental way to address uncertainty and volatility (Banks, 2009).

Despite the Basel framework for banks being in place since 1988 (Basel Accords) and an overhaul in 1994 (Basel II Accords) banks have remained vulnerable to extreme risks. Indeed, notwithstanding the fact that the prudential regime for Basel II was more restrictive than the 1988 Basel Accords, a range of systemic banking crises erupted in the mid-nineties (Asian financial crisis in 1997, collapse of long-term capital management in 1998, Russian financial crisis in 1998, the subprime crisis in 2007 and a couple of banking crises in the EU zone).

And, alas the new Basel regime (aka Basel III) will not be able to prevent another upcoming banking crisis. Indeed, by giving final approval to Basel III capital standards regulators inadvertently exposed the financial system to massive model risk.

Summary of Basel III compared to Basel II:

Officially, the Basel III framework is a central element of the Basel Committee's response to the global financial crisis. It addresses a number of shortcomings in the pre-crisis regulatory framework and provides a foundation for a resilient banking system that will help avoid the build-up of systemic vulnerabilities. The framework will allow the banking system to support the real economy through the economic cycle (Adhikari, 2020). The components of the regulatory framework are as follows (Risk & Compliance, 2018):

- improving the quality of bank regulatory capital by placing a greater focus on going-concern loss-absorbing capital in the form of Common Equity Tier 1 (CET1) capital;
- increasing the level of capital requirements to ensure that banks are sufficiently resilient to withstand losses in times of stress;

- enhancing risk capture by revising areas of the risk-weighted capital framework that proved to be acutely mis-calibrated, including the global standards for market risk, counterparty credit risk and securitization;
- adding macroprudential elements to the regulatory framework, by: (i) introducing capital buffers that are built up in good times and can be drawn down in times of stress to limit procyclicality; (ii) establishing a large exposures regime that mitigates systemic risks arising from interlinkages across financial institutions and concentrated exposures; and (iii) putting in place a capital buffer to address the externalities created by systemically important banks; (BCBS, 2011)
- specifying a minimum leverage ratio requirement to constrain excess leverage in the banking system and complement the risk-weighted capital requirements (BCBS, 2011).

The Committee also introduced an international framework for mitigating excessive liquidity risk and maturity transformation, through the Liquidity Coverage Ratio and Net Stable Funding Ratio (Basel Committee on Banking Supervision, 2017).

Basel III is an extension of the existing Basel II Framework, and introduces new capital and liquidity standards to strengthen the regulation, supervision, and risk management of the whole of the banking and finance sector. The Basel III requirements were in response to the deficiencies in financial regulation that is revealed by the 2000's financial crisis. Basel III was intended to strengthen bank capital requirements by increasing bank liquidity and decreasing bank leverage (Shah, 2018).

The global capital framework and new capital buffers require financial institutions to hold more capital and higher quality of capital than under current Basel II rules. The new leverage ratio introduces a non-risk-based measure to supplement the risk-based minimum capital requirements. The new liquidity ratios ensure that adequate funding is maintained in case there are other severe banking crises. The figure below shows how Basel III strengthens the three Basel II pillars, especially Pillar 1 with enhanced minimum capital and liquidity requirements (Shah, 2018).

Figure 1. Basel II and Basel III pillars

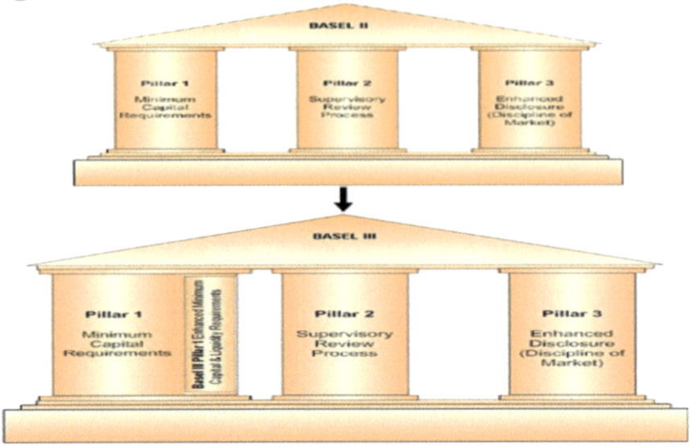

Source: FDIC

The Basel III rule introduced the following measures to strengthen the capital requirement and introduced more capital buffers (Shah, 2018):

- Capital Conservation Buffer is designed to absorb losses during periods of financial and economic stress. Financial institutions will be required to hold a capital conservation buffer of 2.5% to withstand future periods of stress, bringing the total common equity requirement to 7% (4.5% common equity requirement and the 2.5% capital conservation buffer). The capital conservation buffer must be met exclusively with common equity. Financial institutions that do not maintain the capital conservation buffer faces restrictions on payouts of dividends, share buybacks, and bonuses.
- Countercyclical Capital Buffer is a countercyclical buffer within a range of 0% and 2.5% of common equity or other fully loss absorbing capital is implemented according to national circumstances. This buffer serves as an extension to the capital conservation buffer.
- Higher Common Equity Tier 1 (CET1) constitutes an increase from 2% to 4.5%. The ratio is set at: 3.5% from 1 January 2013, 4% from 1 January 2014, and 4.5% from 1 January 2015.
- Minimum Total Capital Ratio remains at 8%. The addition of the capital conservation buffer increases the total amount of capital a financial institution must hold to 10.5%

of risk-weighted assets, of which 8.5% must be tier 1 capital. Tier 2 capital instruments are harmonized and tier 3 capital is abolished.

Basel III additionally introduced a minimum "leverage ratio". The leverage ratio was calculated by dividing Tier 1 capital by the bank's average total consolidated assets; the banks were expected to maintain a leverage ratio in excess of 3% under Basel III. In July 2013, the US Federal Reserve Bank announced that the minimum Basel III leverage ratio would be 6% for 8 SIFI banks and 5% for their bank holding companies.

Basel III introduced two required liquidity ratios: (i) Liquidity Coverage Ratio (LCR) ensures that sufficient levels of high-quality liquid assets are available for one-month survival in a severe stress scenario; and (ii) Net Stable Funding Ratio (NSFR) promotes resilience over long-term time horizons by creating more incentives for financial institutions to fund their activities with more stable sources of funding on an ongoing structural basis. Basel III also introduced capital requirements to cover Credit Value Adjustment (CVA) risk and higher capital requirements for securitization products.

2.1.2. Specific Prudential Environment On Extreme Risks

Basel II mandates the maintenance of bank capital to address three broad categories of risk: credit risk, market risk and operation risk. Basel II methodology assumes that credit risk can be reliably specified with respect to particular asset categories. These projections are based on historical experience, reflected in data sets, which are at times general and at times specific to a particular institution.

Basel II may have failed, however, to identify the strong shift in the correlation of defaults that accompanied the financial crisis. Market risk assessment displays similar issues of under-anticipated correlation under extreme conditions. Of the three categories, operational risk is the least tractable. It is a catch-all category, reflecting both internal failures and external events. The character of risk shifts markedly between 'ordinary times' and extreme events (Atik, 2009). Consider this matrix (Atik, 2015):

	Ordinary times	Extreme events
Credit Risk	Defaults may be predicted based on historical data – no strong correlations of defaults	Inadequate data for robust quantification or risk – strong correlation of default
Market Risk	Loss of value linked to performance of asset	Loss of value linked to type of asset (contagion)
Operational Risk	More likely to be institution specific	More likely to be environmental

Extreme events include events thought to be extremely unlikely and events that are unimagined (and hence ex ante unimaginable). The Basel regulations largely examine risk as faced by individual financial institutions. Yet systemic risk (contagion) is a well-recognized feature of the international financial system. The liquidity crisis of 2007-2008, however, appeared to be a novel (unanticipated) phenomenon. Cross-failure of institutions may be yet another example of unanticipated correlation of outcomes, with a peculiar magnification effect. The Basel regime does not ask – at least not explicitly – whether there is adequate capital across the entire banking system. The current financial crisis may be an instance where this failed to hold. A revised Basel regime might need to account for additional capital stored outside individual institutions to assure adequate capital under extreme conditions affecting the broader banking sector.

This is a distinct critique from the concern that the levels of protection provided were inadequate. Setting a level of protection is always a judgment call. Higher levels of protection require increasingly greater costs. The Basel II Framework reflects a series of such compromises between the limits of protection and tolerated risk. For example, a frequent level of protection found in Basel II is the ability to survive a 10-day time period with a ninety-nine percent confidence level. This is not absolute protection; rather the level of protection admits (and accepts) bank failure in certain cases.

As already indicated, extreme events can be usefully divided as either identifiable outcomes that occur too infrequently to be effectively managed (such as the financial equivalent of 1,000 years flood or hyperinflation). And there are those that are total novel with no historical basis whatsoever and very hard to imagine.

2.1.2.1. Credit Risk And Extreme Events

The Basel systems address credit risk. The chief technique mandated is the maintenance of minimum levels of capital (Prescott, 2001). Regulatory capital acts like a 'cushion', absorbing credit losses without impairing the ability of a financial institution to repay depositors (and otherwise remain solvent). Capital works well where default risks can be reliably forecasted – and when there are not strong default correlations among individual assets. The Basel system thus attempts to set capital adequacy levels high enough to absorb credit losses under reasonably foreseeable conditions.

But, capital adequacy is not a fail-safe system. First, the very setting of a level signals a magnitude beyond which capital will be exhausted (analogous to the relationship between the height of a dike and its effectiveness with respect to storm surges). All a particular level of capital can do is to provide a specific level of protection – the magnitude of loss absorption is directly related to a specified level of capital.

Second, it is vulnerable to error due to the potential 'atypicity' of the historical data that form the basis for setting levels. Third, the assumptions concerning the correlation of asset performances may not hold true for extreme ranges. Indeed, the essence of an extreme event is that adverse performance of particular financial assets becomes strongly correlated. Response to an isolated instance of an individual's disease is distinct from the response to a plague.

If predictions of defaults are based on (relatively) prosperous times, they will greatly understate risk. This appears to be the case with respect to mortgages in the United States during the housing boom. Defaults were low as overall economic conditions were positive, and stressed borrowers were able to manage difficulties by selling the underlying assets during a period of steadily climbing house prices. It was such atypical historical data that served for setting many capital adequacy levels. As such, there was a structured underestimation of the potential for a much larger rate of loss. The loss given default was also underestimated. As we move toward a more extreme event, not only do default rates increase, but so does the magnitude of loss given default. The sharp downturn in collateral value (i.e., house prices) results in bank's being far less able to recover when mortgages default.

Finally, in an extreme event, defaults become positively correlated. Instead of comprising discrete events, individual defaults loom as a unified event (destroying the effect of any risk mitigation attained through holding a portfolio of assets). The pool of performing assets necessarily shrinks, producing a magnification effect.

Positive loss correlation and magnification also results at the level of the overall banking sector. Many institutions simultaneously experiencing stress is much more dangerous than an isolated bank failure (acknowledging the potential for contagion effects in better times). The ability of any particular bank to withstand contagion effects such as an imitative bank run or payment system breakdown is compromised during periods of extreme financial stress. Banks share weakness in a systemic manner. These observed features of the current crisis suggest that considerably more capital is needed when an extreme event occurs. The capital need not be fixed within the banks themselves, however. As the initial management of the financial crisis has demonstrated (might demonstrate?) many banks have been able to call on additional capital from national treasuries in their 'lender of last resort' role.

2.1.2.2. Market Risk And Outliers

Traditionally banks specialized in the generation and holding of illiquid assets. Many if not most originated loans were held until maturity. Accounting conventions permitted these assets to be held at constant (i.e., book) values. Contemporary finance has changed these practices in profound ways. Banks are less likely to hold assets through maturity; rather they increasingly follow the originate-and distribute model, profiting from fee income. Other banks (and other financial institutions) purchase assets. Basel II adopts the distinction between the 'banking book' and the 'trading book'. The banking book lists assets that are being held in the traditional way, where expected return is the present value of periodic interest and principal payments, as well as any final principal payment extinguishing the obligation. The trading book lists assets that are held for indefinite periods of time, where anticipated return derives from capital appreciation, to be realized when assets are disposed of (prior to maturity). Holding assets require different amounts of regulatory capital depending on which 'book' they are assigned. Assets may be assigned to the 'banking book' or to the 'trading book'.

The assignment of assets to a particular book is reflective of an institution's intentions with respect to holding an asset. Assets held to maturity are properly assigned to the banking book; assets destined for sale (including traditional assets intended for distribution or securitization) are properly assigned to the 'trading book'. Banks effectively have considerable discretion in assigning assets to one book or the other – indeed, the possibility of inter-book arbitrage has emerged as a weakness of the Basel II Framework. Basel II presumes that assets will be marked-to-market. This affects all assets, irrespective of the book to which they are assigned. As market values increase, additional regulatory capital is 'created'.

When asset market values decrease, however, capital is consumed. This is true regardless of whether the asset is intended to be held until maturity or not. Marking-to-market has the effect of mandating quasi-instantaneous write-downs. When market prices decline broadly across classes of assets, capital can disappear at an alarming rate, plunging an institution into a capital crisis. This then flows to capital maintenance levels, and the noted counter-cyclicality of Basel II: banks need to raise expensive additional capital precisely when their financial profile is the weakest. There are many identifiable causes of (or situations associated with) decreases in asset value. Among these are liquidity risk, interest-rate risk, exchange-rate risk and migration risk.

Market volatility is itself a source for concern. Again, banks no longer have the facility to try to 'weather the storm' by holding assets until conditions improve. Capital impairment occurs regardless. The trend towards securitization has amplified the risk of an extreme market shift. One of the appeals of securitization is the (apparent) reduction of risk achieved by pooling assets. Any real reduction of risk depends on low correlations of nonperformance by the particular assets forming the pool. In extreme circumstances, where most or all assets in the pool lose value, the pool begins to resemble a single, bad asset.

Securitization vehicles often magnify risk exposure to extreme conditions. First, they may utilize leverage. Depending on the nature of the claim (tranche) a bank might hold, risk exposure may be significantly enhanced. Second, they may be divided into claims where correlation and other magnification effects are underappreciated. Compounding these concerns is the likely unreliability of shadow 'market' prices for claims on securitization pools and other complex products.

These are most often not true prices at which claims are exchanged in thick markets, but rather synthetic prices projected from the (already suspect) prices of the underlying assets. But whether or not these prices are accurate, or even real, they do drive capital demands under the Basel II system. History is simply missing for assets which are novel. Synthetic pricing proved to be a poor substitute for constructing risk assessments. Unanticipated financial performance resembles an extreme event, even if it seems all too probably in hindsight

2.1.2.3. Extreme Operational Risk

Operational risk describes the residual category of identifiable risks beyond credit and markets risks. These include both internal and environmental risks. Internal risks include poor management, losses caused by rogue traders, and fraud. It also includes certain counterparty risks that are not captured under the credit or market risk categories. External risks include those presented by weaknesses in the interlocked financial system, as well as the usual horrors (wars, plagues, insurrections). An operational risk event may be of an unanticipated magnitude – and not adequately provided for. And it may be perversely correlated with other stresses.

Consider the Madoff Ponzi scheme. A Ponzi scheme is subject to collapse even under the most benign conditions, but is much more vulnerable during periods of market pessimism and declining asset values. The recognition of losses from such an event (corresponding to discovery and collapse of the scheme) may well compound simultaneous credit and market losses.

During extreme events salient operational risks are more likely to be external – that is, they cannot be so easily traced to management failures. And so, they are more likely be experienced by many institutions – leading in turn to magnification and systemic risk. Not all risks can be anticipated. Indeed, it is difficult to manage risks that cannot be imagined (those that are outside of experience) although experience teaches that unanticipated and unimagined events do occur. The liquidity crisis had been imagined by some, who – like Cassandra – were ignored. That said, one might credibly say that the 'market' failed to imagine or anticipate such an outcome.

2.1.2.4. Extreme Systemic Risk

Basel II directly controls the activities of individual institutions. That said, like all prudential regulation, Basel II is in some sense more concerned by the spillover effects of an institution's crisis onto the larger banking system (Schwarcz, 2008). In the current financial crisis, bank capital was not only inadequate as measured on an individual institutional basis, it was inadequate on a system-wide basis. There were no sufficiently well capitalized banks that were able to absorb the capital deficits (and negative equity) of the failed institutions. Government response in the United States, United Kingdom and elsewhere demonstrated the existence of severe de facto capital deficits. While institutions remain with well-worn, recognizable names, the effective truth is that the pre-crisis banking sector has been utterly destroyed and what exists today results from an ad hoc public recapitalization.

Schwarcz has argued that a better approach to the problem of systemic risk should be located outside particular banking institutions in a 'liquidity provider of last resort'. In some sense, Schwarcz anticipated the immediate crisis' responses, which might be described as a bundle of state-provided liquidity and capital infusions to the broad banking sector.

2.2. Organizational Governance Of Extreme Risk Management

According to Moody's Analytics (Mizuno, 2015), the global environment for banking is undergoing fundamental paradigm shifts amid slowly progressing structural changes in the world economy, with no sign of a turnaround – if anything, most of these trends are likely to continue for the next 10 years and pose serious challenges to the world's banks.

Due to the financial crisis, numerous banking regulations have been introduced over the last few years, making the process of managing banks' balance sheets more and more complicated. Maximizing revenue while managing risk and regulatory compliance has become increasingly difficult. Moreover, regulators now require that the management of all of an organization's levels be consistent throughout. As more macro-prudential regulations pressure banks to make sure they do not become a threat to global financial stability, banks are finding that raising revenue simply by conducting an already increasingly risky business is becoming more difficult.

From a macroeconomic perspective, the amount of money flowing into the global financial markets owing to quantitative easing has ballooned to an unprecedented scale, as investors seek higher yields and new investment opportunities wherever they can be found. As a result, the world's financial markets have become more volatile, with a growing correlation among asset markets. In addition, the dramatic expansion of China's economic presence has become one of the turbulent factors affecting global growth and the financial markets' stability. Disinflation owing to low growth globally and the slump in commodity prices have also impacted the global economy.

These structural shifts have led to the emergence of new types of risks, which could be difficult to assess accurately with conventional risk management practices. Also, as banks shift away from their core businesses to seek profits, competition will intensify and they will feel even more pressure to maintain their profitability. However, banks will not be able to maintain revenue as easily as in the past. The large global banks in particular will have to address these paradigm shifts and carry out the necessary changes to survive

The financial markets have also experienced structural changes in line with those in the global economy. With enormous amounts of money flowing into the global markets, bubbles have started forming in several asset categories, including equities and bonds, leading to strong concerns among market participants about the risk of price corrections (which tend to overshoot, causing wild ups and downs over short periods as well as more volatility), or a collapse. These risks are not limited to the short-term markets. For example, the sudden crash of the corporate bond market could badly hurt the financing conditions of firms, risking a credit crunch because of resulting liquidity tightening. A credit crunch would first affect firms with weaker liquidity even if they currently look safe or are free of credit risk (benefiting from monetary easing).

Banks should focus more on proactively managing, rather than merely establishing, risk appetite, and making sure that all of the activities of their individual business segments are in sync. Given how quickly market conditions can change – and therefore how quickly financial risks can emerge – banks will need to be nimble and rapidly adapt to conditions as they evolve. Because market risk can so easily lead to credit risk, banks should be especially alert to signs of market volatility or sudden changes in their operating environments. Huge capital inflows make emerging economies vulnerable because of the risk that investment cash flows could disappear at any moment if their economic indices go far below investors' expectations. Such "disappointment risk" could lead to a credit crunch, a further decline in asset prices, exchange rate deterioration and further deterioration of the economy – a downward spiral particularly serious for emerging countries that rely on the issuance of external debt.

The rise in asset prices resulting from quantitative easing has lowered not only interest rates globally, but also risk premiums throughout the markets, which suggests that market participants have developed a strong risk appetite and are requiring less spread for the risks they are taking. As a result, the net interest margins – and therefore the profitability – of most banks in advanced economies have weakened.

The regulatory reforms following the financial crisis have achieved their main objective of preventing crises. Capital requirements have been raised significantly, making most banks more resistant to stress. Despite the emergence of several risks that could trigger global crises, a cascade of bank failures, such as during the financial crisis, is unlikely in the near future.

However, a new phenomenon has emerged, in which market segments such as shadow banking, non-banks, and the fixed income markets (including funds and bonds) have assumed the role of banks in providing financing to the global economy. These segments are not subject to regulations as strict as those for the banking industry and have expanded very quickly, becoming an important source of financing – which has also led to concerns about potential price corrections driven by shocks in those segments. Unfortunately, regulatory reform has also had some undesirable side effects. Because most large banks have downsized their trading operations, liquidity in some fixed income markets has declined considerably, greatly increasing price fluctuations in the government and corporate bond markets in advanced economies.

Another important side effect of quantitative easing is the "masking" of credit risk – that is, the flow of money has made some credit risk more difficult to discern, especially for low-credit-quality corporate firms. For example, global default rates have been very low, suggesting an almost complete lack of credit risk. However, default rates are low partly because the massive quantitative easing money has made financing conditions of corporate firms much easier and financial institutions have strengthened their risk appetite to take credit risks in those firms.

Because of the severe revenue environment, the large global banks have upped their risk appetite and aggressively loosened their lending criteria, as in the US leveraged loan market, where loan covenants have been relaxed significantly. With ample funds flowing into the market, low-credit-quality firms, which would otherwise have been pushed into distress, have instead benefited from vast amounts of available liquidity. In the event of a shock, these large amounts could quickly flow out of the market, causing serious liquidity issues for the low-credit-quality firms. In addition to typical market or liquidity risks, credit risk could be triggered suddenly, causing extreme market volatility and transform into further risks, at least until quantitative easing ends and excess money flows out of the global market. The significant tightening of banking regulations has improved banks' financial strength and diminished the likelihood of similar crises.

However, these banking regulations have also turned bank management into a much more complex process, with implications for the balance sheet management of the large global banks in particular.

- Basel III capital regulations: require banks to hold a certain level of capital, including a variety of capital buffers.
- The leverage ratio regulation: stipulates how banks manage their balance sheet size.
- Liquidity regulations: mandates a certain level of liquidity, from both short- and long-term perspectives.
- Interest Rate Risk in Banking Book (IRRBB): also requires that banks hold a certain level of capital.
- The Total Loss Absorbing Capacity (TLAC) regulation: limits the amount of debt banks can hold on their books.

Once they are fully phased in, these regulations will constrain banks' balance sheets from a variety of directions. In most cases, the regulations will work against the banks when they try to take on more risk to raise profits – the greater the risk, the worse the regulatory results. If banks want to achieve their revenue targets in line with the regulations, they will need to strike a very fine balance between aiming for higher profits and taking on more risk.

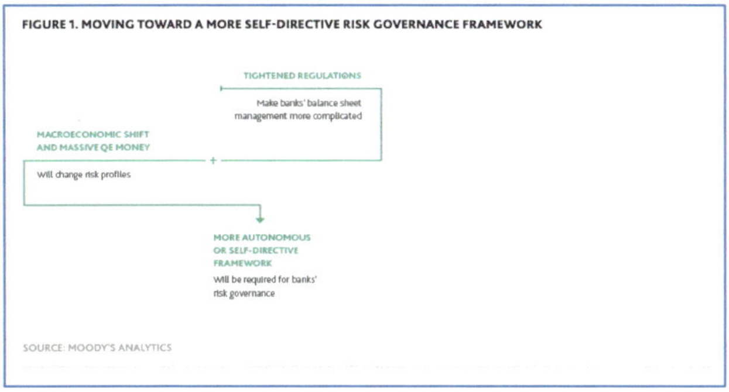

Source: Yuji Mizuno, Moody's Analytics

Regulations that are inconsistent or contradictory can be confusing. For example, a bank buying a government bond with a fixed interest rate would be positive for the liquidity regulations, but negative (because of the required concomitant increase in capital) for the leverage regulation. Moreover, because it is a fixed rate instrument, the IRRBB regulation would stipulate a higher capital requirement for the bank. Thus, determining if a certain business activity is good or bad from the perspective of regulatory compliance will become more complex.

Traditionally, in trying to achieve their revenue targets and minimize risk, banks have been able to comply with most regulations naturally in the course of business. However, with regulations becoming more complex, compliance is turning into a much more demanding task in itself, and banks will have to somehow reconcile three, not just two, competing factors: revenue growth, risk management, and regulatory compliance.

Over the next 10 years, the operating environment for banks will be quite different, especially for two reasons:

1. Macroeconomic and financial conditions: such as low growth, low interest rates, and excess money owing to quantitative easing; a volatile environment owing to rapid market changes; and an increase in hard-to-discern risks that can suddenly pop up.
2. Banking regulations: such as explicit strategies to maximize revenue, manage risk, and comply with regulation.

As a result, banks will have to make changes to their risk governance, revamping their governance frameworks by:

1. Creating an enterprise-wide framework to guide all employees and teams to achieve specific targets.
2. Developing tools to help management discern difficult-to-see risks and improve response speed.
3. Improving data management to enhance data quality.

FIGURE 2. REFORMING RISK GOVERNANCE: ADAPTING TO BANKING CHALLENGES

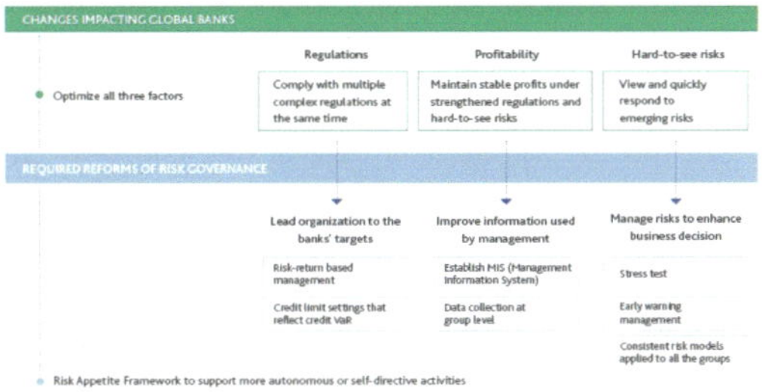

SOURCE: MOODY'S ANALYTICS

Source: Yuji Mizuno, Moody's Analytics

Because of tightening regulations and limited business opportunities, a bank will need to create a comprehensive business strategy that applies to all of its individual business segments. Running operations based on the revenue plans of individual business segments will not allow a bank to maximize group revenue, manage risk consistently, or thoroughly comply with regulations. This has been the main motivation for the introduction of Risk Appetite Frameworks, whereby banks set up overall business plans to accomplish these three tasks.

However, banks should focus more on proactively managing, rather than merely establishing, risk appetite, and making sure that all of the activities of their individual business segments are in sync. Given how quickly market conditions can change – and therefore how quickly financial risks can emerge – banks will need to be nimble and rapidly adapt to conditions as they evolve. And, ideally, each business segment will run as autonomously as possible but always in the direction of the overall strategy.

Additionally, frameworks should include incentives for business segments to meet specific targets. For example, if a bank's goal is to minimize concentration risk in its credit portfolio, setting credit limits that reflect the economic capital or credit value-at-risk will be an effective tool to diminish portfolio concentration. The point is to set up a framework that all relevant employees can adhere to, to de-concentrate a portfolio. Or, if a bank is trying to achieve a better balance between risk and return, it can establish incentives to prioritize trades with a specific risk/return ratio; for example, by disseminating risk information on required spreads for loans or internal fund transfer pricing throughout the organization. These frameworks would guide all employees, so that all business activities would be directed toward achieving the specific targets.

In the areas where building such an autonomous framework proves difficult, firms can use other tools; in this case, enhancing their stress testing capabilities will be particularly important. If a bank can conduct stress tests quickly and flexibly enough, it will help correctly guide management.

Changes in the operating environment will make financial risks challenging to discern, and assessing potential risk using past data or traditional risk management tools will also be more difficult than in the past. For example, when oil prices declined sharply in early 2015, few banks knew how the drop in prices would affect industries other than the energy sector. Many banks tried to conduct an impact analysis to clarify the possible ripple effects of the drop in prices. What is more, no one could foresee how the drop would affect the financial markets. The plunge in oil prices itself was an unprecedented incident and considerable effort was needed to clarify the risk.

Banks will have to establish frameworks to more systematically identify emerging risks and provide early warning signs throughout their organizations. Banks will also have to develop sophisticated risk models to capture and quantify these risks. And all of a bank's business segments should use the same risk models to ensure consistency.

With market conditions changing quickly and new types of risks emerging frequently, quickly obtaining accurate information throughout an organization will be critical, so having a first-rate management information system in place will be paramount. Moreover, that management information system should be the same for all of a group's entities globally. A bank's management team will need to respond rapidly to changes, and they will need the highest-quality data to make good decisions.

The banking industry will be affected by structural changes and will need to implement reforms in risk governance to adapt, requiring additional costs and effort. However, it is also true that "change is a chance." Only banks that can perform the necessary reforms in response to the changes will win the competition. The next ten years will definitely be an important turning point for large banks.

2.2.1. Theories of Corporate Governance

Theories related to corporate governance are discussed in this section. These theories are institutional theories, agency theory, stewardship theory, and stakeholder theory.

2.2.1.1. Institutional Theories

One of these institutional theoretical arguments is that organizations tend to focus on the pressures and constraints of their environment (Oliver, 1991). This is supported by assertions that organizational choice is limited by a variety of external pressures (Meyer et al., 1983), environments are collective and interconnected (DiMaggio and Powell, 1983; Powell, 1988), and organizations must be responsive to external demands and expectations, in order to survive (Meyer and Rowan, 1977). Institutional theorists (DiMaggio and Powell, 1983; Meyer and Rowan, 1977; Zucker, 1987) have suggested further that institutional constituents that exert pressures and expectations include not only formal corporate governance guidelines, but also public opinion regarding good corporate governance (Scott, 1987).

Another argument is that institutional theorists have emphasized the survival value of conformity with the institutional environment, and the advisability of adhering to external rules and norms (DiMaggio and Powell, 1983). Zucker (1987) argues that organizations are predicted to conform to institutionalized beliefs or practices when the "social fact" quality of these beliefs or practices renders them the only conceivable "obvious" or "natural" way by which to conduct an organizational activity. Therefore, in the context of this study, this institutional theoretical argument illustrates that when corporate governance guidelines obtain the status of a social fact, organizations may engage in complying with such guidelines as they are seen as obvious or proper, as opposed to being calculative and self-interested (Oliver, 1991).

This institutional theoretical assertion is used to argue that compliance by commercial banks with corporate governance guidelines may not be linked only to positive organizational outcomes (e.g., higher perceived reliability of financial reporting), but also because it would be unthinkable to do otherwise. In other words, applying corporate governance guidelines may be driven not only by processes of interest mobilization, as explained by DiMaggio (1988), but also by preconscious acceptance of these institutionalized guidelines.

Another aspect of institutional theory is that an organization's survival requires it to conform to social norms of acceptable behavior (Covaleski and Dirsmith, 1988). DiMaggio (1988), DiMaggio and Powell (1983), Meyer and Rowan (1977) and Zucker (1988) suggest that the self-serving advantages of compliance with institutional norms and requirements are revealed in the variety of rewards to which organizational conformity has been related in the institutional literature. Increased prestige, stability, legitimacy, social support, internal and external commitment, access to resources, attraction of personnel, fit into administrative categories, acceptance within professions and invulnerability to questioning are examples of institutional conformity.

The above-noted theoretical institutional assertion is used to argue that commercial banks in Kenya, whether listed or not, comply with corporate governance guidelines so as to conform to social norms of acceptable corporate behavior. Thus, the specific content of these guidelines, relative to risk management and internal control, exerts an important influence on their risk management and internal control practices. In view of the above-noted institutional theoretical arguments the underlying theory assumes that commercial banks adhere to corporate governance guidelines, even though the guidelines are neither mandatory nor limited to a "comply or explain" principle.

2.2.1.2. Agency Theory

Agency theory having its roots in economic theory was exposited by Alchian and Demsetz (1972) and further developed by Jensen and Meckling (1976). Agency theory is defined as "the relationship between the principals, such as shareholders and agents such as the company executives and managers" (Johnson, 2011). In this theory, shareholders who are the owners or principals of the company, hires the gents to perform work. Principals delegate the running of business to the directors or managers, who are the shareholder's agents (Clarke, 2004). The agency theory shareholders expect the agents to act and make decisions in the principal's interest. On the contrary, the agent may not necessarily make decisions in the best interests of the principals (Padilla, 2000). Such a problem was first highlighted by Adam Smith in the 18th century and subsequently explored by Ross (1973) and the first detailed description of agency theory was presented by Jensen and Meckling (1976).

Indeed, the notion of problems arising from the separation of ownership and control in agency theory has been confirmed by Davis, et al., (1997). In agency theory, the agent may be succumbed to self-interest, opportunistic behavior and falling short of congruence between the aspirations of the principal and the agent's pursuits. Even the understanding of risk defers in its approach. Although with such setbacks, agency theory was introduced basically as a separation of ownership and control (Bhimani, 2008). Holmstrom and Milgrom (1994) argued that instead of providing fluctuating incentive payments, the agents will only focus on projects that have a high return and have a fixed wage without any incentive component. Although this will provide a fair assessment, but it does not eradicate or even minimize corporate misconduct. The positivist approach is used where the agents are controlled by principal-made rules, with the aim of maximizing shareholders value. Hence, a more individualistic view is applied in this theory (Clarke, 2004). Indeed, agency theory can be employed to explore the relationship between the ownership and management structure.

However, where there is a separation, the agency model can be applied to align the goals of the management with that of the owners. Due to the fact that in a family firm, the management comprises of family members, hence the agency cost would be minimal as any firm's performance does not really affect the firm performance (Eisenhardt, 1989). The model of an employee portrayed in the agency theory is more of a self-interested, individualistic and are bounded rationality where rewards and punishments seem to take priority (Jensen & Meckling, 1976). This theory prescribes that people or employees are held accountable in their tasks and responsibilities. Employees must constitute a good governance structure rather than just providing the need of shareholders, which maybe challenging the governance structure.

2.2.1.3. Stewardship Theory

Stewardship theory (Johnson, 2011)has its roots from psychology and sociology and is defined by Davis, et al., (1997) as "a steward protects and maximizes shareholders wealth through firm performance, because by so doing, the steward's utility functions are maximized". In this perspective, stewards are company executives and managers working for the shareholders, protects and make profits for the shareholders. Unlike agency theory, stewardship theory stresses not on the perspective of individualism (Donaldson and Davis, 1991), but rather on the role of top management being as stewards, integrating their goals as part of the organization.

The stewardship perspective suggests that stewards are satisfied and motivated when organizational success is attained. Agyris (1973) argues agency theory looks at an employee or people as an economic being, which suppresses an individual's own aspirations. However, stewardship theory recognizes the importance of structures that empower the steward and offers maximum autonomy built on trust (Donaldson and Davis, 1991). It stresses on the position of employees or executives to act more autonomously so that the shareholders' returns are maximized. Indeed, this can minimize the costs aimed at monitoring and controlling behaviors (Davis, et al., 1997). On the other end, Daily et al. (2003) argued that in order to protect their reputations as decision makers in organizations, executives and directors are inclined to operate the firm to maximize financial performance as well as shareholders' profits. In this sense, it is believed that the firm's performance can directly impact perceptions of their individual performance.

Indeed, Fama (1980) contend that executives and directors are also managing their careers in order to be seen as effective stewards of their organization, whilst, Shleifer and Vishny (1997) insists that managers return finance to investors to establish a good reputation so that that can re-enter the market for future finance. Stewardship model can have linking or resemblance in countries like Japan, where the Japanese worker assumes the role of stewards and takes ownership of their jobs and work at them diligently.

Moreover, stewardship theory suggests unifying the role of the CEO and the chairman so as to reduce agency costs and to have greater role as stewards in the organization. It was evident that there would be better safeguarding of the interest of the shareholders. It was empirically found that the returns have improved by having both these theories combined rather than separated (Donaldson and Davis, 1991).

2.2.1.4. Stakeholder Theory

Stakeholder theory was embedded in the management discipline in 1970 and gradually developed by Freeman (1984) incorporating corporate accountability to a broad range of stakeholders. Wheeler et al, (2002) argued that stakeholder theory derived from a combination of the sociological and organizational disciplines. Indeed, stakeholder theory is less of a formal unified theory and more of a broad research tradition, incorporating philosophy, ethics, political theory, economics, law and organizational science. Stakeholder theory can be defined as "any group or individual who can affect or is affected by the achievement of the organization's objectives". Unlike agency theory in which the managers are working and serving for the stakeholders, stakeholder theorists suggest that managers in organizations have a network of relationships to serve - this includes the suppliers, employees and business partners. This group of networks is important other than owner-manager-employee relationship as in agency theory (Freeman, 1999). On the other end, Sundaram and Inkpen (2004) contend that stakeholder theory attempts to address the group of stakeholders deserving and requiring management's attention.

Whilst, Donaldson and Preston (1995) claimed that all groups participate in a business to obtain benefits. Nevertheless, Clarkson (1995) suggested that the firm is a system, where there are stakeholders and the purpose of the organization is to create wealth for its stakeholders. Freeman (1984) contends that the network of relationships with many groups can affect decision-making processes as stakeholder theory is concerned with the nature of these relationships in terms of both processes and outcomes for the firm and its stakeholders. Donaldson and Preston (1995) argued that this theory focuses on managerial decision-making and interests of all stakeholders have intrinsic value, and no sets of interests are assumed to dominate the others.

2.2.2. Concept Of Corporate Governance

From a generic perspective, banks are viewed as any firm with a broad range of stakeholders. In the case of banks, the group of claimants includes shareholders, who contribute to the formation of capital, as well as other categories that have a direct interest, such as: creditors, employees, general public, governments and regulators. Referring to corporate governance models and viewing a comparison between the Anglo-American and the Franco-German models, Macey and O 'Hara (2003) note the strange fact that paradigms of corporate governance differ on the basis of national boundaries rather than on the basis of the indigenous characteristics of the firms being governed.

The Anglo-American corporate governance approach focuses on the interests of maximizing shareholder value, while the Franco-German model considers the interests of all stakeholders. In the case of banks, the two authors find a hybrid approach, in which most firms are governed according to the US model, while banks are governed according to the Franco-German paradigm. The governance of banks (Johnson, 2011) is targeted at the interest of its shareholders, employees, creditors, local communities, customers and regulators. There is a significant public dimension to the banking firm. In the banking context, depositors' savings and government interests are at stake (Macey and O'Hara, 2003). When the social costs of an outcome exceed the private costs of an outcome, there is a negative externality effect. In this case the failure of a bank can influence the functioning of the entire banking system. The positive externality effect is also acknowledged: good individual performance improves the health of the banking system, which benefits all stakeholder groups. In this context, the corporate governance model argues that shareholders are not the exclusive beneficiaries of fiduciary duties. Non-shareholder constituencies claim fiduciary duties from management, in certain circumstances requesting higher protection than the duty performed in relation to shareholders.

The special nature of banking requires that management duties are more extensive than those of other directors. Managers function in the light of two distinct sets of interests: one is the private interest internal to the firm and the other is the public interest external to the firm. From the banks' governance perspective, the agent seeks that behavior beneficial to the firm's interest does not compromise the public interest (Ciancanelli and Gonzales, 2000).

Corporate governance includes all types of firms and its definitions could extend to cover all of the economic and non-economic activities. Literatures in corporate governance provide some form of meaning on governance, but fall short in its precise meaning of governance. Such ambiguity emerges in words like control, regulate, manage, govern and governance. Owing to such ambiguity, there are many interpretations. It may be important to consider the influences a firm has or affected by in order to grasp a better understanding of governance. Owing to vast influential factors, proposed models of corporate governance can be flawed as each social scientist is forming their own scope and concerns (Khusboo, n.d.).

2.3. Gaps in the knowledge of measuring risk

The theory of the knowledge of risk is predicated on two definitions of risk:

- Risk can be expressed as a combination of : (i) a range of potential scenarios about what could happen; (ii) the likelihood that an event might happen; and (iii) the consequence if the event does happen. One would think that if a risk manager applies this triplet of risk, whereby it would determine a range of probabilities and consequences for all types of scenarios, a risk could be assessed. However, the way how these types of information on scenarios, probabilities and consequences could be obtained is less straightforward.
- If one adds the element of time in the equation and the dynamic response of a system, risk can be described as a function of time, probability of initiating events and their specificity, the condition of the system, and the

probability and severity of the consequences. In this definition, the state of the system is central to the determination of the consequences and their probabilities. However, this assumes a knowledge or understanding of the system.

Linking both definitions reveals difficulties in assessing risk subsequent to knowledge gaps in three domains: complexity, uncertainty about probabilities, and ambiguity of consequences.

The notion of complexity in a context of risk assessment is driven by the complexity that is inherent not only to knowledge about the activities, but also to the consequences of these activities (such as events, scenarios, and outcomes). Significant hazards can be identified provided that the risk analyst studies the probability of occurrence of the hazard as well as the severity of the potential negative effect (Wallace, 2014). Risk can only be assessed when both the underlying system and the assumptions about the elements of the system, such as processes, components, events, hazards, or conditions, are properly understood by the risk analyst. Complexity is related to uncertainty and complements the latter. It can be described complexity as "the difficulty of identifying and quantifying causal links between a multitude of causal candidates and specific adverse effects". Putting risk assessment in this context of complexity leads to a definition whereby risk assessment is seen as an interactive complexity: "those of unfamiliar sequences, or unplanned or unexpected sequences, and either not visible or immediately comprehensible." What characterizes complexity are concepts such as diversity and multiplicity, and these notions call for a multidisciplinary approach to risk assessment.

Another aspect of complexity are nonlinearity and interactivity. Components of a system do not act in silo but interact with each other, and the links between cause and effect in a complex system are not direct in a linear way, but on the contrary, effects of an action can be amplifying or damping (Perl, 2009). Complexity is also characterized by the inability by the operators as well as risk analysts to gain a full knowledge of the system. However, it is part of human nature to be confronted with such complexity; bounded rationality refers to the fact that individuals are bound to devise actions that are based on an incomplete understanding of the system, potentially leading to sub-optimal actions. A solution to this is what is known as sense-making, namely being vigilant to early warning systems of unexpected events thereby reducing the aspect of surprise. Alas, extreme risk events take place mainly because analysts and operators tend to rely on simple, possible, and known facts. They lack the creativity and suffer from a failure of imagination.

Similar to other risk management related terms, there is no universally accepted definition for the term complexity. However, a good guidance is the one provided by the Federal Reserve and the Basel Committee on Banking Supervision. They relate the notion of complexity to the expansion of banks outside their core business lines.

Risk analysis involves quantifying the probability of an extreme event and tracking the diffusion of uncertainty through a system to its outcome. Events that are more certain than others can be given probability measures. A probability can be defined as "a numerical measure of a state of knowledge, a degree of belief, or a state of confidence." But, extreme events have a low probability and thus by definition are hard to predict and thus difficult to assign a measure of likelihood. Existing data are unreliable, and this makes the measurement of probabilities highly uncertain, particularly when various participants are involved and different interests are at stake.

Given that risk analysis is driven by concerns about future outcomes of decisions taken today, these consequences are the results of judgments by the analysts and operators consider as crucial. And the ambiguity resides in the choice for deciding which consequences are more important. But, the quantification of extreme events can be imprecise, and thus the inaccurate measurement of an extreme event can have very severe consequences. Even thresholds and model predictions do not facilitate the decision making as they may carry different meanings and interpretations to each of the operators or analysts. This means that the ambiguity in the severity of the consequences results in difficult decision making.

The above-mentioned definition of risk leads banks to design a risk process framework that is very common, namely the classification of risk into risk categories, thereby compartmentalizing risk too much to the detriment of a more holistic approach that fosters the understanding of interrelationship among the individual risks and engineers overall resilience of the banking organization. The Basel Committee has determined four main categories of risk in the scope of the banking supervision: credit, market, liquidity, and operational risk.

Chapter 3. Existing Risk Management On Extreme Events

Notwithstanding the good intentions of the Basel Committee, while higher capital requirements will certainly prevent financial institutions from engaging in too risky activities, it will not shield them from future unexpected events. And that's where Basel III provides a false sense of security—there is no such thing as safety in numbers. Safety goes beyond numbers—it's a question of building a resilient business model.

Therefore, there is no rapport between expected losses from normal risk and the maximum potential losses from extreme risk, as these are two self-governing factors. Both must be managed concurrently and plainly, as they affect firms very differently. The price of a mistake in relation to normal risk is the loss of profits; the price of a mistake with extreme risk can be mortal to organizations. Treating severe risk as an annex of normal risk and relying merely on more robust capital requirements is a calamity waiting to happen.

Recall that what triggered the failures in 2008 was not "too much risk," but rather "too much (extreme) tail risk"—a key distinction. While recent actions have targeted "too much risk," none has fully addressed the "extreme risk" vulnerability. Today there are not even metrics to quantify it, without which one cannot demonstrably tackle how much severe risk is too much or how much capital is needed to protect against it.

Financial firm failures in a crisis always come as a surprise because, without a measure, even management does not know how close to the edge of the extreme risk precipice their institution is, and thus senior executives remain unaware of their firm's vulnerability (e.g., London Whale at JPMorgan Chase Bank in a different setting). Capital guidelines based on objective and transparent metrics of extreme risk would fundamentally address the risk to ensure financial institutions' sustainability in crises and thus strengthen the financial system. Anything less leaves the problem unaddressed, with the real culprit lurking around unwittingly at best and compounding risks over time at worst.

But unfortunately, such quantitative guidelines to tackle unexpected events do not yet exist. In the meantime, in the absence of such extreme risk metrics, we shall do well with qualitative risk metrics. Financial crises are just part of economic cycles and will happen again. The only sure way to survive them is to grasp extreme risk now and manage it proactively. Financial firms have precise metrics for profits and volatility from normal risk. Should there not be one for extreme risk that causes devastation in financial crises? As already mentioned, the answer is simply no.

A better way to manage these extreme risks in the case of a black swan event is to develop and build a more resilient business model that focuses on reinforced business and control processes combined with a strong risk awareness culture.

3.1. Problem #1: Basel Too Focused On Quantitative Measures

While many see in the current Basel III regulations a reduction in the use of risk management models - partly a response to the perceived failure of risk models during the financial crisis: "misplaced reliance on sophisticated math" (Turner, 2009, p.22), the Basel Accords continue to rely on three pillars whereby the mission of the second pillar is to supervise the compliance with the first pillar, and the third pillar heralds additional reporting and transparency requirements about the first pillar.

Basel Committee on Banking Supervision reforms - Basel III

Strengthens microprudential regulation and supervision, and adds a macroprudential overlay that includes capital buffers.

	Capital					Liquidity
	Pillar 1			Pillar 2	Pillar 3	
	Capital	Risk coverage	Containing leverage	Risk management and supervision	Market discipline	Global liquidity standard and supervisory monitoring
All Banks	**Quality and level of capital** Greater focus on common equity. The minimum will be raised to 4.5% of risk-weighted assets, after deductions. **Capital loss absorption at the point of non-viability** Contractual terms of capital instruments will include a clause that allows – at the discretion of the relevant authority – write-off or conversion to common shares if the bank is judged to be non-viable. This principle increases the contribution of the private sector to resolving future banking crises and thereby reduces moral hazard. **Capital conservation buffer** Comprising common equity of 2.5% of risk-weighted assets, bringing the total common equity standard to 7%. Constraint on a bank's discretionary distributions will be imposed when banks fall into the buffer range. **Countercyclical buffer** Imposed within a range of 0-2.5% comprising common equity, when authorities judge credit growth is resulting in an unacceptable build up of systematic risk.	**Securitisations** Strengthens the capital treatment for certain complex securitisations. Requires banks to conduct more rigorous credit analyses of externally rated securitisation exposures. **Trading book** Significantly higher capital for trading and derivatives activities, as well as complex securitisations held in the trading book. Introduction of a stressed value-at-risk framework to help mitigate procyclicality. A capital charge for incremental risk that estimates the default and migration risks of unsecuritised credit products and takes liquidity into account. **Counterparty credit risk** Substantial strengthening of the counterparty credit risk framework. Includes: more stringent requirements for measuring exposure; capital incentives for banks to use central counterparties for derivatives; and higher capital for inter-financial sector exposures. **Bank exposures to central counterparties (CCPs)** The Committee has proposed that trade exposures to a qualifying CCP will receive a 2% risk weight and default fund exposures to a qualifying CCP will be capitalised according to a risk-based method that consistently and simply estimates risk arising from such default fund.	**Leverage ratio** A non-risk-based leverage ratio that includes off-balance sheet exposures will serve as a backstop to the risk-based capital requirement. Also helps contain system wide build up of leverage.	**Supplemental Pillar 2 requirements.** Address firm-wide governance and risk management; capturing the risk of off-balance sheet exposures and securitisation activities; managing risk concentrations; providing incentives for banks to better manage risk and returns over the long term; sound compensation practices; valuation practices; stress testing; accounting standards for financial instruments; corporate governance; and supervisory colleges.	**Revised Pillar 3 disclosures requirements** The requirements introduced relate to securitisation exposures and sponsorship of off-balance sheet vehicles. Enhanced disclosures on the detail of the components of regulatory capital and their reconciliation to the reported accounts will be required, including a comprehensive explanation of how a bank calculates its regulatory capital ratios.	**Liquidity coverage ratio** The liquidity coverage ratio (LCR) will require banks to have sufficient high-quality liquid assets to withstand a 30-day stressed funding scenario that is specified by supervisors. **Net stable funding ratio** The net stable funding ratio (NSFR) is a longer-term structural ratio designed to address liquidity mismatches. It covers the entire balance sheet and provides incentives for banks to use stable sources of funding. **Principles for Sound Liquidity Risk Management and Supervision** The Committee's 2008 guidance *Principles for Sound Liquidity Risk Management and Supervision* takes account of lessons learned during the crisis and is based on a fundamental review of sound practices for managing liquidity risk in banking organisations. **Supervisory monitoring** The liquidity framework includes a common set of monitoring metrics to assist supervisors in identifying and analysing liquidity risk trends at both the bank and system-wide level.
SIFIs	In addition to meeting the Basel III requirements, global systemically important financial institutions (SIFIs) must have higher loss absorbency capacity to reflect the greater risks that they pose to the financial system. The Committee has developed a methodology that includes both quantitative indicators and qualitative elements to identify global systemically important banks (SIBs). The additional loss absorbency requirements are to be met with a progressive Common Equity Tier 1 (CET1) capital requirement ranging from 1% to 2.5%, depending on a bank's systemic importance. For banks facing the highest SIB surcharge, an additional loss absorbency of 1% could be applied as a disincentive to increase materially their global systemic importance in the future. A consultative document was published in cooperation with the Financial Stability Board, which is coordinating the overall set of measures to reduce the moral hazard posed by global SIFIs.					

Source: Deloitte

Indeed, the Consultative Document of the BIS states that (p. 1): "*supervisory review process (embedded through Pillar 2) is explicitly recognized as an integral part of the Basel Capital Accord. It is intended to ensure not only that banks have adequate capital to support all the risks in their business, but also to encourage banks to develop and use better risk management techniques in monitoring and managing these risks. Such supervisory review enables early intervention by supervisors if banks' capital does not sufficiently buffer the risks inherent in their business activities*" (BIS, 2001).

Thus, the second pillar is the supervisory response to the first pillar, and the Internal Capital Adequacy Assessment Process (ICAAP) is itself the result of Pillar 2 of Basel Accords. The Basel Accord stipulates that the supervisory review process is based on four key principles (BCBS, 2019):

1. Banks should have a process for assessing their overall capital adequacy in relation to their risk profile and a strategy for maintaining their capital levels.
2. Supervisors should review and evaluate banks' internal capital adequacy assessments and strategies, as well as their ability to monitor

and ensure their compliance with regulatory capital ratios. Supervisors should take appropriate supervisory action if they are not satisfied with the result of this process.

3. Supervisors should expect banks to operate above the minimum regulatory capital ratios and should have the ability to require banks to hold capital in excess of the minimum.
4. Supervisors should seek to intervene at an early stage to prevent capital from falling below the minimum levels required to support the risk characteristics of a particular bank and should require rapid remedial action if capital is not maintained or restored.

These principles clearly indicate that the supervisory review process (Pillar 2) revolves around the measurement and compliance with the capital adequacy/ liquidity/ leverage requirement. As for Pillar 3, this pillar aims to complement the minimum capital requirements (Pillar 1) and supervisory review process (Pillar 2) by developing a set of disclosure requirements that will allow the market participants to gauge the capital adequacy of an institution.

In other words, while the first pillar is about minimum capital requirements (as well as liquidity and leverage requirements) aimed at taming credit/ market/ operational risk, the second pillar will be about the supervisory review process (through amongst other bank stress testing) intending to ensure that the banks have adequate capital to support all the risks associated in their business. And, finally, the third pillar will aim to divulge more information about capital structure of a bank, tier-I and Tier –II Capital and the composition of the liquidity/ funding/ leverage ratios. Additionally, pillar three will also increase the transparency about the underlying methods and approaches to assess the capital adequacy and compliance with the liquidity/ funding/ leverage ratios.

In a nutshell, pillar two and pillar three mainly revolve around the existence of pillar one; without the latter the former two would not exist. This shows that these Basel Accords essentially owe their existence to the design of these quantitative tools that the capital ratios and the various liquidity/ funding/ leverage ratios. The underlying idea of pillar two and pillar three is to support pillar one.

While writing prudential provisions is already an arduous task, implementing these robust capital standards that give individual institutions sufficient buffers from extreme events and protect the system at-large (Rossi, 2013) is an even bigger challenge for regulators and the Basel Committee since the inception of risk-based capital charges years ago. However, overreliance on analytic methods that failed miserably during the crisis puts the entire system at risk while creating enormous burdens on institutions and regulators to closely oversee these models.

The Basel capital rules feature essentially two types of requirements: leverage ratios that do not make adjustments for specific risk types; and risk-based standards that do account for such differences. In the past, critics of simple leverage ratios have called out the potential for such measures to be overly simplistic. Without differentiating, risk leverage ratios may artificially lead to market distortions and misallocations of capital across sectors. Eventually, Basel got around to adding risk-based standards for credit risk and then components for market and even operational risk. The concept of imposing a set of risk-based capital standards spanning these major risk types is sensible in theory, but turns out to be extraordinarily cumbersome at best and systemically risky at worst in practice.

Tagging Basel III as overly complex is hardly a revelation. Prominent regulators such as Andrew Haldane of the Bank of England (Jones, 2012) and Thomas Hoenig (Zibel, 2012), a director at the FDIC, have been vocal critics of Basel III's over-engineering for some time. Both have been proponents of leaning more on leverage ratios than on the risk-based capital standards driven by complex models that played a role in vastly underestimating the buildup of risks before the crisis and remain prone to a host of governance and technical weaknesses. Three areas that highlight Basel's overreliance on models are treatment of operational risk; the use of value-at-risk models for determining capital requirements; and counterparty valuation adjustment computations for derivatives.

Operational risks stemming from breakdowns attributed to people, process and technology have become increasingly apparent in banking over the years. Measuring a bank's average exposure to such risks does not easily lend itself to strict quantification due to inherent challenges in measuring events that occur very infrequently but generate large losses when they happen. However, statistically-based models are used in estimating Basel operational risk capital under the advanced measurement approach for the largest banks. Generating loss distributions, which describe the range of potential losses that a bank could experience, from inherently stable internal data sources is challenging enough. It becomes almost a form of alchemy when applied against noisy operational risk data sets. Applying the latest statistical techniques to operational risk measurement lulls us into a false sense of analytic security and desensitizes management to the important qualitative aspects of controlling these risks.

While the Basel 3 document transpires that although the importance of the quantitative aspects of risk measurement may be quite apparent the importance of the qualitative aspects may be less so, in practice, though, the qualitative aspects of risk management are deemed no less important to the successful operation of a banking business (Schmidt-Bies, 2004). These aspects of qualitative risk management are related to experience & judgment in relation to the make-up and use of financial models. The aspect of sound risk management in building internal models is equally important, not to mention the need for improved disclosures in relation to risk reporting or the way how internal models have been developed, provision for loan losses are being calculated, for example. Qualitative risk management is also about the need for data integrity and data quality that underpin a strong risk management.

Basel also permits the application of VaR models, but there are notorious for vastly underestimating bad scenarios during the mortgage crash, such as misestimating credit, market and even operational risk. Even today issues with VaR models remain, as evidenced by last year's JPMorgan Chase derivatives trading incident, where changes in VaR models and errors in measurement of trading losses contributed to misidentification of emerging risk. VaR models and extensions of these methods (referred to as stress VaR models) heavily depend on stable data and assumptions about model inputs. Moreover, there is a tendency to become overly enamored with modeled outcomes given their intellectual rigor and empirical basis, but that doesn't make them right.

Another example of misplaced emphasis on models occurs in estimating counterparty risk for derivatives activities, or CVA calculations. The financial crisis underscored the need to strengthen counterparty risk assessment. However, this is an area where models replete with mathematical elegance are notoriously sensitive to a number of critical assumptions and data. And if this weren't enough, VaR for CVA is allowed under advanced measurement methods for Basel, further subjecting the CVA results to inherent flaws in estimating extreme loss events using VaR techniques.

Unfortunately, despite impressive advances in computational and technical risk estimation, our ability to accurately measure complex risks over extreme outcomes remains elusive in many instances. By no means should we cease research and development on risk quantification. However, despite all the advances in modeling, we need to admit that it is simply not practical to cement these technologies in bank capital rules.

The risk management of financial institutions and oversight of that risk by regulators is too complex for 'risk management by Excel' (van Deventer, 2010) to be the standard. Effective risk oversight recognizes these realities:

- The devil is in the details. Risk should be analyzed on a transaction-level basis, one by one, spanning even the 700 million transactions held by the largest banks in China.
- Risk should recognize the potential adverse effects of a long list of factors: movements in home prices, commercial real estate prices, commodity prices, correlated corporate credit risk, stock indices — not just traditional areas of focus like interest rate risk and foreign exchange risk.
- Best-practice analysis of this risk cannot be fully specified in a 7-page press release or even the 300-plus pages of the original Basel II pronouncements. Attempts to do so are complete folly.
- Rules-based regulations are constrained by the ability of non-specialist bankers, regulators and politicians to understand them. These regulations lead either to a collapse of the attempted regulation, like

the Fed's proposed interest rate rules, or a dramatic simplification like the Basel III. This simplification creates "Risk Management by Excel" and triggers gross inaccuracies.

- Only principles-based regulation is ultimately effective in bringing highly accurate transaction-level analysis to regulators and bank management. This takes technology and smarts on the part of regulators and banks.
- Principles-based regulation and limited-purpose banking are by definition intimately intertwined with national culture, domestic banking practice, and regulatory organization. We note that more than 99% of banking assets in almost every major country (we exclude international banking centers like Singapore and Bermuda) are domestic. One would conclude, then, that the role of Basel in principles-based regulation is less than useful. "One world" in banking regulation is a concept whose time has not yet come.

3.2. Problem #2: Basel Regulations Are Pro-Cyclical

One of the key elements of Basel III is maintaining risk-sensitive bank capital ratios and putting in place a countercyclical buffer.

Despite numerous refinements and revisions over the last two decades, the weights applied to asset categories seem to have failed to fully reflect banks' portfolio risk (Acharya and Richardson, 2009; Vallascas and Hagendorff, 2013). To tackle this problem the new regulatory framework of Basel III has introduced a minimum leverage ratio, defined as a bank's Tier 1 capital over an exposure measure, which is independent of risk assessment (Ingves, 2014).

The aim of the leverage ratio is to act as a complement and a backstop to risk-based capital requirements. It should counterbalance the build-up of a "risk-taking channel" by limiting the effects of risk weight compression during booms (Borio and Zhu,

2012). Given that the leverage ratio weights all exposures equally and does not depend on estimated default probabilities, it is expected to act counter-cyclically, being tighter in booms when banks increase their activities and looser in busts when they deleverage. Such behavior of regulatory bank capital over the cycle should produce not only a reduction in the probability of a crisis but also a general reduction in the amplitude of fluctuations in output. The countercyclical buffer has been introduced in order to increase capital requirements in good times and decrease the same in bad times. The buffer will slow banking activity when it overheats and will encourage lending when times are tough. The buffer will range from 0 to 2.5 percent, consisting of common equity or other fully loss-absorbing capital.

Indeed, notwithstanding this countercyclical objective, Basel III is wrong about mitigating procyclicality in the sense that, firstly, regulatory risk weights change countercyclicality—that is, risk weights increase during economic downturns and decrease during upturns. This shows that countercyclical regulatory risk weights only serve to further exacerbate any accounting leverage procyclicality. And secondly, the Basel III higher capital buffers will amplify even more business cycle fluctuations, forcing banks to restrict their lending even further when the economy goes into recession. Additionally, during periods of economic boom, financial institutions tend to have their lending portfolios increasing, while when there is an economic downturn, those same financial institutions will try to curtail their lending activities.

In reality, banks anticipate the cyclical position of the economy and may hold capital in excess of the regulatory requirements. Poorly capitalized banks that face materializing credit risk in a bust have two options in order to avoid falling below the minimum capital requirement. They can either raise capital, or they can increase their capital buffers through a reduction of risk-weighted assets. Both options have drawbacks. Consequently, a decrease in risk-weighted assets can be attained through a decrease in lending. If this reduction in lending is stronger than the decrease in loan demand, then the recession is further amplified.

The basic argument about the procyclical effects of bank capital requirements is well-known. In recessions, losses erode banks' capital, while risk-based capital requirements, such as those in Basel II, become higher. If banks cannot quickly raise sufficient new capital, their lending capacity falls and a credit crunch may follow. Yet, correcting the potential contractionary effect on credit supply by relaxing capital requirements in bad times may increase bank failure probabilities precisely when, because of high loan defaults, they are largest. Given the conflicting goals at stake, some observers think that procyclicality is a necessary evil, whereas others think that procyclicality should be explicitly corrected. Basel III is a compromise between these two views. It reinforces the quality and quantity of the minimum capital required to banks, but also establishes that part of the increased requirements be in terms of mandatory buffers—a capital preservation buffer and a countercyclical buffer—that are intended to be built up in good times and released in bad times (Small, 2013).

Indeed, more recently, the predominant role of the Basel II framework has been the subject of many research studies. Some scholars claim that the recent global financial crisis highlighted the weaknesses of the Basel II regime whole others have argued that the Basel II provisions even accelerated the domino effect thereby increasing the effects of the GFC. And, in response to these findings, the Basel Committee on Banking Supervision issued a new framework called the Basel III regime with new standards that would better shield banks from a future systemic crisis. Indeed, the new Basel III regime would incorporate new standards on capital requirements, liquidity, leverage, more robust reporting requirements (Pillar 2 guidelines), cross-border supervisory cooperation, and enhanced disclosures on off balance sheet activities and derivatives.

But, these proposals, which constitute what is commonly known as Basel III, are unlikely to be adequate for dealing with anything of the magnitude of the global financial crisis, let alone something bigger. The first proposal is concerned with the quality, consistency and transparency of the capital base to ensure that high-quality capital is present to absorb losses. Redefining capital to exclude items that do not remotely represent or resemble capital is a positive move. However, redefining capital does not solve the problems associated with the calculation of the capital ratio on the basis of risk-weighted assets. The risk weights are arbitrary, and the whole system boosts the procyclicality of the banking industry without solving the problem of regulatory arbitrage (Moosa, 2011).

Granted, countercyclical capital buffers will be introduced to promote the build-up of capital in "good times" that can be drawn upon in periods of stress ("bad times"), hence reducing the procyclicality of the banking industry. The problem is that identifying "good times" and "bad times" is subjective at worst and rather difficult at best. There is no way of coming up with a figure for the capital buffer that will absorb losses in bad times.

It is some sort of "Mission Impossible" to calculate (basic) regulatory capital Basel-style, which makes the task of calculating countercyclical capital buffers "Mission Impossible 2". The bottom line is that the banking industry is procyclical, and no-one can change this fact of life. But at least we know what not to do—that is, boosting the procyclical tendencies of the banking industry, which is what Basel II does and what Basel III will also do. In short the Basel III proposals do not deal with some of the most fundamental problems of Basel II: allowing banks to use internal models to calculate regulatory capital, reliance on rating agencies, the implementation problems, and the exclusionary and discriminatory aspects of Basel II.

3.3. Problem #3: Too Much Emphasis On Stress Testing Exercises

3.3.1. What Is A Bank Stress Test?

The term 'stress test' refers in generic terms to *"A test designed to assess how well a system functions when subjected to greater than normal amounts of stress or pressure"*, (Oxford Living Dictionaries, 2016). A bank stress test is an exercise based on a study of the balance sheet of a banking institution where an instrument (f. ex. a portfolio of loans or investments) is tested under a credit risk, market risk, operational, concentration, or liquidity risk stress scenario. The Basel Committee defines a stress test as "*a risk management tool used by financial firms, as well as a tool for supervisors, central banks and international financial institutions/organizations to assess the impact of potential risks on the financial system, individual banks, or specific portfolios*" (BIS, 2017).

Typical examples of stress test scenario cases are, for instance:

- What happens if annual GDP growth rate falls by x% in a given year?
- What happens if energy prices rise by x%?
- What happens if unemployment rate rises to x% in a specific year?
- What happens if stock markets crash by more than x% this year?
- What happens if interest rates go up by at least x%?
- What if half the instruments in a portfolio terminate their contracts in the fifth year?

The bank (Thun, 2013) will model the impact of the stress scenarios on risk parameters (cf. the probability of default (PD), loss given default (LGD), exposure at default (EAD), loan loss provisions, refi costs, etc.), and see what the effect is on VaR, economic capital, liquidity gap, etc.

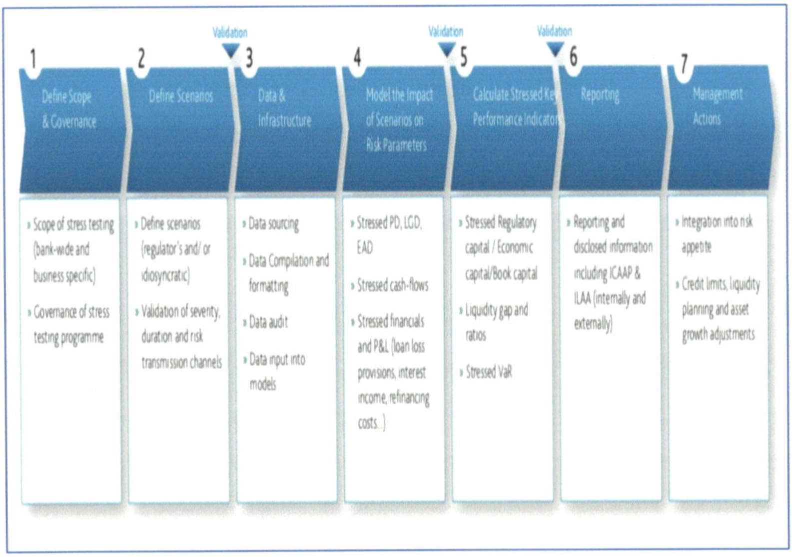

Source: Moody's Analytics - Common Pitfalls in Stress Testing (2013)

3.3.2. Bank Stress Tests And Regulators

Sizeable global banking institutions started applying internal stress tests at the beginning of the 1990s. In 1996, the Basel Capital Accord was amended to demand banking organizations to run their own stress tests to establish their capacity to provide a response to market incidents.

And, up until 2007, banking institutions themselves run those stress tests solely for internal self-assessment purposes, as it was not a regulatory requirement. However, at the start of 2007, governmental prudential agencies started to show interest in running their proper stress tests to reassure themselves about the efficacy of the business activities of banking institutions.

> List of bank stress test in the US Federal Reserve System (Board of Governors of the Federal Reserve System, 2018):
>
> Supervisory Capital Assessment Program (SCAP): 2009 (Note: there was no 2010 stress test in the USA)
>
> Comprehensive Capital Analysis and Review (CCAR) for larger banks: 2011 – 2018
>
> Dodd-Frank Act Stress Tests (DFAST) for smaller banks: 2013-2018

In 2009, the U.S. federal authorities prescribed the first battery of bank stress tests known as the Supervisory Capital Assessment Program, which was an assessment of capital conducted by the Federal Reserve System and thrift supervisors to determine if the largest U.S. financial organizations had sufficient capital buffers to withstand the recession and the financial market turmoil. That stress test was only conducted in 2009.

Two years later, in 2011, the U.S. regulatory authorities came up with a new set of bank stress test colloquially known as the Comprehensive Capital Analysis and Review (CCAR). This assessment has been conducted annually and consists of two related programs:

- Comprehensive Capital Analysis and Review (targeting larger banks)
- Dodd–Frank Act supervisory stress testing (targeting smaller banks)

Ever since that time, stress tests have been routinely conducted by financial regulatory bodies in various countries or regions, to make sure that a banking organization falling under their scrutiny was not engaging in practices that would lead to adverse outcomes. The bank-wide stress tests define standardized scenarios that the banks have to use for their calculations.

The US Federal Reserve Bank provides three different sets of scenarios, namely baseline, adverse, and severely adverse scenarios for both the Comprehensive Capital Analysis and Review (CCAR – for larger banks) and the Dodd-Frank Act Stress Tests (DFAST – for smaller banks).

The complexity increases with each regulatory stress test, as well as the data requirements and reporting obligations for the individual banks. Trading and banking book assets are subject to stress at the highest level of consolidation of the banking group. Banking organizations are now better equipped to show regulators the quality of their risk methods and controls, and have made significant advancements over the past few years toward designing stress test tools. Though, even with the significant progress that has been made to the technical application of stress testing frameworks, a lot remains to be done to reinforce the quality of the data mining, the operational delivery, and the need to embrace stress testing to the next (strategic) level.

3.3.3. Conditions Under Which Bank Stress Tests Operate

The credibility of stress tests is dependent in good measure on the bank's design (Ong and Pazarbasioglu, 2014), including:

- The coverage of global systemically important banks and connections between these banks and large nonbank financial institutions/ industries;

- The resources, legal authority, and independence of the regulator conducting the stress test simulation;
- The importance and severity of the adverse scenarios analyzed in the stress tests;
- The quality of models utilized by the regulators to measure the impact of shocks on bank capital;
- The definition and level of the capital target that banking organizations must meet under stressed conditions; and
- The mechanism for linking test results to recapitalization actions.

General speaking, while stress testing is a risk management tool that banks can use based on their judgment and needs, under Pillar 2 of the Basel II framework (i.e., Risk Management and Supervision) (BIS, 2017), banks are expected to perform "rigorous, forward-looking stress testing that identifies possible events or changes in market conditions that could adversely impact the bank". (BIS, 2009).

Furthermore, banks are required to have a routine, robust process for stress testing and scenario analysis in order to support their decisions on measures of capital adequacy, such as establishing a risk mapping of events or environmental changes that could result to unfavorable development, identifying the effect of such events given current positions, and determining the strategy and processes for managing their portfolios and risks given such events. According to the Federal Reserve guidelines, the processes for stress testing should cover events such as economic or industry downturns, market events, and decreased liquidity (Federal Reserve, 2012). Likewise, under Pillar II, banks are expected to substantiate that their current capital levels are sufficient to resist a "range of severe but plausible events" (BIS, 2009) and that different approaches are utilized to determine the bank's overall capital needs.

3.3.4. Strengths And Weaknesses Of Bank Stress Testing

Stress tests can demonstrate whether the viability of a banking organization is safeguarded within a range of predetermined scenarios (i.e., the banking institution is liquid and in compliance with minimum prudential and economic capital as defined in the first and second pillar of the Basel Accords).

Topics that are covered by the recent stress-test research literature are, amongst others, macro stress tests (see, for instance, Wong et al, 2008), worst-case studies (see, for example, Breuer, 2006), calculation of confidence intervals for risk factors (see, for instance, Rösch and Scheule, 2007) and stress tests for (credit) risk concentrations (see, for instance, Bonti et al, 2005). Stress testing has also been successfully used to mitigate bank opacity (Kapinos, Martin, and Mitnik, 2015); quantify systemic risk under extreme but plausible stress (AMF, 2017); keep the participants mindful of severely adverse shocks thereby mitigating "disaster myopia" and joint financial instability (Patel, 2017); and improve the data collection and analytical capabilities of financial institutions (Mazingo et al, 2014).

However, stress testing does not look at the most likely scenario that exhausts, for example, the bank's equity; it looks at scenarios where macroeconomic (interest rates, GDP, unemployment, inflation, etc.) or market (equity prices, bond yields) factors are being stressed and then the impact onto the bank's capital is being studied. In other words, the traditional bank stress tests do not address extreme risks. It is crucial to indicate that stress tests only indicate the bank's risk exposures to a specific event and not the probability of such an event occurring.

Stress testing attempts to answer questions such as "how much would be lost given the event occurring?" However, it does not answer the question "how much is likely to be lost?" Besides, assumptions must be made in the specification of a stress test. These assumptions rely, to a greater extent, on the subjective judgment and experience of those who conduct the stress tests. There is thus no guarantee that the "right" scenarios and methods will be chosen, or that the results are interpreted in a satisfactorily way. Stress tests may also impose a high computational cost, particularly in collecting data from diverse business units and the need to revalue multiple options-based positions.

In a nutshell, these are the main challenges embedded with the use of stress tests:

- The mining and reconciliation of data continues to represent one of the major hurdles to banking institutions. Stress tests cause a toll in terms of high computational cost, especially in the data mining from the various business units and from the necessity to revalue difficult options-based positions.
- Traditional bank stress tests are executed in silo lacking the enterprise-wide integrated approach. Organizations are not in a capacity to integrate in an orderly fashion their stress tests on credit with the ones on liquidity, operational risk, concentration or market risks.
- A stress test measures the exposure to a specified incident, but not the likelihood of such an event ever taking place. That hurts a lot the reliability and credibility of stress test.

Additionally, many decisions in the design of a stress test must be made that rely on the expertise and experience of the risk executive (i.e., the cognitive aspect of human behavior). There is thus no certainty that the risk executive will select the "right" scenarios or analyze the findings adequately.

3.4. Problem #4: No Holistic Treatment Of Extreme Risk Events

One of the elements that the Basel Accords has attempted to frame is operational risk. Indeed, the initial Basel Accords of 1988 do not explicitly address risks other than credit and market[3]; the 1994 New Basel Capital Accord wanted to rectify this by recommending specific operational risk management tools.

[3] *It is worth mentioning that under the 1988 Accord, the Committee recognized that the capital buffer related to credit risk implicitly covered other risks. The broad brush approach in the 1988 Accord delivered an overall cushion of capital for both the measured risks (credit and market) and other (unmeasured) banking risks. To the extent that the new requirements for measured risks are a closer approximation to the actual level of those risks (as a result of the proposed changes to the credit risk calculation) less of a buffer will exist for other risks. It should also be noted that banks themselves*

It is important to make one side-note on this: while it is relatively straightforward for a banking organization to collect data through probability models on specific levels of credit and market risk, it is however much more cumbersome to generate similar data on operational risk. Many organizations assume that suffering operational losses is an unavoidable cost of running a business, even though today's data analytical tools allow companies to better comprehend and measure operational risk. And, notwithstanding the fact that these data tools in turn enable organizations to determine a capital reserve against future operational losses, it remains very difficult to properly measure operational risk in an organization. Either these losses are too small to be noteworthy or viewed as too seldom to ever taking place.

The international compliance regime for banks, Basel II, requires that such risks be quantified using a mixture of statistical theory, such as extreme value theory, and scenario analysis conducted by internal committees of experts. While the use of quantitative based risk tools gives the potential to avoid as far as possible the problems caused by the paucity of data and the bias of pure expert opinion, these same quantitative risk methods rely on a set of assumptions and historical data that are commensurate with the complexity of reality.

As indicated in the chapter defining the notion of extreme risk, the latter is very much associated with in the banking industry with operational risk (even though strategic risk – the risk of a loss arising from a poor strategic business decision – is excluded from the Basel definition[4] of operational risk).

While strategic risk is not included in the realm of operational risk, the strategic risk faced by banking organizations has gained prominence in the aftermath of the financial crisis, with the Basel III Accords identifying strategic risk as a potentially significant risk and requiring that banks hold capital buffers, or economic capital to

typically hold capital well in excess of the current regulatory minimum and that some are already allocating economic capital for other risks.

[4] *The risk of direct or indirect loss resulting from inadequate or failed internal processes, people and systems or from external events*

mitigate against strategic risk (Chockalingam et al., 2018). Similar to all business organizations, banking institutions need to take risks when conducting a business. It is by now a public secret that what distinguishes risk-taking in banking organizations from risk-taking in the corporate world is the fact that the collapse of a bank, as a consequence of these risks, can have a systemic domino effect on the global economy, as evidenced by the 2007-2008 global financial crisis.

While credit, market and operational risk are the most prevalent risks within a banking organization, the risks associated with the design and execution of a strategy or the implementation of a business model is arguably the greatest risk facing banking institution, given today's great uncertainty in the global economy. Strategic risk also pertains to disruptions in the environment in which the banks operate in. Strategic risk is highly prevalent in current market conditions, with the entrance of online banks and Fintechs, and looming deregulations. Yet, despite its significance in the risk framework, strategic risk has received scarce coverage in the literature. To the best of existing knowledge, there exists no measurable definition of strategic risk in the literature.

And, hence here again, alas, given that the majority of the cases involving extreme risks are very different from existing experience, there may be no relevant guide in the past data when addressing strategic risk. Given that the frequency and impact of totally unexpected events is generally underestimated, there is no prospect of predicting them. And, that's why embracing qualitative risk methods to manage strategic risk events may seem as a supplemental way to address uncertainty and volatility.

3.5. Problem #5: Instability Financial Markets Environment

Adam Smith in his theory of the invisible hand postulates that when the supply and demand curves intersect, the market is in equilibrium. This is where the quantity demanded and quantity supplied are deemed to be equal; the corresponding price is the equilibrium price or market-clearing price, the quantity is the equilibrium quantity. In other words, thanks to the invisible hand market forces will push the market towards equilibrium. Indeed, markets tend toward equilibrium because when a shortage exists, consumers who are unhappy about not being able to purchase the products or services they want will tend to bid the prices higher, moving the market toward equilibrium.

The general equilibrium analysis is based on the following assumptions:

- There is perfect competition both in the commodity and factor markets.
- Tastes and habits of consumers are given and constant.
- Incomes of consumers are given and constant.
- Factors of production are perfectly mobile between different occupations and places.
- There are constant returns to scale.
- All firms operate under identical cost conditions.
- All units of a productive service are homogeneous.
- There are no changes in the techniques of production.
- There is full employment of labor and other resources.

Given these assumptions, the economy is in a state of general equilibrium when the demand for every commodity and service is equal to the supply for it. It implies perfect harmony of the decisions made by all the market participants.

But, notwithstanding the equilibrium assumptions, in the case of financial markets, they do not reflect the underlying conditions accurately due to behavioral bias (Bhamra & Uppal, 2016) and lack of efficiency (Ingber, 1984) (Fama, 1970). They provide a picture that is always biased or distorted in some way or another. More importantly, the distorted views held by market participants and expressed in market prices can, under certain circumstances, affect the so-called fundamentals that market prices are supposed to reflect (Thoma, 2008).

Indeed (Crotty, 2011), the radical deregulation of financial markets after the 1970s was a precondition for the explosion in size, complexity, volatility and degree of global integration of financial markets in the past three decades. It therefore contributed to the severity and breadth of the recent global financial crisis. It is not likely that deregulation would have been so extreme and the crisis so threatening had most financial economists adopted Keynes-Minsky financial market theory (Keynes, 1973) (Minsky, 1980), which concludes that unregulated financial markets are inherently unstable and dangerous. Instead, they argued that neoclassical efficient financial market theories demonstrate that lightly regulated markets generate optimal security prices and risk levels, and prevent booms and crashes (Crotty, 2011). Efficient market theory became dominant in spite of the fact that it is a fairy-tale theory based on crudely unrealistic assumptions. It could only have been adopted by a profession committed to Milton Friedman's (1953) fundamentally flawed positivist methodology [5], which asserts that the realism of assumptions has no bearing on the validity of a theory. Keynes argued persuasively that only realistic assumptions can generate realistic theories.

As a result of widespread deregulation since the 1970s, increasing interconnectedness thanks to technological advances, never ending globalization, and increased financialization of the economy the environment of banks has over the years changed dramatically (Foster, 2008) (Palley, 2017). Additionally, political and geopolitical changes across the globe equally influence the trajectory of the banking environments globally (vander Straeten, 2018). In other words, the operating environment of the banks has become more volatile, uncertain, complex and ambiguous.

In the aftermath of the financial collapse in the US that began in 1929 (Radford, 2020), it was almost universally believed that unregulated financial markets are inherently unstable, vulnerable to fraud and manipulation by insiders, and capable of triggering deep economic crises and political and social unrest. These economic and political events were compatible with the theories of endogenous financial instability created by John Maynard Keynes (Keynes, 1973) and augmented by Hyman Minsky (1980). To protect the country from financial instability, the US government created a strict regulatory system that worked effectively through the 1960s. Economic and financial turbulence in the 1970s and early 1980s led to both a paradigm and a policy regime shift. The neoclassical theory

---

[5] for example, MF claims that the realism of assumptions has no relevance in judging the validity of a theory is assessed and found wanting

of 'efficient' or 'perfect' financial markets and new classical macro theory (which assumes that markets always generate full employment) replaced the theoretical visions of Keynes and Minsky. The government, influenced by the belief that efficient financial market theory was sanctioned by economic 'science,' – embodied by Milton Friedman positivist approach - radically deregulated US financial markets after 1980.

Many factors contributed to the recent financial crisis. Instability is built into modern financial markets, a historical fact incorporated in the financial market theories of Keynes, Minsky, Marx (1959) and others. In recent decades, financial innovation, bonus-driven compensation systems, rising leverage and global integration led to fast financial market expansion and excessive risk-taking that generated a series of dangerous financial crises. Government intervention to shorten and limit the depth of these crises in turn created moral hazard that induced even greater risk-taking that accelerated the long-term financial explosion.

Nevertheless, there is no doubt that radical financial market deregulation was a necessary condition for the generation of a secular financial expansion this long and this strong, and for the creation of a global crisis as severe as the one we are still living through. Excessive deregulation is based on a misleading theory of financial markets constructed on obviously unrealistic assumptions and has little empirical support. As the world recently observed, predictions based on efficient financial market theory turned out to be catastrophically wrong. The idea that markets are self-correcting received a mortal blow in the recent financial crisis and should be buried once and for all.

For example, mainstream financial theory assumes that financial products and institutions are perfectly transparent; this is a precondition for efficient pricing. In fact, deregulation and financial innovation made the portfolios of the giant bank conglomerates that are at the center of the global financial system so complex that it became impossible for anyone to make a reliable estimate of their risk. In 1998 the Bank for International Settlements sanctioned the idea that regulators, who were now incapable of assessing the riskiness of large banks, should shift responsibility for setting limits on giant banks' risk to the banks themselves, who might be better informed. Banks were allowed to manage their own risk through a statistical exercise known as Value at Risk

(VaR). They were, in effect, permitted to set their own capital requirements. Not surprisingly, they used this freedom to minimize them. VaR is an estimate of the highest possible loss in the value of a portfolio of financial assets and liabilities over a fixed time interval with a specific statistical confidence level. Mimicking the CAPM and options pricing models, VaR models assume that the probability distribution of future security prices is predetermined and knowable - they are characterized by risk rather than uncertainty. They also assume that expectations can be adequately represented by a 'normal' distribution. "All the models in the financial economics edifice assume a normal distribution".

There are three fundamental flaws in this mode of risk assessment.

First, a VaR calculation uses historical data to forecast future financial market performance, typically data from the past year or less. If this calculation is done in the midst of a boom, the data will reflect the 'perfect calm' of the period – corporate profits will be high as will capital gains on securities, while interest rates, defaults and asset price volatility will be low. The possibility of the outbreak of crisis will not be considered because there are no crises in the database. VaR analysis implicitly assumes this ideal environment is permanent.

Thus, the risk associated with boom-induced high leverage and excessively optimistic expectations will be severely under-estimated. VaR's rosy risk-estimates allowed banks to hold dangerously low capital cushions and therefore enabled them to use extra leverage to continue to add risky securities to their portfolio. However, even if the data were extended to cover crises in past decades, growth and innovation would have changed the system so substantially that there would be little likelihood that the future would resemble the past extrapolated (Crotty, 2011).

Second, while VaR models assume that security price movements conform to the normal distribution used in canonical financial models, in fact they follow a distribution in which the preponderance of observations are 'normal,' but on occasion observations far from the mean appear – the well-known 'fat tail' phenomenon. The standard exercise calculates VaR under negative conditions likely to occur only 5% of the time. In a normal distribution the likelihood that an observation several standard deviations beyond a 95% confidence interval will occur is infinitesimal. Yet, extreme events inevitably occur from time to time.

The use of normal distributions allowed banks to assume that serious future crises were impossible. Thus, VaR risk estimates let banks minimize required capital and maximize leverage and lending capacity. This maximized profits and bonuses in the boom even as it sowed the seeds of a future crisis.

Third, the asset-price correlation matrix is a key determinant of measured VaR. The lower the correlation among security prices, the lower the portfolio's risk. VaR models assume that asset prices are jointly normally distributed and that future asset price correlations will be identical to those of the recent past. However, in crises most prices fall together as all investors run for liquidity and safety, creating a high positive correlation and dangerously high risk unaccounted for in VaR calculations.

Another example of how the equilibrium model is distorting reality in the financial markets: the canonical models of optimal financial markets assume that leverage is never dangerous because fully-informed agents rationally choose an optimal debt position. In fact, under radical deregulation debt had risen to systemically dangerous levels by 2007.

From the mid 1990s until the onset of the crisis economic growth was largely driven by rising household borrowing and the stimulus to consumption provided first by a booming stock market and, later, by an enormous increase in housing prices augmented by an explosion in home equity loans. In 1981 household debt was 48% of GDP, while in 2007 it was 100%. This meant that if job or wage growth slowed, the ability of households to sustain heavy debt loads would be compromised. It also meant that if interest rates rose or credit tightened, or if stock or housing prices declined, consumption spending and aggregate demand would decelerate, threatening job and wage growth. The economy had become extremely financially fragile.

Financial firms were also excessively indebted; financial sector debt rose from 22% of GDP in 1981 to 117% in late 2008. The spectacular leverage and financial fragility of key financial sectors along with the gross overvaluation of the securities they held made a severe financial crisis almost inevitable. Excessive household debt and boom-augmented household wealth ensured that the real-sector fallout from a financial sector crisis would be severe, but this threat was hidden by neoclassical fairy tales about market efficiency.

It is estimated that half of the spectacular rise in investment banking return on equity in the four years ending in mid 2007 was attributable not to clever investment strategies or even to super-heated boom conditions, but simply to higher leverage with higher risk. Moreover, about half the debt of the big investment banks consisted of overnight borrowing that would evaporate in a crisis. Commercial banks appeared to be adequately capitalized during the boom, but only because a high percent of their assets – for some more than half – was kept off-balance-sheet, and the prices of all their assets were inflated by the bubble. In fact, banks were dangerously leveraged. When the crisis hit, the value of these assets, and therefore of bank capital, plummeted, causing a frantic global search for new capital, a spike in interest rates and a tightening of credit standards. The initial decline in security prices triggered a de-leveraging process in financial markets in which liquidity disappeared. Asset price declines led to margin calls, which led to forced assets sales and more margin calls in a dangerous downward spiral.

The shrinking availability and rising cost of credit brought on by the crisis, a strong negative wealth effect on consumption, and a declining construction industry led to a slowdown in economic growth and a rise in unemployment. This is turn, led to lower profits and wages, which triggered rising defaults on both business and household loans, especially residential mortgages. Real- and financial-sector problems were mutually infectious.

Excessive leverage, rising defaults, deteriorating expectations, evaporating liquidity and a destructive interaction between the real and financial sectors drove the downturn. These phenomena are integral components of the KM theory of financial market dynamics but are invisible in the mainstream financial market narrative about why radical deregulation is the best policy.

And, then there is the tell-tailing illustration about how everyone acted as if the theory of optimal financial markets applied to all major financial products, but it could not possibly apply to the inherently non-transparent securities at the center of the recent boom and bust. Financial innovation has proceeded to the point where important financial products such as mortgage-backed securities (MBSs) and collateralized debt obligations (CDOs) are so complex and so opaque that they are inherently nontransparent. As such, they cannot be traded on standard competitive financial markets, but are sold instead through negotiation between the originating investment bank and a buyer – "over the counter." It has been estimated that half of all securities are privately traded. Nontransparent securities traded privately cannot possibly generate 'optimal' prices as defined in mainstream theory.

For this reason alone, no one should have put any credence in efficient market theory as a guide to regulatory policy. According to the Securities Industry and Financial Markets Association (SIFMA), there was $7.4 trillion worth of MBSs outstanding in the first quarter of 2008, more than double the amount outstanding in 2001. Over $500 billion dollars in CDOs were issued in both 2006 and 2007, up from $157 billion as recently as 2004 (SIFMA website).

The explosion of complex MBSs and derivative products created large profits and bonuses at giant banks and other financial institutions, but also destroyed the transparency necessary for any semblance of market efficiency. Since these securities were nontransparent, so were the institutions that held them. Exchange-traded securities are sold in highly competitive and transparent markets with low profit margins accruing to the market-making institution.

Thus, banks had a strong incentive to create products so complex that they could not be sold on exchanges at all. By the mid-2000s, eighty percent of derivatives were sold over-the-counter in private deals. Such agreements are characterized by oligopoly pricing power, asymmetric information and unequal bargaining power that allow banks to generate high profit margins. Consider the collateralized debt obligation. A mortgage-backed CDO converts the cash flows from the mortgages in its domain into tranches or slices with different risk characteristics. Several thousand mortgages may go into a single MBS and as many as 150 MBSs can be packaged into a single CDO.

The risk associated with mortgage-backed CDOs cannot possibly be priced correctly. Ratings agencies and the investment banks that create these securities rely on simulation models to assess their risk, but these models are unreliable and easily manipulated, and these institutions have strong incentives to produce unrealistically high ratings. The models are 'black boxes': data is fed in and millions of lines of computer code spit out a rating. It should come as no surprise that market operatives referred to the process through which investment banks and ratings agencies priced or marked CDOs as marking to 'magic' or to 'myth.' The fact that neoclassical financial theory obviously cannot generate its signature optimality conclusion when no one knows the properties of a security somehow never came up in the deregulation debate

Above elements clearly highlight that the banking environment contrary to popular beliefs is unstable and inefficient, and hence that the future is an unknown risk rather than a known risk. This shifting, highly unpredictable environment is creating uncertainty among global banks that are scrambling to identity what the future might hold on the regulatory front. What can banks expect for the time being? We look for three key conditions to prevail amid today's volatile environment (Caplain et al., 2017):

- High expectations on banks: Banks can be certain that regulators will continue to maintain high expectations and intense scrutiny on the industry. That should not be surprising for a global industry that has paid an estimated US$160 billion in fines since the financial crisis 10 years ago. Scrutiny by regulators has been intense and will remain exceptionally high.
- Greater focus on bank conduct and culture: Look for a broader focus by regulators as they move beyond enforcement and course-correcting, placing greater emphasis on governance, compliance and the need for banks to maintain highly reliable infrastructure and controls. Regulators' focus will transcend traditional retail banking and insurance products to include investments, savings and pensions, and to the fairness of commercial lending practices.

- Bank 'safety' is a leading priority: Thirdly, the industry can expect continued emphasis on the need for financial organizations to keep their capital safe. This will include increased reliance by regulators on `stress testing' and response planning - creating `worst-case scenarios' for which banks will be required to provide detailed strategies, responses and solutions.

3.6. Problem #6: Lack of Imagination

Corporate leaders have tarnished the concept of extreme risk over the last three decades, as whenever an event occurs that appears to be unexpected, they tend to quickly brand the event as extreme.

Financial failures have many causes: for example, they can be determined by credit risk variables (Samad, 2012), triggered by a shortage of liquidity, or caused by fraudulent activities. Nevertheless, human decision processes or organizational policies, such as flaws in internal processes and procedures can also cause financial calamities. Similarly, technological incidents, such as a cyber-attack on an IT system, and external events, such as changes in the political, regulatory and legal environment, can present extreme risks.

However, failures can also be triggered by insufficient imagination, in the sense that organizations may lack sufficient preparedness when facing a crisis. Bank executives have often claimed that they did not foresee the global financial crisis of 2007-2008. Is this the case, or is it because they were complacent and lacked imaginativeness?

In the aftermath of a disaster, senior executives in governmental and business organizations typically use the term 'black swan' too liberally, as if the extreme event had come from nowhere (Huang et al., 2003). Aside from understanding the complexity and connectivity of extreme risks, it is also essential to propose solutions and tools that help organizations prepare for extreme events and increase their resilience.

This classification of these underlying causes of extreme and rare events has a two-fold benefit:

- It helps better understand the nature of tail risk
- It also gives clues on how organizations can in some ways prevent extreme and rare events going forward

Only the first driver of extreme and rare events, namely cases originating from unknown unknowns, is unavoidable. Organizations will not be able to protect themselves from hazards about which they have no knowledge. They will always be an unavoidable fact of life.

3.7. Problem #7: Coincidence Of Multiple Noncritical Errors

While some technical and human errors might in isolation not be critical, but when they do happen simultaneously, they can cause a full-scale disaster. Extreme risks can be engineered by sequences of multiple non-critical failures and errors, or in other words, when poorly acknowledged events (such as failures and errors that carry low individual probability) take place at the same time, they can together have a devastating effect.

The existence of multiplicative processes combined with stochastic reset phenomena can give rise to black swans. Unlike individual risks, extreme and rare events are not additive in the aggregate but multiplicative in nature. From a Bayesian perspective, coincidence is viewed as an event that is not yet supported as an alternative due to its low likelihood, even though that event is supporting an alternative to a current advocated perspective on things. The inability in noticing seemingly non-salient events can result in major accidents. The human logic behind such blindness rests on two approaches:

- the change blindness that is supported by the fact that organizations fail to notice the occurrence of unexpected event, and even less diagnosing and responding to it.
- Hick's theory postulating that an organization's response time to an extreme and rare event will be driven by the number of alternative choices. Indeed, the higher the number of choices, the longer the decision time.

3.8. Problem #8: ORM, ERM, and SRM

Generally speaking, gaining a better understanding of the behavior of extreme events allows for a better understanding of the behavior of the market during extreme events, and in turn, the latter is also useful for understanding the behavior of the market both under ordinary and extraordinary conditions. In other words, it is crucial not to separate extreme events from other events.

As a reminder, the Basel Committee identifies the following risk types:

- Risk in Pillar I (minimum capital requirements): credit risk, market risk, and operational risk.
- Risk in Pillar 2 (Internal Capital Adequacy Assessment Process (ICAAP)): liquidity risk, interest rate risk, and concentration risk.

Given the likelihood for confusion because of the myriad of analogous terms, there is a need to establish boundaries as to the use of term 'extreme risk'. I want to delineate the scope of the term extreme risk by restricting it to those unlikely events that can strike the business community, meaning both the corporate world as well as the banking industry. Colloquially, some confuse tail or extreme risks with operational risks, while others believe that they are part of enterprise risk management or strategic risk management. And, then finally, extreme risk is many times used as a synonym for event risk, systemic risk, and emerging risk. I will briefly describe each of these risks and how they interact with extreme risk. In the first instance, I will delve into the fields of operational, enterprise, and strategic risk management. And, below graphic illustration highlights how extreme risk interacts with each of these three specific fields of risk management.

3.8.1. Operational Risk Management

The risk management of disruptive events is partly dealt with by operational risk management. Indeed, "operational risk can be created by a wide range of different external events, ranging from power failures to floods or earthquakes to terrorist attacks." (vander Straeten, 2017) Similarly, operational risk can arise as a result of internal events, such as the potential for failures or inadequacies in any of the bank's processes and systems (e.g., IT, risk management, or human resource management processes and systems), or those of its outsourced service providers.

Under typical operational risk management (ORM) framework, the financial firm assesses the potential risk for such events to happen and designs and implements disaster recovery systems and procedures to ensuring continuity of activity (also known as the business recovery plan). Additionally, against the monetary loss derived from such operational events, the firm evaluates the potential cost and puts in place proper mitigation techniques. Operational risk can equally arise from human resource mismanagement, such as mismanaged or poorly trained employees, employee negligence or willful misconduct, conflicts of interest, fraud, and rogue trading. Therefore, failure to communicate, low morale, the emergence of mistrust, increased turnover, and cynicism among staff members are regarded as early-warning signs for a potential increase in operational risk.

In the scope of the banking industry, I will grab the definition from the Basel Committee as it relates to operational risk (BCBS, 2016): "the risk of a change in value caused by the fact that actual losses, incurred for inadequate or failed internal processes, people and systems, or from external events (including legal risk), differ from the expected losses".

Research on operational risk is a vast scientific discipline, close to quality management. In a similar fashion, operational risks affect reputation, client satisfaction, and shareholder value, all while business volatility is increasing. The Basel II definition of operational risk excludes, for example, strategic risk – the risk of a loss arising from a poor strategic business decision. However, from an extreme risk perspective, strategic mistakes are part of the scope. Overall, these delineations of scope illustrate that extreme risk is a grab bag of many kinds of risk that are rare and/or extreme nature. Rare and regular operational risk events illustrated with a loss distribution.

3.8.2. Enterprise Risk Management

Enterprise risk focuses on the risks generated in the scope of achieving an entity's objectives. Most organizational objectives can be subdivided into four main categories for enterprise risks: strategic, operational, reporting, and compliance. Strategic risks are one of the components of enterprise risks. So, in practice, this means that the ERM function will have an overall helicopter view on all the risks that affect the financial firm (credit risk, market risk, liquidity risk, funding risk, operational risk, interest rate risk, legal risk, IT risk, reputation risk, etc.) and will integrate the findings of each risk area with concepts on internal controls and strategic planning. Given its scope, ERM is deemed capable of addressing "the needs of various stakeholders who want to understand the broad spectrum of risks facing complex organizations to ensure they are appropriately managed" (Bardin, 2007).

Typically, this involves pinpointing specific events or circumstances relevant to the objectives of the organization (risks and rewards), evaluating them in terms of likelihood and severity, determining a strategy to respond, and monitoring progress. Unfortunately, many of these organizations that do embrace an ERM framework tend to continue to focus mainly on near-term (predictable and quantifiable) risks without paying adequate attention to "emerging risks" (i.e., those risk issues that have not manifested themselves sufficiently to be managed using the tools commonly applied to more developed exposures and with those that have a low likelihood).

The traditional ERM process that revolves around principles such as risk identification, evaluation, relief, and monitoring have its foundation on a somewhat simplified view of the world (Fiksel, et al., 2014). Each risk is identified and addressed independently, and hidden interactions and correlations are rarely revealed through this method. This procedural method can soothe organizations into a false sense of security that could be blasted by a random event (for example, an oil spill in the Gulf of Mexico). Given its scope, ERM is deemed capable of addressing the needs of various stakeholders who want to understand the broad spectrum of risks facing complex organizations to ensure they are appropriately managed.

Typically, this involves identifying particular events or circumstances relevant to the organization's objectives (risks and opportunities), assessing them in terms of likelihood and magnitude of impact, determining a response strategy, and monitoring progress (Narvaez, n.d.). Unfortunately, many of these organizations that do embrace an ERM framework tend to continue to focus mainly on near-term (predictable and quantifiable) risks without paying adequate attention to "emerging risks" (i.e., those risk issues that have not manifested themselves sufficiently to be managed using the tools commonly applied to more developed exposures and with those that have a low likelihood).

Hence, there is a "cry in the dark" for allowing ERM to evolve in the near future into emerging risk management rather than traditional enterprise risk management. Emerging risks are those risks an organization has not yet recognized or those that are known to exist but are not well understood (Diebold, 2010). These are Donald Rumsfeld's famous "known unknowns" and "unknown unknowns."

Nowadays, an ERM program that does not address the potential challenges created by the existence and development of emerging risks will not meet its goal of protecting and generating opportunity for the organization. Indeed, the recent GFC, which was identified early by some risk managers as an emerging risk, raised many serious questions, some of which focused on the effectiveness of risk management practices and, more specifically, ERM.

There was a failure to use enterprise risk management to inform management's decision making for both risk-taking and risk-avoiding decisions. There was also a failure to embed the best practices of ERM from the top all the way down to the trading floor, with the mistaken assumption that there is only one way to view a particular risk (SEC, 2009).

3.8.3. Strategic Risk Management

Strategic risks are risks that affect or are created by an organization's business strategy and strategic objectives, or in other words risks relating to formation or implementation of a business strategy. Operational risks are major risks that affect an organization's ability to execute its strategic plan. Strategic risk can be broken down into strategic positioning risk and strategic execution risk. Strategic positioning risk refers to the whether the bank is headed in the right direction with its strategy.

Strategic execution risk refers to whether the strategy is being executed properly, and if the objectives are still meaningful. Despite its significance, the coverage of strategic risk in the academic literature has been rather scarce. While the other forms of risk described above have clear definitions, there is no single, unified definition of strategic risk or business risk. In addition to having clear definitions, the other forms of risk, especially credit risk, also have been treated extensively from a risk management perspective. One possible reason for the scarcity in the coverage of strategic risk could be that it has been considered as a part of operational risk, as in Schroeck (2002). Another contributing factor could be that from a practical perspective, the question of who is responsible for the management of strategic risk in a bank arises (Stulz, 2014).

While processes such as ORM/ ERM/ SRM can help companies avoid financial market and supply chain disruptions, as well as recover normal operations quickly, they also have serious limitations (Fiksel, 2015):

First, they rely too heavily on risk identification. In a complex and turbulent global supply network, many of the risks that a company faces are unpredictable or unknowable before the event happens. These "emergent" risks are often triggered by improbable events whose causes are not understood, and their potential cascading effects are difficult to understand a priori. Clearly, it would be impractical for companies to identify and investigate all the potential risks that may be hidden in their global supply chains.

Second, they depend on statistical information that may not exist. Risk assessments are limited by the quality and credibility of the assumptions on which they are based, and faulty assumptions or data can lead to misallocation of resources. Of particular challenge are low-probability, high-consequence events for which there is little empirical knowledge; managers may underestimate the probabilities of these events or the magnitudes of their consequences because they have never experienced them.

Third, the traditional process of risk identification, assessment, mitigation, and monitoring is based on a simplified, "reductionist" view of the world. Each risk is identified and addressed independently, and hidden interactions are seldom recognized. This procedural approach can lull organizations into a false sense of complacency that could be shattered by an unexpected event (for instance, an oil spill in the Gulf of Mexico).

The complex, dynamic nature of global financial markets and supply chains requires constant vigilance to discern systemic vulnerabilities, as well as exceptional agility and flexibility when disruptions occur. Organizations need to improve how they deal with financial market and supply chain complexity and unexpected disruptions so that they can prosper in the face of turbulent change. Organizations tend to become less resilient as they grow more complex. However, they can cultivate resilience by understanding their vulnerabilities and developing specific capabilities to cope with disruptions.

They can try to emulate some of the behaviors seen in natural systems—tolerance for variability, continuous adaptation, and exploitation of opportunities created by disruptive forces. Depending on the type of disturbance, the adaptation can be rapid or gradual.

3.9. Banking Risks Affected By Extreme Events

Generally speaking, banking regulators have defined the following types of risks that banks typically face: credit risk, country and transfer risk, market risk, interest rate risk, liquidity risk, operational risk, legal risk and reputational risk. In the U.S., the OCC in the scope of its prudential objectives has described nine types of risks, namely: credit, interest rate, liquidity, price, foreign exchange, transaction, compliance, strategic and reputation.

But, many of these risk categories can be summarized as follows, as mandated by the Basel Committee: credit, market, liquidity and operation risk, with the latter being a catch-all basket. Extreme events affect each of these risk categories, and the 2007 financial crisis has highlighted the unanticipated character of such extreme events.

As outlined in previous sections, extreme events can be categorized either as:

- rare phenomena that can have known extreme effects (based on experiences from history, such as wars, natural disasters, hyper economic conditions, etc.)
- unknown events for which there is no historic experience and imagination lacks

While the former can be anticipated, the latter cannot, as it is restricted by a lack of experience or foresight. Risk managers need to look both backwards and forwards when contemplating extreme events. However, habits that assume continuity of past events and a check-the-box risk management approach remains, alas, durable. A bank can be confronted with several kinds of potential losses: expected losses, unexpected losses, and exceptional or extreme losses.

- The expected loss from a statistics perspective is determined as the average of the credit losses expected from an individual exposure (or portfolio of exposures) over a given time given normal market conditions.
- The unexpected loss is defined as the mean total loss beyond the average loss, and it is measured as the standard deviation from the mean within a specific confidence level given normal market conditions.
- The exceptional or extreme loss is the total loss beyond the loss percentile defined by a confidence level. Extreme losses are in excess of the sum of expected loss plus unexpected loss, and can go up to the total value of the exposure.

Market risk suffers from a similar pathology correlation effects can be unanticipated, hence rendering them difficult to trace. Other sources of extreme events affecting market risk can be with respect to volatility), warehousing risk, or reputation risk. Similar to credit risk and market risk, liquidity risk models have demonstrated their inability to value extreme events, in turn impacting the market risk and funding risk under global scenarios. Lastly, operational risk within the banking industry include also extreme events that can result in significant losses, and not merely in terms of immediate cash flow impact, but also in terms of reputation.

3.10. How Do Extreme Events Affect Credit Risk?

Whether it is Basel I, Basel II, or Basel III – all these Basel regimes cope with measuring and managing credit risk chiefly by compelling banks to uphold regulatory capital cushions aim to absorb losses caused by credit events through the measurement of the credit risk. Banks are relying on historical data to assess the likelihood and severity of a credit loss, and inherently assume reasonably foreseeable conditions with no strong default correlation among individual risk assets (loans, securities, credit facilities). In other words, under ordinary conditions, the prediction of credit defaults is determined by the use of historical data whereby there is also no strong default correlation and assuming relatively prosperous market conditions. However, in an environment of extreme events, credit risk quantification will be impaired as a result of the absence of adequate data and the failed assumptions that default correlations will remain low.

Thus, the existing Basel regimes, such as the Basel II framework (International convergence of capital measurement and capital standards) struggle to create a failsafe environment. Many scholars have already indicated that the blind application of mathematical theories have destroyed the financial markets. The Deputy General of the Bank for International Settlements also stated: it is now clear that quantitative finance methodologies and internal risk modelling techniques based on normality assumption and historical statistical relationships have failed to capture the extreme events which occur in periods of systemic stress.

The BIS pinpoints to the inability of risk models to apprehend extreme events because the hypotheses on market liquidity, volatility, and correlations are backward-looking. One can refer to the tenacious refusal of these models to formulate market conditions where extreme and rare events could even be assumed as a distant likelihood. Mandelbrot indicated that that extreme events dominate real-life economic systems the extreme cases, where with the techniques advocated by Basel III techniques the determination of the capital level is determined by historical and current data, even though very few data exists on extreme events. Granted, Basel in its most recent release advocates for the first time the use of forecast data based on, for example, surveys. "The effects of possible future credit loss events on ECL must be considered" . However, these forecast data are known to be sticky, in the sense that professional forecasters and survey respondents do not always take into account incoming information. In other words, the level of regulatory capital assumes a certain level of risk; however, under extreme conditions, those levels of risks become equally extreme rendering the existing capital buffer as insufficient.

The underlying hypotheses on default correlations do not hold through as extreme market conditions cause defaulted assets to exhibit high correlations. An extreme event affects a large number of individual assets concomitantly where the response to a cohort of default becomes totally different from a response to an individual default. Not only does the probability of default increase under an extreme event, but the loss given default becomes equally more severe as a result of a deep drop in collateral values, and thus in recovery rates.

Risk mitigation under an extreme scenario does no longer apply, particularly because of the nature of the banking industry. Banks tend to mimic each other's investment policies (not only driven by risk return rationale, but also by regulatory environment due to similar risk weights being allocated to certain assets (f.ex. under the standardized approach, claims on sovereigns rated AAA to AA- are risk weighted at 0%, or corporate AAA to AA- set at 20%) (SEC, 2019). Banks are incentivized to use similar risk models to measure credit risk causing a herd effect as a result of the model risk. This has an amplifying effect on destabilized markets, as … "existing risk management models treat the risks of positions as exogeneous and are therefore of little use to financial institutions in evaluating the risks created by model-driven behavior, either their own behavior or that of other institutions".

It has been shown that the use of internal risk models (under the IRB approach) is also an incentive for banks to game, manipulate and calibrate their own models in order to minimize the amount of capital. Despite progress, the ongoing adoption of quantitative models by banks to calculate capital requirements is subject to critique not only by banking regulators, but also by scholars. All these separate observations tend to lead to the conclusion that the existing level of regulatory capital is inadequate to shield banks from the effects of extreme conditions. The minimum capital requirements are merely illusive and do not mirror the reality.

Or, in other words, banks would need to substantially increase their capital levels, thereby hurting their profitability, particularly that historically speaking banks used to hold more capital. While banks in the early 1900s were less diversified and could not rely on a deposit insurance mechanism, and thus could not be compared to today's banks, it is noteworthy to observe that U.S. and British banks used to have a higher risk-weighted capital, oscillating around 16-24% compared to 6% since the 1950s making them more vulnerable to financial crises. Additionally, the comparison is even more rude, when highlighting the capital ratio of nonfinancial companies (cf. it was at approximately 30-40% on the eve of the 2007 global financial crisis).

But, even with the implementation of Basel III and recent amendments to it, banking systems seems to be more prone to financial crises. In other words, the wide spread adoption of the international Basel regulations (cf. even the recent Basel III) has caused banks to sing the same tune as it relates to the use of risk management techniques (Strickland, 2017) and is not shielding them from a future systemic crisis.

It is the nature of the Basel regulations themselves with respect to leverage and capital rules that is making banks more susceptible to disruptions and shocks. The FDIC came up with a study arguing that the leverage ratio should be at least twice what is being implemented as the prescribed 3% ratio is deemed to inadequately take into account the mispricing of risks, not to mention the variations in weighting in the trading book. Not only do the recent Basel III rules bring an economic cost to banks, and the economy overall (such as the impact in terms of funding cost and credit spreads, for instance), but the overall requirements in terms of capital and leverage are deemed insufficient given the rising debt level on the global stage, particularly in the wake of the coronavirus pandemic.

3.11. The Extreme Loss

All areas of risk management are affected by extreme risk phenomena, including credit risk. One of the most significant questions for a risk manager is therefore how to design a risk management framework that not only contemplates the existence of extreme risks, but also the ramifications of an extreme risk event to be measured.

Extreme loss is also labeled as exceptional loss or stress loss, and this is the loss beyond the confidence level for an unexpected loss. The exceptional loss is not included in the unexpected loss as it equals the loss beyond the loss percentile determined by a given confidence level. Exceptional losses are above and beyond the sum of expected loss and unexpected loss (and that sum is equal to the loss percentile). The use of extreme risk models or stress scenarios may help find the range and severity of these losses.

As it relates to credit risk, the objective of risk management is to determine risk capital that is sufficient to absorb unforeseen losses from credit events, such as for example rating downgrades and defaults. The volume of risk capital, retained by banking organizations in line with the Basel agreements, is related to the risk at the portfolio level, and the two typical risk measures adopted to assess such risks are the Value at Risk and Expected Shortfall methods.

The modelling of extreme risk relies on the typical mathematical method that is articulated around the notion of a probability distribution where the extreme risk is situated at the tail of the distribution. While a bank might compute a variance or mean of a risk, the latter measure does not say much about an extreme risk event. Therefore, banks will embrace two popular techniques to measure extreme risk, namely Value at Risk and expected shortfall.

Generally speaking, a risk measure endeavors to determine a single numerical value to a potential random financial loss. Thus, it is of great significance to design a good risk measure that is meaningful both for the risk manager and the regulator. Within the literature, there is a couple of must-haves for good risk measures, aka coherent risk measure, such as:

- monotonicity
- translation invariance
- positive homogeneity
- subadditivity

Bearing in mind above criteria that define a 'good' measure, the VaR measure shows flaws only in terms of subadditivity. Indeed, a drawback of the VaR method is that it is not sub-additive, i.e., the VaR of two sub-portfolios can be larger than the VaR of the total portfolio, thus not taking into account the pooling and diversification effects.

The incoherence of the VaR method can be an issue for a risk management governance that is based on VaR limits of individual loan books or investment portfolio. Like any other mathematical model, a VaR measure is only as good as the underlying hypotheses and the data inputs. Note also that different VaR methods will result to different VaR measures for the same portfolio, because the VaR can be calculated using a historical VaR, a variance-covariance parametric VaR or the Monte Carlo VaR approach.

The expected shortfall (ES) method for quantifying risk was put into existence as an alternative to the VaR that is insufficiently sensitive to the shape of the tail of the loss distribution. The VaR is adopted as a statistical method to quantify the volume of potential loss due to market changes that could affect an investment portfolio over a given time period. The popularity of the VaR method resides in the fact that it aggregates all risks into a single measure.

Even the Basel Committee has indicated that there is an alternative to the drawbacks of the VaR approach, namely by shifting the attention to the ES measure, to be adopted both for the standardized and internal rating-based methods. The VaR method is being discussed in the section on market risk. Shocks impact the shape of the tail of the loss distribution in distinct ways. The ES method measures the risk of an investment in terms of expected return in the worst x% of cases, however bearing in mind a specific confidence level and assuming a Gaussian distribution of the asset returns. In practice, an expected shortfall is equal to the average amount lost over, for example, a 10-day period, and that is greater than the 99th percentile of the loss distribution.

The ES is also known as the expected tail loss, Conditional Value at Risk, and Average Value at Risk. The ES is defined as the expected loss that is greater than the VaR at a specific confidence level. The ES method is known to be more suited to capture extreme risks in the tail of the loss distribution under both normal and stressed market conditions. The ES is sub-additive, meaning that by taking into account, amongst others, the diversification effect, the sum of two individual sub-portfolios is smaller than the ES of the total portfolio. However, while the ES approach is a risk measure that provides more information on extreme losses, similar to the VaR, different estimation models for the ES will yield different ES measures. Note that in order for the ES approach to yield a risk measure that is as accurate as the VaR measure, typically larger data sets are needed. In other words, the ES measure is less trustworthy than the VaR for meager sets of data.

In terms of retrospective testing, while it is challenging to back-test one-day 99% risk measures yielded by the ES approach, there are some methods available to back-test the ES. ES estimates can in some cases be less accurate than VaR measure, meaning that the required capital derived from ES measures may be less stable than capital determined by VaR measures. Noteworthy is that in order to apprehend the impact of market behavior under extreme events, the implementation of the VaR and ES will take place under the assumption of Extreme Value Theory (EVT).

Both the VaR and ES risk measurement approaches take into account changes in the market only very slow, and thus these relatively static methods do not sufficiently consider recent changes in terms of market conditions. This also means that for either risk measure, the back-testing of a stressed model is very difficult as the risk manager does not have another stressed period to use for back-testing. Indeed, while some of the calculation methods for each of these risk measures assume a distribution of asset returns that follow a Gaussian distribution, in reality market crashes exhibit extreme changes in asset returns that are not compatible with the assumption of normality.

Apart from expected shortfall, stress scenarios are an alternative method to assess the worst possible losses under extreme conditions in the scope of portfolio risk management. Stress scenarios can either be static or dynamic, and are adopted as a method by banks for the quantification of the resilience of the loan books and investment portfolios to both historical and hypothetical adverse market conditions.

The distinction between static and dynamic stress testing resides in the sense that dynamic stress tests focus on forecasts for macroeconomic and financial variables that are directly mirrored in the projections for the financial statements of the bank. A static stress testing is articulated around balance sheets that do not change through the forecast horizon.

In the aftermath of the global financial crisis, the use of bank stress tests has become more prominent and established as a critical tool in the arsenal of bank regulators.

In practice, the underlying idea is that a stress tests enables to assess how a system or an asset will cope under pressure and impact the balance sheet and profitability of the banking organization.

Stress scenarios first emerged in the 1990s as a supplement to existing mathematical models to quantify risks on the banks' trading books and was formalized by the Basel Committee in the scope of the prudential capital framework for market risk (Basel Committee on Banking Supervision, 1996). A couple of years before the occurrence of the global financial crisis, Basel II had determined the need for additional stress testing, namely in the scope of credit risks, albeit this development was still in its infancy.

These post-GFC stress tests focused on providing banking institutions with early warning signals helping them fend off funding gaps and deficits in liquidity, unexpected losses, and plausible insolvency. In the U.S., it was the Federal Reserve Bank that first adopted in 2009 stress test with the US Supervisory Capital Assessment Program (SCAP) which was a much more adverse macro-economic stress scenario than the anticipated path of the economy in those days. Subsequently, the SCAP has been acknowledged as a crucial vector in helping stabilizing the US banking system.

Over the last years, U.S. regulators have introduced a new annual assessment consisting of the Comprehensive Capital Analysis and Review (CCAR) and the Dodd-Frank Act Stress Tests (DFAST), as a way to help regulate and supervise bank holding companies. These testing programs, that have both a qualitative and quantitative aspect, aim to assess the capital adequacy given a range of stress test scenarios and determine the opportunity for these bank holding companies to distribute dividends. Together with the Basel III stress testing, these assessments help assess the risks that may threaten the viability of these banks as a going concern.

However, stress testing can be challenging when attempting to exhaustively modelize systemic risks, as it is difficult to assess the impact of a bank's results onto other banks. Integrating liquidity risk, or funding risk, particularly the non-linear relationship with the solvency of bank, can also prove to be difficult. Noteworthy is that, similar to the VaR and ES risk measures for potential losses, stress tests can provide a false sense of security by applying preferred stress scenarios, and thus overestimating the absorption capacity of the banks' capital (Gross and Población, 2015). Likewise, risk managers and regulators alike tend to suffer from a lack of imagination and fail to take the findings of these stress tests seriously.

3.12. How Do Extreme Events Affect Market Risk?

Generally speaking, the VaR can give a misleading false sense of security and does not say much about the maximum possible losses beyond the confidence level. The VaR method is best applicable under stable market conditions, as in times of crisis extreme changes in market prices are greater due to the amplification of spillovers.

Another drawback of the VaR method relates to its inability to adequately calculate the correlation effect for large portfolios, particularly that when under stress correlation between asset prices tend to breakdown. Scholars have found that the " VaR error increases significantly as the correlation error increases, particularly in the case of well-diversified linear portfolios"

Given that the Basel rules assume that assets held in the trading book are marked-to-market, extreme changes in market prices can result in sudden changes in capital, and hence the mark-to-market accounting can have a destabilizing effect. The consequence of fluctuations in market prices is that assets held under M-t-M (or fair value) will cause capital to also fluctuate: a decrease in market values results in capital consumption (and vice versa) with unrealized gains and losses accounted under "accumulated other comprehensive income" within the equity section of the balance sheet.

From a capital maintenance perspective, when market prices fall broadly abruptly across all asset classes, the bank may suffer a sudden drop in capital, and hence the need from a regulatory perspective to raise additional capital. However, the latter will be more costly, literally because the bank's financial profile is at its most frail status. In other words, subsequent to the M-to-M rule that no longer allow for banks to weather the storm until market conditions ameliorate, the ruination of capital will occur despite everything. Drop in market values can be caused by multiple sources, such as liquidity risk, FX risk (Melvin and Taylor, 2009), interest rate risk (Hull et al., 2005), rating migration risk, and credit spread risk.

In the scope of the originate-distribute model, banks have been embracing the securitization as a one of the risk tools to reduce risk (apparently) through asset pooling. However, securitization can magnify the effects of extreme market conditions during a financial crisis. For example, in the case of securitized real estate assets, they are deemed "riskier than the broader stock market during a financial turmoil". Additionally, the nature of some of the underlying assets (i.e., leveraged assets) of the securitized assets (cf. in a SPV structure) coupled with the level of seniority (tranche) held by the bank can markedly increase the vulnerability of the bank.

Compounding the risk even further are the so-called mark-to-market prices of these securitized assets (cf. for example, MBS), that are mostly synthetic prices derived from mispriced underlying assets (cf. such as CDO assets) (Deng et al., 2011, p. 28), further illustrating that synthetic pricing cannot be a substitute to robust credit underwriting. Such drop in market prices under mark-to-market accounting may cause significant drops in capital, in turn requiring higher demands for capital.

Extreme events can also expose previously underappreciated risks, such as pipeline risk (i.e., where markets are no longer receptive for warehoused assets held by banks meant for distribution due to a precipitous drop in asset values. Such involuntary longer than expected warehousing can subject a bank to these mark-to-market driven losses, such as illustrated by the $23.9 billion write-off Wachovia suffered in the wake of the global financial crisis in 2008 in relation to its real estate financing business.

With the onset of the global financial crisis, a statistical tool has gained in popularity in dealing with the measurement of market risk under extreme conditions: Extreme Value Theory. EVT is has been adopted for the calculation of risk measures, such as Value at Risk or Expected Shortfall, that need to be computed, even when market conditions are extreme. And, numerous scholars and have documented that EVT provides a far-reaching theoretical framework on which statistical models characterizing extreme scenarios can be defined. Recent studies show that historical methods tend to overestimate the VaR (thus requiring more capital) while the variance-covariance tend to underestimate the VaR for extreme events. Instead, EVT provides adequate distributions to fit extreme events, as unlike VaR and ES, EVT makes no hypotheses on the nature of the distribution of all observations.

Notwithstanding the advantages that the adoption of the EVT brings, such as complementing the VaR model, supported by a rigorous body of mathematical theory, or providing robust means of modelling, there are also some drawbacks, such as:

- EVT is not a cure for risk management as numerous theoretical issues remain unaddressed (f.ex. multiple dependent risk factors)
- EVT implicitly postulates that today's extreme losses are not worse than those more than a decade ago

Chapter 4. Alternatives

4.1. Alternative #1: Three Lines Of Defense

As they navigate volatile conditions, banks have been advised to adopt or maintain a more holistic, integrated approach to managing risk and uncertainty. This was meant to include ongoing emphasis of the 'three lines of defense' framework. This framework is designed to help organizations:

- Clearly identify the roles and responsibilities of their business unit (first line).
- Practice ongoing risk management using standard-setters or risk-oversight groups that are responsible for establishing policies and procedures (second line).
- Sustain effective risk-management activities via independent assurance providers who report independently to the board or the board's audit committee (third line).

Properly implemented, the three lines of defense is meant to create dialogue and analysis aimed at preventing banks from overlooking emerging risk that could ultimately cause financial disaster, while also prompting banks to effectively manage ongoing risk across the organization.

In the "three lines of defense" model, business lines are the first lines of defense in risk management, as they own the risk, while the various control and compliance oversight functions resting with the risk management function act as the second line of defense, and independent assurance is the third line of defense.

Within the financial services sector, risk management traditionally takes the form of erection of external defenses through global and national regulations. Internal defenses habitually take the form of the three lines of defense model, which portrays three parties as the core to good risk management:

- Operational staff within the business who take frontline responsibility for assessing, measuring, and monitoring risks
- Risk management function
- Internal auditing whose role is to provide board-level assurance on the effectiveness of internal controls

However, there are several problems. This model is not what usually happens, and it would not be desirable if it did (Bonish, 2013):

First, managers in these control functions seldom collaborate with operations managers. Control processes are usually developed in isolation from operating managers and other control functions. Collaboration is rare and coordination more so.

Second, control processes do not constitute a line of defense in most circumstances. Most controls are detective rather than preventive. Only preventive controls constitute a line of defense and then only at the operating level (therefore, they are an essential element of the "first line of defense"), which is where the metaphor breaks down. Detective controls allow intervention and workarounds to address a problem after the fact. That is not a line of defense; it is a line of remediation.

Third, the role of the internal audit is also not a line of defense. It is, or should be, the provision of comfort that operating functions are properly specified from a control perspective; that preventive controls, where feasible, are developed and operating effectively; and that, where they are not, detective or compensating controls are instituted and monitored and remedial action is subsequently taken.

Lastly, to think of an internal audit as a line of defense is asinine. It does not and should not do any such thing. It is not operating either preventively or "detectively" at a transactional level. It is there to provide assurance that operating management is fulfilling its control job and that support managers are supporting operating managers to do so. It is not there to intervene in the normal transaction flow as a control stage.

That is why in Australia and New Zealand, for example, internal auditing is not part of the third line of defense; instead, there is a dedicated department called assurance that embodies the third line of defense. While the "three lines of defense" model for risk management has been accepted as a best practice by banking regulators and the Basel Committee on Banking Supervision, the internal audit function should be replaced by a risk assurance function.

The assurance department's responsibilities include the following, among others:

- Assisting in the development of the overall strategy and approach to risk and compliance assurance in line with the risk management framework, anti–money laundering (AML), and compliance management framework
- Developing the AML and compliance assurance plan and ensuring this takes a risk-based approach in identifying areas to be assessed and monitored throughout the year
- Collaborating with managers and peers to ensure that the AML and compliance assurance plan is coordinated with other risk assurance classes to minimize gaps and overlaps and to provide end-to-end coverage across organizational boundaries
- Reviewing and revising plans to reflect changes in the risk and compliance environment
- Ensuring delivery of AML and compliance assurance in accordance with the plan
- Reporting to management on findings of substance and working with them to resolve issues and improve operational risk management in their area
- Tracking the resolution of significant issues identified during assurance activity
- Providing concise, integrated risk reporting on the effectiveness of AML and compliance risk management

- Assisting to develop and maintain strong relationships with external and internal auditors to achieve a coordinated and integrated program of assurance for the division

The Swiss cheese model portrays risk management as a series of slices of cheese that act as defenses against the impact of "holes" or ineffective controls that may arise because of either active failure in control systems (e.g., IT breakdown) or latent conditions that can cause holes in the defense slices. These latter conditions are caused by inherent weaknesses in the defenses that increase their susceptibility to failure, such as an organizational culture that does not see risk management as important.

In other words: defenses, barriers, and safeguards occupy a key position in the system approach. High technology systems have many defensive layers: some are engineered (alarms, physical barriers, automatic shutdowns, etc.), others rely on people (surgeons, anesthetists, pilots, control room operators, etc.), and yet others depend on procedures and administrative controls. Their function is to protect potential victims and assets from local hazards. Mostly they do this very effectively, but there are always weaknesses.

In an ideal world each defensive layer would be intact. In reality, however, they are more like slices of Swiss cheese, having many holes—though unlike in the cheese, these holes are continually opening, shutting, and shifting their location. The presence of holes in any one "slice" does not normally cause a bad outcome. Usually, this can happen only when the holes in many layers momentarily line up to permit a trajectory of accident opportunity—bringing hazards into damaging contact with victims.[6]

The holes in the defenses arise for two reasons: active failures and latent conditions. Nearly all adverse events involve a combination of these two sets of factors. Active failures are the unsafe acts committed by people who are in direct contact with the patient or system. They take a variety of forms: slips, lapses, fumbles, mistakes, and procedural violations. Active failures have a direct and usually short-lived impact on the integrity of the defenses.

A recent illustrative example of an active failure is the infamous incident that took place in Fukushima, Japan, in March 2011 when operators (TEPCO) did a poor risk assessment and collateral damage management, leading to a domino effect with the tragic consequences we all know. Followers of the person approach often look no further for the causes of an adverse event once they have identified these proximal unsafe acts. But virtually all such acts have a causal history that extends back in time and up through the levels of the system. Indeed, latent conditions arise from decisions made by not only designers and builders but also top-level management. Such decisions may be mistaken, but they need not be. All such strategic decisions have the potential for introducing viruses into the system (Behm and Powell, 2014).

Latent conditions—as the term suggests—may be a sleeping disease that lurks beneath the surface within the system for many years before combining with active failures and local triggers to create an accident opportunity. The good news is that latent conditions can be identified and remedied before an adverse event occurs; understanding this leads to proactive rather than reactive risk management.

With respect to active failures, while we cannot alter the human condition, we can change the conditions under which humans work. To use another analogy: active failures are like rodents. They can be killed one by one, but they still keep coming. The best remedies are to create more effective defenses and to clean up the sewers in which they breed. The sewers, in this case, are the ever-present latent conditions.

The risk imbalances may occur within a company's control environment, risk architecture, or the overall information and understanding of risk. If the imbalances are redefined, then one-off holes may not matter. A company can manage isolated failures in its control system.

If, however, many different holes occur together and are aligned, then the overall system comes under threat of failure, even if the individual lines of defense are in place. That is the risk with the Swiss cheese model. Citibank, Barclays, RBS, Fortis, UBS, and so on provide examples of how seemingly good defense systems can be undermined by risk imbalances.

The powerful latent forces of a segmented business model, combined with a lack of common purpose about risk management across the firm, ultimately produce the ingredients for failure. There is an element of hazard in the fact that the holes may or may not align, but if they do align, then problems abound. The central lesson of the Swiss cheese model is that defense structures alone are not sufficient. How they interact is also of critical importance, but this is a matter of human relations and issues of relative knowledge and power.

4.2. Alternative #2: Basel 3.5

For more than two years now, supervisors, banks and policymakers have been discussing draft proposals from the Basel Committee to change the international requirements for the risk models used by banks. In these proposals (known as 'completion of Basel III' or 'Basel IV', we will stay with 'Basel 3.5' in this paper) there is a radical new view of risk models and supervisors will impose additional limitations on the banks in their modelling of risk (Rabobank, 2018).

Where are we now? The Basel Committee for Banking Supervision (BCBS, hereinafter: 'the Basel Committee') has drawn up a package of new prudential rules for banks, consisting of a revision to the standard approach to credit risk, the introduction of a capital floor based on standardized approaches, the use of internal models, limitation of options for modelling operating risks, and new rules for the establishment of risk-weighted items and unused credit lines at the banks. The separate elements of the package are now (largely) completed at a technical level, and the debate in Basel is turning to the final calibration. The proposals are connected and their effects are cumulative. The total capital effect should be moderate (agreement in the G20) and the different elements should strengthen each other and not contradict each other.

The Basel Committee therefore already stated in advance that it wished to present the proposals to the 'Group of Governors and Heads of Supervision' (GHOS) as an integrated package. This proved to be difficult and the presentation has been postponed several times. If the Basel Committee and GHOS reach agreement, then this does not yet mean that the recommendations will be implemented, as a parliamentary process will then follow. This will happen in all the jurisdictions that normally implement Basel guidelines. Broad-based support is essential for this.

The proposals are controversial because they do not take proper account of collateralization and differences in markets and legal systems between countries. The result may be less lending, or more expensive lending than otherwise would have been the case. The first problem concerns the possible introduction of an international minimum capital floor that prescribes that the result of calculations of internal bank models must amount to a certain minimum fixed percentage of the result on the basis of a standard model. For banks with an international 'average' portfolio of loans on an 'average' bank balance sheet and with an 'averagely robust' system of bankruptcy law in the country in which they operate, this is not a problem. It is also not a problem for loans with a high-risk profile, since high risk weights already apply. Paradoxically, it is mainly a problem for loans with relatively 'secure' collateral and for banks with a low risk profile.

The standard capital floor will have disproportionate consequences for European mortgage banks and agricultural banks with strong collateral security and low loss ratios. The banks most unduly affected will actually be those with a high proportion of low-risk banking activities and which also use internal modelling. Regarding mortgages, there is also no account taken of the existence of a (statutory or otherwise) maximum loan principal for households in a country or the presence of a good social security system so that there is more certainty that households will be able to continue to afford a mortgage. In this case the financing risk of mortgages is lower than the international average risk norm set by the capital floor.2 Despite the fact that increasing the level of capital in a banking system and an even more prudent estimation of risk will be welcomed by many, it is extraordinary that the package will seriously affect loans that are well collateralized. We consider this to be an indication that the package has not been properly calibrated.

Apart from mortgages and agricultural loans, Basel 3.5 will also increase the minimum capital reserves for trade and project finance. Given the social and economic importance of these activities, there needs to be further consideration of whether this is indeed proportional for all countries. Trade and commerce are important for the economy.

Furthermore, and probably unintentionally, the package will have damaging effects on operations of banks in developing countries and emerging markets. The proposals do not make sufficient distinction between different situations. For project and trade finance, in practice it makes a great deal of difference that a bank has many years of expertise in a market segment and is a large professional party. This is why banks have invested for years in increasing their expertise, knowledge of sectors and knowledge of risk modelling. This needs to be better reflected in the proposals than currently is the case.

Moreover, the requirements could lead to incentives for making an incorrect evaluation of risk and return. As was the case after Basel I, it will become attractive to dispose of low credit risks that are affected by the minimum floor to external investors and keep high risk loans on the book. If the regulator's calibration is not correct, the markets will arbitrage this. This emphasizes the importance of accurately establishing these criteria. Banks and supervisors from many European countries, Canada, Australia and Japan have urgently called for improvements to the proposals. Despite compromise proposals by the Basel Committee and from Ingves, its chair, several attempts to reach an agreement in the GHOS that is acceptable to all supervisors have failed (Rabobank, 2017).

4.3. Alternative #3: Basel IV

Basel IV is a contested term for the changes agreed in 2016 and 2017 to the international banking standards known as the Basel Accords; regulators argue that these changes are simply completing the Basel III reforms, agreed in principle in 2010-11, although most of the Basel III reforms were agreed in detail at that time. Critics of the reform, in particular those from the banking industry, argue that Basel IV require a significant increase in capital and should be treated as a distinct round of reforms.

The purpose of the Basel reform package ("Basel IV") was to establish a global minimum standard for dealing with the past financial crisis and at the same time to prevent new crises by increasing the capitalization of the institutions. The finalization took place in December 2017 by the Group of Central Bank Governors and Heads of Supervision (GHOS).

Basel IV introduces changes that limit the reduction in capital that can result from Banks' use of internal models under the Internal Ratings-Based approach. This includes:

- A standardized floor, so that the capital requirement will always be at least 72.5% of the requirement under the Standardized approach;
- A simultaneous reduction in standardized risk weights for low-risk mortgage loans;
- Requiring banks to meet higher maximum leverage ratios (an initial leverage ratio maximum is likely to be set as part of the completion of the Basel III package);
- A higher leverage ratio for Global Systemically Important Banks (G-SIBs), with the increase equal to 50% of the risk adjusted capital ratio
- More detailed disclosure of reserves and other financial statistics.

British banks alone may have to raise another £50Bn in capital in order to meet Basel 4 requirements. The average Common Equity Tier 1 (CET1) capital ratio for major European banks is estimated to fall by 0.9%, with the biggest impact on banks in Sweden and Denmark of 2.5% - 3%. Basel III's rules increased the amount of capital that banks must hold, and set a core tier 1 capital ratio of 6%. The technical implementation deadline for Basel III is 2019, but recent developments in the banking market have suggested that even stricter rules may be applied by a later framework, which has been dubbed "Basel 4". The Basel Committee on Banking Supervision released a consultative paper, seeking out views on the Committee's plan to change how capital requirements and market risks are calculated

Indeed, since Basel III was rolled out (McKinsey, 2017), the Basel Committee on Banking Supervision (BCBS) has been reviewing risk-measurement approaches internationally and among banks. One outcome of this review was the new standardized measurement approach (SMA) for operational risk, which was proposed in 2016. The committee also began a discussion on aggregated internal-rating model floors, concerned about the wide variation in the levels of risk-weighted assets (RWA) issuing from banks' internal models. The committee finalized standards for minimum capital requirements for market risk—the fundamental review of the trading book (FRTB)—in January 2016.[1] The committee plans to make technical revisions to this framework in 2017–18, however, and the country-level implementation is still under discussion.

Together, the changes are part of a Basel III amendment now more commonly referred to as Basel IV. The Group of Central Bank Governors and Heads of Supervision (GHOS) indicated that it does not intend to increase the total regulatory capital requirements in the industry as a whole. It did, however, acknowledge that the impact "may well be significant" for some banks. Recent McKinsey research has gone further, suggesting that the impact of Basel IV will be significant throughout the banking industry

Chapter 5. Making Banks' Business Models Resilient

Currently, within the financial services industry, most of the knowledge concepts about extreme events are either too much tainted by the traditional risk management methods that attempt to predict the future occurrence and severity of an extreme event using quantitative models. Or, otherwise, the knowledge tools are too much geared on Big Data in trying to map all possible scenarios and hazards that have taken place in the past, and that could affect companies in the future.

Firms need to be proactive to ensure that they are ready to handle any risky situations that can interfere with their operations. The concept behind the research, therefore, focuses on making a firm agile, resistant, resilient and be able to recover quickly when an extreme event takes place rather than predicting times when the firm is likely to encounter risks and reacting when the events turn up. A resilient business model is not just about being to resist the impact of an extreme event, but also how fast the firm can recover from the impact of an extreme event.

This study will enable firms and researchers to understand how extreme risk management is very different from traditional risk management because it will show that extreme risks will be addressed through the prism of strategic planning and business resiliency rather than using probability theories. Therefore, this research will focus much more on the governance, business processes, qualitative methods, and risk mitigation techniques surrounding extreme risk management than on the quantitative approaches, such as using as hedging techniques and distributions of probabilities. The work on antifragility (Nassim Taleb, 2012) indicates that it is an increase in resilience and agility that will help organizations become less fragile (i.e., antifragile). Therefore, institutions should, in fact, be embracing instead of avoiding stressors, such as shocks, volatility, noise, mistakes, faults, attacks, or failures. It is through these experiences that organizations become more robust when facing emerging risks (Sheffi, 2015).

The key, when trying to understand extreme risk events and how to manage them, is to build a multi-dimensional model that not only embraces resiliency and complexity but also where irrational human behavior plays a vital role. Here too mathematical principles behind quantum mechanics could be used to understand better the notoriously tricky human behavior that sometimes causes extreme events (Khrennikov, 2010).

However, one should always keep in mind that in the aftermath of a disaster senior executives in governmental and business organizations typically tend to use the term Black Swan too lavishly (Paté-Cornell, 2012). Aside from understanding the complexity and connectivity, it is also essential to propose solutions and tools that will make organizations more resilient (Comfort, L., A. Boin, and C. Demchak, 2010). Such means can be risk maps, vulnerability analysis (Bankoff, 2004), reverse stress testing (Kiedtke and Monkiewicz, 2011), supply chain resilience (Olson 2014), financial contingency planning (Paul, 2013), and sustainable business models (Spinelli and McGowan, 2014).

It seems the world is becoming more turbulent faster than most companies are becoming more resilient. The past 20 years has produced a rising tide of corporate write-offs, a growing number of prolonged profit slumps and an ever-expanding catalog of wrenching turnarounds. Few companies seem prepared for a world that is all punctuation and no equilibrium. In the past, executives could safely assume that business models were more or less immortal. No longer. Today, the only way to sustain success is to reinvent it. This is the challenge facing Coca-Cola as it struggles to raise its "share of throat" in noncarbonated beverages. It's the task that bedevils America's old-style airlines as they compete against Southwest and JetBlue. It's the hurdle for Sun Microsystems as it searches for ways to protect its high-margin server business from the Linux onslaught. And these companies are hardly unique (Hamel and Valikangas, 2003).

How can companies close the resilience gap? They must start with a new aspiration: zero trauma. This implies an ability to dynamically reinvent business models and strategies as circumstances change - with no calamitous surprises, no convulsive reorganizations and no colossal write-offs. Sound impossible? So did the notion of zero defects when it was first proposed. Zero trauma involves undertaking a strategy that is constantly evolving to fit into emerging opportunities and budding trends, with the organization continuously creating its future instead of justifying its past. Furthermore, resilience enables organizations to experience revolutionary change in rapid, evolutionary steps without any disastrous shocks, paroxysmal restructuring, massive write-offs and indiscriminate retrenchment (Hamel and Valikangas, 2003).

But, zero trauma is much more than merely 'reengineering', 'enterprise resource planning', or 'Six Sigma' (Hamel & Välikangas, 2003). While the ideology of optimization is creating a lot of wealth, optimization is sufficient only as long as there's no fundamental change in what has to be optimized. An accelerating pace of change demands an accelerating pace of strategic evolution, which can be achieved only if an organization cares as much about resilience as it does about optimization. Any company that can make sense of its environment, generate strategic options, and realign its resources faster than its rivals will enjoy a decisive advantage. This is the essence of resilience. And it will prove to be the ultimate competitive advantage in the age of turbulence—when companies are being challenged to change more profoundly, and more rapidly, than ever before.

While there is no simple recipe for building a resilient organization, a decade of research on innovation and renewal allows us to suggest a few starting points:

- Supply chain risk management
- Business model reverse stress testing
- High reliability organization

First, what is the definition of resilience?

The resilience is usually defined as the actual ability of a system or an organization to adapt itself to the consequences of internal or external changes and threats. It also means a capacity to anticipate disruptions, adapt to events, and create lasting value (Wieland and Wallenburg, 2013: 300- 320). This definition is synonymous with the broad approach to defining financial system stability.

The Financial System Inquiry 2014 sets out its fundamental belief:

The inquiry believes the financial system [performs its role] most effectively when it operates in an efficient and resilient manner and treats participants fairly. This occurs when participants fulfill their roles and responsibilities in a way that engenders confidence and trust in the system. The inquiry defines resilience as: 'the financial system's capacity to adjust to both the normal business cycle and a severe economic shock' (p. 4). It emphasizes that 'A resilient system does not preclude failure' and, more controversially, 'nor necessarily imply price stability'. Building on that statement, the report indicates: Rather, a resilient system can adjust to changing circumstances while continuing to provide core economic functions, even during severe but plausible shocks. In a resilient system, individual institutions in distress should be resolvable with minimal costs to depositors, policy-holders, taxpayers and the real economy.

5.1. Solution #1: Supply Chain Risk Management

The last thirty years have been aberrant for risk managers working in the banking industry as a myriad of financial disasters have been affecting the banking industry and financial markets as a whole. Notwithstanding new and advanced mathematical models to calculate the probability and severity of a sequence of risk events that might affect banks, not to mention a string of new harsh regulatory provisions, many banking executives continue to feel that the business models of their banks remain vulnerable to the rise of emerging risks. Indeed, albeit the lion share of the U.S. banks is nowadays in compliance with the prudential regulations (Gray & Jopson, 2018), virtually all of these rules (not to mention internal functions within the bank) ignore a series of emerging risks, amongst which supply chain risk.

Also, a recent survey by EY and co-sponsored by the IIF (Jackson & Schlich, 2013) shows that banking executives remain wary about the range of risks facing the industry in the short and long term. Broader technological, geopolitical, economic, social and environmental concerns are regarded as materially menacing further underpinned by signs of increased global regulatory fragmentation. As a result, competition among financial actors is becoming acuter notwithstanding banks' balance sheets that are deemed to show for it. In other words, as a result of increased financialization of the economy, globalization, and interconnectedness, banking executives feel that the banks ‘ business models are insufficiently inclusive failing to take into account a range of emerging risk factors. This brief memo gives an overview of how a better supply chain risk management can help achieve stronger resilience and business continuity for G-SIBs.

5.1.1. Context Of Supply Chain Risk Management

One way to better understand the risk environment into which banks need to operate is through the theories of supply chain risk management (SCRM) and supply chain resilience (SCR). In essence, a banking organization can be viewed as supply chain due to the myriad of actors that interfere in the delivery of services to the banks' clients. And, these actors can be either internal (cf. different departments within the bank (IT, back-office, front office, middle office, risk management, etc.)) or external (third-party vendors and contractors). However, when the words ‘supply chain’ and ‘supply chain risk management’ come to mind, casual observers will typically associate these concepts with the world of manufacturing, logistics, and resources, and not immediately with the realm of banking. Indeed, in the corporate world the definition for the concept of supply chain risk management is (Felea & Albāstroiu, 2013) “the risk management of the flow of goods and services that includes the movement and storage of raw materials, work-in-process inventory, and finished goods from the point of origin to the point of consumption."

In essence, SCRM draws heavily from the areas of operations management, logistics, procurement, and information technology, and strives for an integrated approach.

With the exception when the media talks about cyber-attacks affecting the infrastructure of financial organizations or the growing importance of software vendors supplying financial organizations, interestingly enough, within the financial services industry nothing comparable to an integrated supply chain (risk management) exists (Camerinelli, 2017).

In the corporate world, traditional methods for managing supply chain risk rely on (Simchi-Levi et al., 2014) "knowing the likelihood of occurrence and the magnitude of impact for every potential event that could materially disrupt a firm's operations. For common supply chain disruptions —poor supplier performance, forecast errors, transportation breakdowns, and so on—those methods work very well, using historical data to quantify the level of risk". However, it is a different story altogether for low-probability, high-severity events such as the 2007-2008 GFC, Hurricane Katrina in 2005, the 2003 SARS outbreak, or significant outages due to unforeseen events such as geopolitical upheavals. Since historical data on these exceptional episodes are scarce or even nonexistent, their risk is hard to measure utilizing conventional mathematical models.

As a result, many organizations do not adequately prepare for them. That can have disastrous consequences when calamities do strike and can compel even operationally savvy organizations to scramble after the fact (Simchi-Levi et al., 2015). To address this challenge, in addition to investing resources in designing a mathematical model that focuses on determining the likelihood that any specific risk will take place, it is equally appropriate to center on the description of the supply chain. This would put the onus on analyzing the impact of potential failures at points along the supply chain (cf. such as the impact of a sudden default of a swap counterparty during the closing of a loan), rather than again the cause of the disruption (Simchi-Levi, 2013). This type of analysis removes the requirement to determine the probability that any specific risk will occur - a savvy approach since the mitigation strategies for disruption are equally valid regardless of what caused it.

5.1.2. Application Of The Concept Of 'Supply Chain' To Banks

As such, one interesting angle to adopt a fresh perspective (Kim et al., 2016) is by looking at how leading consumer business (CB) organizations efficiently move goods through their supply chains, and apply it to the banking world. Indeed, transposing this concept to today's banks (cf. be it commercial or investment banks), one can readily associate cash as goods, whereby banks can apply proven CB strategies to reduce excess inventory, lower handling, and processing costs, improve operating efficiency and optimize their network of ATMs.

The Bank as User for SCM

4 Flows:

1. Material.	Money (Cash)	Banks are the solvency meter in societies. House of trust for several parties.
2. Capital.	Investments	Private Investments. Public Financial Needs.
3. Information.	Economic - Financial	Economic information to protect outside. Financial information to improve inside. Other Specific information (Legal, HR, ..etc.)
4. Man power	Employees	

2 Ends:

1. Suppliers.	Depositors
2. Customers.	Investors

Source: QNB Alahli

Indeed, when you think about it, the granting of a loan, for instance, is the essence of a banking activity as it is through these lending activities those banks generate revenues. And, this is the primary root of banking, namely transforming money by collecting deposits and in turn lending them to the economy (cf. be it households, firms, and governments).

However, banks do not have an integrated approach (Jackson & Davis, 2015) in managing the different phases to deliver an end-product/service to a customer failing to view, for example, the lending process as an integrated supply chain from the front to end. Yes, they have a B2B paperless computer driven lending process in the case of a mortgage loan where the consumer can purchase or refinance a home without ever signing or handling a piece of paper. But, the life cycle of a loan goes much further than merely an online application (cf. infra: Example of (absence) of an integrated supply chain within a bank). Again, banks do not have a streamlined fully integrated chain of supply of services that involve back office, middle office, risk management, business developers, finance, IT, etc. (Davis, 2017). All these departments work in a silo with, yes, bridges between themselves, but without really thinking about their service as being part of an integrated chain. In other words, what is missing is the risk management of front-to-back processing for all banking activities. Granted, some banking areas have adopted this train of thought such as Treasury or Trade Finance, but these are more the exception than the rule.

Traditional activities such as corporate banking, retail banking, and institutional banking still operate in silo architectures and lack integrity of operations, making them not only quite onerous (and hence inefficient), but, even worse, exposing them to potential disruptions. In an ideal world, the workflow of the sales desk should, through technology platforms, be integrated with the middle office, risk management, back office (in relation to settlement and confirmation), accounting, reporting, and inquiries (Davis, 2017). A simple proof of this segregation is the mere existence of different (and not always compatible) IT architectures and software tools for each of those activities causing an absence of effective bridges among these areas of operations.

The closest thing that banks have to supply chain risk management is maybe operational risk management, and more specifically Business Continuity Management; but that does not suffice. The first step for banks to comprehend and embrace this concept of SCRM (and SCR) is acknowledging that the various business lines within banking organizations also operate as supply chains. The next step, similar to what happens in the manufacturing world, is the understanding of the banks' exposure to supply chain risk – both up and down the stream, thereby helping to identify the weakest links. In today's globalized and interconnected world that keeps on stubbornly focusing on concepts of 'lean' and 'cost-cutting,' there is alas little spare capacity in the supply chains. Complex, multi-stakeholder, outsourced and even cross-border delivery schedules mean that few banks (and businesses overall) can claim accurate visibility to any significant depth in the supply chains of their various business lines. SCRM and SCR resilience are therefore essential risk mitigation approaches that should underpin any decision to optimize supply chains in the long run, and hence help build more resilient banking business models. Alas, today's operational risk management within banks does not embrace nor comprehend that view of supply chain risk management.

More critically, if banks were to manage their cash supply chain more effectively, they would also be able to improve resiliency and better position themselves to compete in the marketplace (Kim et al., 2016). However, this approach within banks is still in its infancy. Also, banks like many other corporates outsource a growing number of their activities, hence relying on third parties to deliver specific services to internal or external stakeholders. In other words, the risks in a supply chain are critical because of increasing outsourcing, off-shoring, product variety, lean 'production', and supply chain security issues (Blos et al., 2012). Moreover, organizations are at a higher risk of system failure because of the massive interdependency throughout the global supply chains. Due to those facts, resilience is becoming the primary concern of any banking organization, and SCRM can be one of the tools to achieve this resilience.

5.1.3. The 'What' Of SCRM And SCR

A definition by Wieland and Wallenburg (2012) about supply chain risk management (SCRM) yields the following: SCRM is "the implementation of strategies to manage both every day and exceptional risks along the supply chain based on continuous risk assessment with the objective of reducing vulnerability and ensuring continuity." To put it differently, SCRM is to apply risk management process tools, with either external partners in a supply chain or the bank's own internal service providers, to deal with risks and uncertainties caused by, or affecting, service delivery-related activities or resources in the supply chain (Brindley, 2004). With SCRM, through a coordinated, holistic approach, all supply chain stakeholders (both internal and external) identify and analyze the risk of failure points within the supply chain (Trowbridge, 2017). Typical risks that might affect the supply chain oscillate from unpredictable cataclysmic threats to cyber-attacks and fraud, third party failures, and reach across quality, security, to resiliency and product integrity. Supply chain risk management is cause-oriented as it typically involves four processes: identification, assessment, controlling, and monitoring of supply chain risks (Wieland & Wallenburg, 2012).

Though, as a result of the increasing complexity of many supply chains and their environments, these processes might not suffice to warrant that for all eventualities a contingency plan exists. That is why supply chain risk management needs to be combined with the concept of supply chain resilience (Christopher & Peck, 2004), as the latter which aims to ensure that the supply chain can bounce back from risks irrespective of their cause. Supply chain resilience is, therefore (Ponomarov & Holcomb, 2009) "The adaptive capability of the supply chain to prepare for unexpected events, respond to disruptions, and recover from them by maintaining continuity of operations (Caddick & Buchanan, 2011) at the desired level of connectedness and control over structure and function". Similar to the typical methodology for quantifying risk, supply chain risk can be defined as a function of the probability of an event's occurrence and its severity. The main disadvantage of applying this approach to measure supply chain risk is that it necessitates quantifying the occurrence or probability of many different event types for n number of supply chain locations (which can be tens of locations in a large banking organization). In that respect, an interesting metric to measure supply chain resilience is what is called Time To Recover. TTR is the time it takes an organization to restore 100% of operational output following a significant supply chain disruption. The determination of TTR assumes that the facility is virtually unusable due to a significant event, and would need substantial reconstruction and re-sourcing used in banking operations. As such, financial market players - be it financial institutions (banks, insurance companies, asset managers, brokers) and/or prudential authorities - could learn a lot from how the corporate world is coping with the risk management of disruptive events (yes, we have operational risk management but that only covers part of the problem).

The top supply chain vulnerabilities of banks are (Jackson &Davis, 2015):

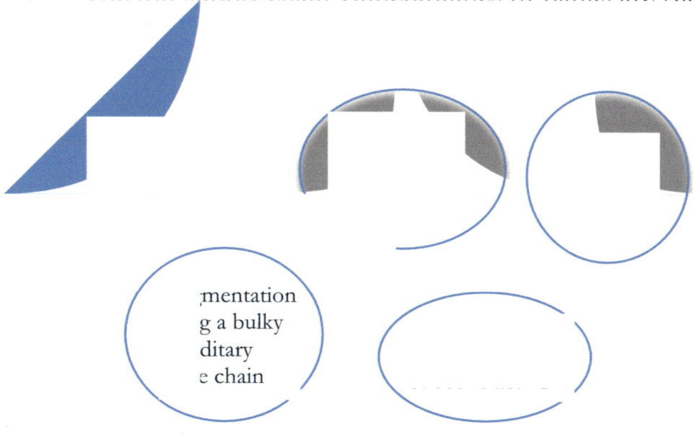

Source: EY

The reliance on wholesale funding affects mostly the smaller banks that need to rely on brokered deposits to support loan growth, while concomitantly larger commercial banks have reduced their dependency on short-term borrowings (i.e., these short-term borrowings typically include federal funds and securities sold under agreements to repurchase, commercial paper as well as other borrowings from FHLB and other market participants). While before the GFC they typically represented 25-30% of total liabilities, nowadays they have fallen to 10-15% (which is still meaningful in absolute numbers when considering a bank with close to one trillion of USD in assets). Other vulnerabilities affecting the supply chain of banks are the increasing reliance on subcontractors (causing a third-party risk), the lack of inter-compatibility between databases from different departments (look at the reconciliation efforts that are necessary every quarter as well as by year end between finance and risk management, for example).

5.1.4. The 'Why' Of SCRM And SCR

The objectives of SCRM and SCR for banks and the benefits of an integrated supply chain include:

- Ensuring 'production' (such as the origination of loans, the collection of deposits, the signing of asset management agreements in the scope of private banking, etc.) and delivery capabilities.
- The avoidance of revenue losses in case of disruptions and reduction of costs.
- The fulfillment of regulatory requirements and compliance.
- Safeguarding the corporate image and customer satisfaction.

Such approach also provides some extra benefits (vander Straeten, 2016). It:

- Identifies hidden exposures. The approach helps managers identify which nodes in the network create the most significant risk exposure—often highlighting previously hidden or overlooked areas of high risk. It also allows the firm to compare the costs and benefits of various alternatives for mitigating the impact.
- Avoids the need for predictions about rare events. The approach determines the optimal response to any disruption that might occur within the supply network, regardless of the cause. Rather than trying to quantify the likelihood that a low-probability, high-severity incident will strike, organizations can focus on identifying

the critical exposures and putting in place risk mitigating strategies (Simchi-Levi, 2014).

- Reveals supply chain dependencies and bottlenecks. These analyses can also help banks make better sourcing decisions that increase the resilience of the supply chain. This includes taking into account the likely struggle among competing banks to lock in alternative sources of funding (liquidity) if a liquidity provider's disruption affects several banks in the market. Such cross-firm impacts of a crisis are often underestimated. For example, also, sourcing contracts with backup vendors can be negotiated to grant a company priority over others in the event a disruption with the primary vendor would take place. Such decisions could then decrease time to recovery after the disruption and hence the financial impact for the banking organization.
- Fosters a culture of 'stakeholders', learning, and discussion. In the scope of analyzing the supply chain in this way, managers engage in discussions with vendors as well as internal suppliers of data or services about acceptable levels of TTR for critical services and share insights about best-practice processes to reduce recovery time. These discussions are then put into stone through service level agreements. As a result, the effect of disruptions is brought to a minimum, and thus also the financial impact for the bank.
- A resilient supply chain is a competitive advantage, reduces customer perception of assumed risks and moves organizations from simple risk management to risk resilient growth (Turner, 2011). It is not just playing defense — it is also about playing offense — finding competitive advantage by shaping a supply chain resilience strategy focused on sustained performance that remains agile and fundamentally operations-focused. It is about balance.

Incentives as mentioned above should convince banks about the need to adopt and embrace these concepts of SCRM and SCR. In other words, these approaches should be transposed to the banking industry, thereby not only assisting 'Risk' on the ways how it manages disruptions caused by low probability - high severity extreme events but foremost supporting the executive leadership in designing more resilient banking business models.

5.1.5. Recent Trends In Supply Chains Affecting Banks

Over the last several decades, supply chain networks in the corporate world have on an ongoing basis evolved to deliver speed, capacity, efficiency not to mention customer service through organizational trends such as volume consolidation, specialization, globalization, and information availability (Appel, 2012). The emphasis on relentless cost optimization has highlighted the tension between cost cuts and supply chain resilience – with the removal of traditional buffers such as excess capacity, redundancy, and safety stock.

Trend	Example	Risk Impact
Globalization	Outsourcing, offshoring	Local concentrated risks become globally diffused, involving multiple actors
Specialization	Geographical concentration of production	Efficient process can be easily disrupted by localised event
Complexity	Product/network complexity	Reliance on multiple parts/players in diverse locations reduces visibility and adds latency into monitoring systems
Lean processes	Single sourcing, buffer stock reduction	While initially efficiency is improved and costs are lowered, fewer alternatives in case of disruption
Information availability	Track and Trace	Systems increasingly reliant on information flow

Source: World Economic Forum

Also, when you think about it, these developments have also affected the banking industry and shifted risk distributions. As a result, their effects have often included sharing risk more broadly around the world (cf. through the effects of the Basel Accords, for instance, or the existence of central counterparty clearing (CCP)), reducing high-frequency risks and focusing risk within individual business lines (real estate, proprietary trading, commodities, securitization, etc.). Another common feature has been to separate risk from responsibility, twist incentives and manufacturing moral hazards – the notion that a party that is secluded from risk will behave differently from how it would act if it had taken full exposure to risk (cf. Look at how Basel III requires banks to maintain an interest in their securitizations (Sarkisyan & Casu, 2013), based on the assumption that retaining "skin in the game" induces banks to improve screening and monitoring of borrowers. Examples of the proposed rules requiring securitizes to retain a portion of the credit risk in the assets that they securitize[7]).

As organizations, including banks, look for efficiencies and cost reduction opportunities in supply chain and delivery processes (f. ex. Online banking), they need to be aware of the potential impact on their risk profile. The increasing vulnerability of supply chains (Peck, 2006) requires a new focus on managing and mitigating risk, which extends beyond the walls of a single organization. It necessitates a much higher level of consciousness of where the risks lie.

5.1.6. Who Should Be The Owner Of SCRM And SCR?

As already indicated previously, technology should facilitate the integration of workflows within a banking organization making it more inclusive. For instance, IT platforms should connect the workflow of the front office with the middle office AND risk management AND back office (about settlement and confirmation) AND accounting AND reporting. A simple proof of this existing segregation is the mere existence of difference IT architectures and software packages for each of those activities lacking useful bridges among these areas of operations and therefore causing bottlenecks when trying to produce reporting data that is consolidated and exhaustive.

The objective of an effective SCRM program is therefore to smoothen these workflow chains connecting all the dots from front-to-end so that professional services can be rendered to the clients irrespective of the (challenging) environment into which a bank can be in (momentarily as a result of an unexpected event). In other words, leadership guidance is essential to any successful SCRM program. A committed leadership not only helps identify risks well before they become the source of a disruption;

[7] It includes Article 122a of the Capital Requirements Directive (CRD II) in the EU and Section 941 of the 2010 Dodd-Frank Act in the US.

additionally, such as an engaged team also provides a swift and thorough response to any incidents that might take place (SCRLC, 2011).

Ultimately, leadership, reporting, and ownership of supply chain risk should rest with operational risk management (Borghesi & Gaudenzi, 2012) and the board. Indeed, according to the two authors "operational processes represent the core business of most organizations, and therefore the proper assessment of operational and supply chain risks is critical to effective and efficient prevention and protection of an organization". However, a capable SCRM steering team should be composed of leaders of not only ORM, but also of the following functions (non-exhaustive list): Front/ middle/ back office, risk management group (incl. governance), business continuity, enterprise risk management, finance (incl. accounting, reporting), logistics, audit, security, and vendor management. These different functions should have representation on both the executive steering team and the implementation team.

Going back to the corporate world, conventional techniques for managing supply chain risk rely on knowing the probability of occurrence and the severity of impact for every potential event that could critically hamper an organization's business operations. For typical supply chain disruptions, such as poor supplier performance, forecast errors, delivery failures, etc., those techniques are robustly relying on historical data to quantify the level of risk (Simchi-Levi, 2014). However, it's a different story for low-probability, high-impact events—mega-disasters like Hurricane Katrina in 2005, viral epidemics like the 2003 SARS and 2014-2015 Ebola outbreaks, or significant outages due to unforeseen events such as factory fires and political upheavals. These black swans, such as the 2007-2008 GFC and the 2010 Eurozone crisis, too have affected the banking industry for instance. Because historical data on these rare events are limited or nonexistent, their risk is hard to quantify using traditional models. As a result, many companies do not adequately prepare for them, and that can have calamitous consequences when catastrophes do strike and can force even operationally savvy companies to scramble after the fact.

To address this challenge, aside from developing a financial model that focuses on determining the probability that any specific risk will occur, it is equally appropriate to center on the description of the supply chain that puts the emphasis on the impact of potential failures at points along the supply chain (such as the sudden lack of liquidity to fund a corporate loan or close a securitization, or the imminent default of a partnering syndicated bank in a project finance deal, or the fall-out of a swap provider) rather than again the cause of the disruption. This type of analysis removes the need to determine the probability that any specific risk will occur—a valid approach since the mitigation strategies for disruption are equally valid regardless of what caused it (Simchi-Levi et al., 2014). Using this approach, banks can quantify what the financial and operational impact would be if a critical funding supply were suddenly out of commission for, say, two weeks—whatever the underlying reason in the market. Proper mapping of the supply chain is therefore crucial since supply chains are in a continual state of flux.

5.1.7. Methods And Tools Of SCRM & SCR

Banks need to move from a fragmented and decentralized supply chain risk management (cf. in the best case, if they already have a description about such a supply chain) to a centralized resource management structure in order to better leverage synergies and increase the overall maturity level of an organization. Implementation of standardized roles and responsibilities, and global policies and procedures has to be supported by an extensive change management program.

5.1.7.1. Heat Maps

One tool to manage supply chain risks efficiently is by drawing 'heat' maps showing risk-events on a matrix defining likelihood and consequence levels. This technique (SCRLC, 2011) "allows managers to see the relative likelihood and consequence of differing risks easily." To use this method effectively, it is paramount to be in possession of well-defined and consistently used criteria for the different likelihood and consequence levels.

LIKELIHOOD	insignificant	minor	moderate	major	critical
almost certain	Moderate	Major	Critical	Critical	Critical
likely	Moderate	Major	Major	Critical	Critical
possible	Moderate	Moderate	Major	Major	Critical
unlikely	Minor	Moderate	Moderate	Major	Critical
rare	Minor	Minor	Moderate	Moderate	Major

CONSEQUENCE

Source: SCRLC

The next step is for any banking organization, having prioritized its risks, determine how it may seek to address them. Once an organization understands its supply chain and has analyzed its potential risks, it can implement an effective supply chain risk management program with its partners, that is, its various internal and external suppliers of data and services. Nowadays there are vendor companies that provide supply chain software and content product category based on combining massive third-party datasets, with graphical views into an organization's data/ service-supply base, and role-based alerting. The ability to map risks across multiple data/ service supplier tiers and business lines in near real-time can give banks a powerful new tool to manage their supply chains far more intelligently and proactively.

5.1.7.2. TTR And REI

A central characteristic of this SCRM approach is also the notion of Time To Recovery (TTR) (Simchi-Levi, 2015), namely the time it would take for a particular node in the chain (cf. such as the sudden absence of funding or a default problem with a swap provider) to be restored to full serviceability after a failure.

To conduct the analysis, the approach removes one node at a time from the supply network for the duration of the TTR. It then determines the supply chain response that would minimize the performance impact of the disruption at that node—for instance, relying on emergency liquidity sources, finding a new swap provider through the intermediation of a central clearing party, taking on a temporary basis a more prominent exposure on the books until the bank finds a new participating bank in the syndication, etc. In other words (Sonnier, 2014), by breaking a supply chain into nodes of interaction, banking organizations "can determine the financial and operational impact of each node, and then calculate the repercussions of disruption if a node were to be out of operation for a certain period.

The model assesses costs induced by potential disruption based on the estimated Time To Recovery (TTR), determining the financial impact" a particular risk node might have. From the optimal response (Zsidisin et al., 2004), it generates a financial or operational performance impact (PI) for the node. An organization can choose different measures of PI: lost units of loan production, revenue, or profit margin, for instance. The approach analyzes all nodes in the network, assigning a PI to each. The node with the most massive PI (in lost revenues, for instance, or lost units of loan production) is assigned a risk exposure index (REI) (Simchi-Levi, 2013) score of 1.0.

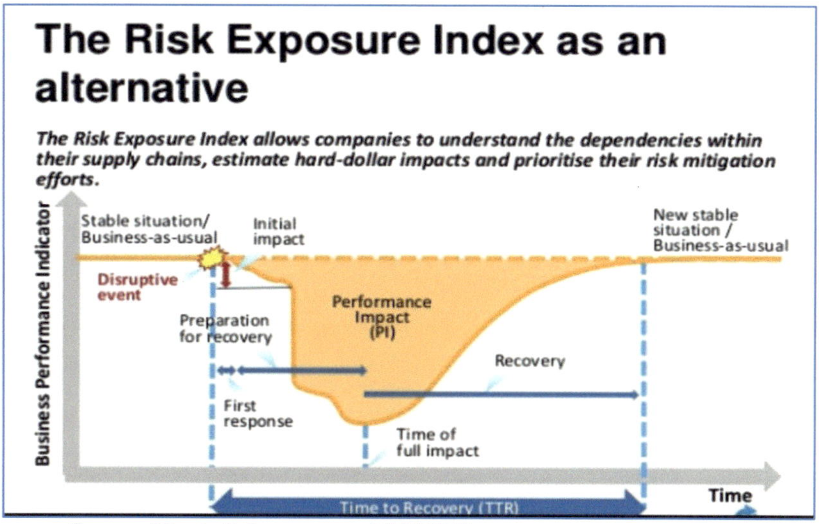

Source: Danie Schoeman and SAPICS

All other nodes' REI scores are indexed relative to this value (cf. a node whose disruption would bring about the least impact gets a value close to zero) (Sonnier, 2014). The indexed scores allow the organization to identify at a glance the nodes that warrant the most attention from risk managers.

5.1.7.3. Third Party Risk Management

Today's business landscape is loaded with significant pitfalls such as data loss, like cyber threats, cataclysm, and corruption that may result in supply chain disruption. Therefore, it is critical to have in place a formal risk management framework within the banking organization that heralds the conduct of a thorough due diligence of new vendors, monitors existing third parties, and makes sure these contractors are following appropriate procedures failing which it will affect not only the reputation of the bank, but potentially cause a disruption of activities, and hence a loss of revenues.

While there is a regulatory guidance about third party risk management in the banking industry, the latter is still in its infancy (Park et al., 2015) with organizations deploying different methods, some less effective. From a governance perspective, and based on survey conducted by EY in 2018 (i.e., Global financial services third-party risk management survey: Is it time to shift your perspective of third-party risk?) there is no governance ruling that stipulates which function within the bank is the owner of responsibility for third party risk management. With less than 50% of the banks TPRM resides with the procurement function, and the remainder is split between IT security, operational risk, enterprise risk and business lines. However, having TPRM owned by procurement is similar to a situation where in a context of lending the front office would also be the one rating the borrower and deciding on the loan (cf. in other words, there would be a conflict of interest and a lack of impartiality and independence). In other words, there is very little consistency in the responsibility and ownership of different functional components of TPRM, showing that organizations are unique in deploying ownership structures and operating models that reflect the structure and culture of their own organizations. While the survey shows that procurement is the most likely home for TPRM, it should instead be the responsibility of ORM. While regulators need to step up their game regarding how banks protect themselves against third party issues (cf. regulatory scrutiny prioritizes reporting and not risk measurement nor risk management programs), banking executives should not be complacent either and instead be proactive.

Primary responsibility for TPRM functions
Which functional area has primary responsibility for the execution of the following components of your organization's third party risk management program?

	Third-party risk management responsibility								
	Procurement	Information security	TPRM	Legal/ general counsel	Operational risk	Compliance	LOB	Other	Not Conducted
Design and administration of the inherent risk assessment	26%	2%	**43%**	0%	20%	0%	4%	6%	0%
Completion of inherent risk assessment	13%	2%	17%	0%	6%	0%	**59%**	4%	0%
Business reputation and qualification review	**35%**	0%	19%	0%	9%	4%	28%	4%	2%
Anti-corruption/ anti-bribery review	9%	0%	9%	4%	7%	**44%**	**4%**	13%	9%
Anti-money laundering (AML)/ economic sanction review	13%	0%	9%	4%	9%	**45%**	4%	13%	2%
Performance monitoring	6%	0%	4%	2%	0%	0%	**87%**	2%	0%
Exit strategy	7%	0%	7%	6%	0%	0%	**74%**	2%	4%
Financial viability assessment	**40%**	0%	15%	2%	6%	0%	15%	23%	0%
Country risk assessment	13%	4%	19%	2%	9%	2%	15%	11%	25%
Information security assessment	2%	**85%**	9%	0%	2%	0%	0%	2%	0%
Business continuity assessment	2%	24%	9%	0%	15%	2%	22%	24%	2%
Service organization controls (SOC) report review	4%	26%	15%	2%	6%	0%	33%	7%	7%
Regulatory compliance procedural assessment	2%	2%	7%	2%	9%	**50%**	17%	4%	7%
Regulatory compliance transactional review	0%	0%	6%	2%	6%	**41%**	26%	4%	17%
Issue management/risk treatment	4%	8%	15%	0%	13%	4%	**51%**	4%	2%
Review and update of contract terms as part of ongoing monitoring	37%	2%	0%	22%	2%	0%	30%	4%	4%
Review of issues identified in reviews as part of update to contract terms	24%	4%	4%	11%	6%	0%	**43%**	4%	6%
Identification of expired contracts	**66%**	2%	4%	9%	2%	4%	11%	2%	0%
Notification of upcoming contract expiration	**66%**	4%	6%	11%	0%	2%	9%	2%	0%
Termination of contracts	**57%**	2%	2%	11%	0%	0%	24%	4%	0%

Source: EY

5.1.8. Absence Integrated Supply Chain Within A Bank

Below are two figures as an example of a workflow that is not interconnected. One workflow concerns a mortgage loan application (origination) highlighting that different actors at each step of the way are not indeed interconnected (FDIC, 2018):

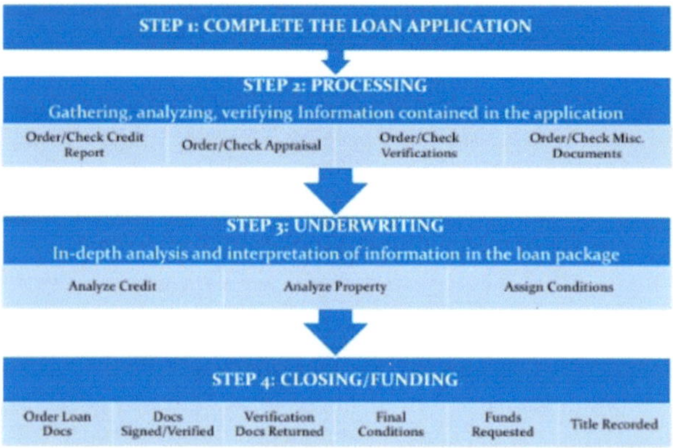

Source: FDIC

And, another workflow concerning the secondary market and servicing:

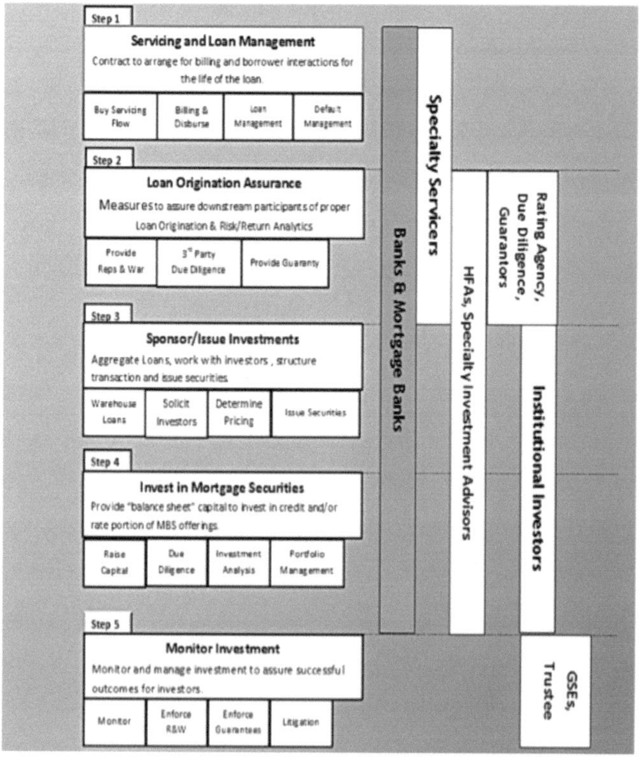

Source: Davis

In practice, for a bank, one could map out the supply chain (front-to-back) process that involves the provision of a loan to a household or business entity or the settlement of payment, and look at how external events could disrupt the provision of this service to the end customer. Again, these events could involve the lack of funding due to dry out of the interbank market or a lack of confidence from fixed income investors; the occurrence of a system defect that would prevent the bank to close the deal (obviously physical disruptions would be covered by operational risk management); the default of a swap counterparty involved in the transaction; exacerbated FX movements or a sovereign crisis affecting international payments; etc.

Now, granted, the risk management of disruptive events is partially covered by operational risk management. Indeed, operational risk can be created by a wide range of different external events ranging from power failures to floods or earthquakes to terrorist attacks. Similarly, operational risk can arise due to internal events such as the potential for failures or inadequacies in any of the bank's processes and systems (e.g., its IT, risk management or human resources management processes and systems), or those of its outsourced service providers. Operational risk arising from human resources management may refer to a range of issues such as mismanaged or poorly trained employees; the potential of employees for negligence, willful misconduct; conflict of interests; fraud; rogue trading; and so on.

Therefore, the emergence of mistrust, failure to communicate, low morale and cynicism among staff members, as well as increased turnover of staff, should be regarded as indicative for a potential increase in operational risk. However, financial events are not covered by operational risk management, such as a market crash, the spill-over effects of the bankruptcy of a systemically important financial institution, the impact of a Grexit and/or Brexit, a very hard landing of the Chinese economy, a trade war between the US and China, etc. All these events will in one way or the other from a supply chain management perspective also disrupt the provisions of financial services to the end-customer.

As such, it is highly useful not only to map the process that allows a description of the front-to-back process in relation to payments, lending, investments, etc., and look at how a disruption would impact one of the nodes alongside the supply chain for each of those financial activities, and how long it would take for the system to recover its senses, i.e., re-conduct the business as a going concern to the benefit of the customers. However, it is even more interesting to use today's technological developments to build IT platforms that allow for the establishment of an integrated supply chain within the bank.

An excellent example of an already operational well-oiled and integrated supply chain is the one in place with a small fintech lender (i.e., Springboard Home Loans):

Source: Springboard CDFI

Generally speaking, by gaining a better understanding of the threats that could impact a supply chain, the latter would be able to anticipate better, react to, and recover from the unexpected (Wu & Blackhurst, 2009). And, ultimately, the bank would emerge as more resilient as a result. Focusing on building supply chain resilience as part of a bank's risk management strategy allows the organization to transform its view of risk to create value rather than merely manage it.

5.1.9. Conclusion

Most banking organizations have operational risk management policies that can cope with localized disruptions. However, recent high-profile events have put into the limelight how risks outside the control of individual banking organizations can have unintended spillover effects that can no longer be mitigated by one banking organization alone.

Given that operational processes represent the core business of banking organizations, therefore the proper assessment of operational and supply chain risks should be viewed as critical to effective and efficient prevention and protection of an organization. And, ultimately, operational risk management should own the risk management of the supply chain.

Now granted, disruptions should no longer be viewed as the 'sacred domain' only of operational risk managers, even in the realm of banks. Already, changes to governance models in the wake of the 2008 Global Financial Crisis have pushed banking organizations to review their approaches to identifying and mitigating systemic risks. C-suite level leadership and corporate boards are ought to increasingly understand and being held accountable for the many aspects of organizational risk, including supply chain risk management.

And, while regulators have not been stepping up their game cf. regulatory scrutiny prioritizes reporting and not risk measurement nor comprehensive and dedicated risk management programs in relation to the supply chain), banking executives should not be complacent either and instead be proactive. The geopolitical, macroeconomic and systemic implications of regulating in a complex banking environment necessitate new approaches to mitigating risks that might affect the supply chain. Systemic risks within supply chains of banks (and other corporate organizations) are characterized by an unexpected trigger event and a supply chain setup that cannot absorb the shock and knock-on effects. The initial event can result in a domino effect causing massive disruption or failure across an entire industry or even region.

However, having the resiliency in place for effective response, no matter what the cause, it felt more important than forecasting of specific disruptions. While highlighting banking industry resilience in the face of recent shocks, it is critical to identify the most concerning vulnerabilities that damage the resilience of supply chains. The goal of SCRM and SCR is not to forecast what or when – but instead helping organizations (i.e., in this case, banks, also) in getting better prepared and able to timely respond in a thorough and planned manner to minimize the consequences of a disruptive event.

While likely types of disruption can be identified, the precise nature of systemic disruptions to supply chains within banking organizations and their delivery modes is hard to predict. Therefore, planning for a specific trigger event is not as important as having the inherent resiliency, flexibility and adaptability within banking organizations to be able to respond and recover regardless of the type of disruption quickly, and SCRM and SCR are one of the best tools for that.

5.2. Solution #2: Business Model Reverse Stress Testing

5.2.1. Context

To stave off another system-wide collapse as witnessed in the 2007-2008 Global Financial Crisis (GFC), banking regulators and political authorities around the globe put the screws on prudential standards thereby putting stress testing in the limelight. Many banking organizations have expressed their consternation that the seemingly never ending-increasing data requirements revolving around stress tests have not much to do with their unique risk profile but more with a desire from the regulators to possess as much as data as possible. Although banks have to obey and allocate massive resources to comply with the regulatory deadlines, they continue to feel that the costs related to the stress tests outweigh the benefits. Banks spent on average around $50 million annually in relation to stress testing exercises (Hinchliffe and Smith, 2016). As an illustration, the graph below highlights the average annual stress testing budgets for the period 2012–2015:

Source: KPMG International – Stress Testing, A benchmark analysis of systemically important financial institutions (2016)

Notwithstanding the latter, banks should view stress testing as a robust risk management tool that provides a significant opportunity to incorporate stress test end-results into strategic decision-making. Fortunately, there is a growing trend indicating that many banking organizations start to view prudential stress testing no longer as a dead weight and thus as a unique opportunity to better understand their business and focus on the areas where weakness could lead to potentially harmful situations to the entire banking organization.

Stress testing – survey and current state
Actively used for many purposes

Uses	Use now	Plan to use
Calibration of risk tolerances and limits	71%	29%
Strategic planning	53%	42%
Regulatory impact assessment	64%	16%
Strategic asset allocation	36%	31%
Shaping emphasis/de-emphasis on different business lines	33%	33%
Reinsurance	40%	22%
Model validation	33%	27%
Dividends, share-repurchase and similar capital planning	49%	9%
M&A	33%	25%
Product development, design and pricing	29%	25%
Underwriting	18%	25%
Resource allocation decisions	11%	27%
Distribution planning and sales compensation levels and design	4%	25%
Provider contracting	2%	25%
Other	7%	2%

Source: PwC – Trends in stress testing (2016)

With the collapse of Lehman Brothers at the end of third quarter of 2008, markets got fixated on the severity of the GFC, and the crisis raised a greater awareness on stress testing exercises that, for a long time, often had a minor influence in risk management. Indeed, even though prior to the GFC banking organizations had already been utilizing stress test tools internally for several years (e.g., to stress market risk factors such as equity prices or yield curves), the test findings had little-to-no impact on the general business decisions of bank institutions. As a result, up to the eve of the GFC, banking institutions accumulated large risk positions without incorporating in the strategic decision-making the assessment of how exposed they would be if the market would turn against them.

5.2.2. Bank Stress Testing framework

The term 'stress test' refers in generic terms to *"A test designed to assess how well a system functions when subjected to greater than normal amounts of stress or pressure"*, (Oxford Living Dictionaries, 2016). A bank stress test is an exercise based on a study of the balance sheet of a banking institution where an instrument (f. ex. a portfolio of loans or investments) is tested under a credit risk, market risk, operational, concentration, or liquidity risk stress scenario. The Basel Committee defines a stress test as "*a risk management tool used by financial firms, as well as a tool for supervisors, central banks and international financial institutions/ organizations to assess the impact of potential risks on the financial system, individual banks, or specific portfolios*" (BIS, 2017). Typical examples of stress test scenario cases are, for instance:

- What happens if annual GDP growth rate falls by x% in a given year?
- What happens if energy prices rise by x%?
- What happens if unemployment rate rises to x% in a specific year?
- What happens if stock markets crash by more than x% this year?
- What happens if interest rates go up by at least x%?
- What if half the instruments in a portfolio terminate their contracts in the fifth year?

The bank (Thun, 2013) will model the impact of the stress scenarios on risk parameters (cf. the probability of default (PD), loss given default (LGD), exposure at default (EAD), loan loss provisions, refi costs, etc.), and see what the effect is on VaR, economic capital, liquidity gap, etc.

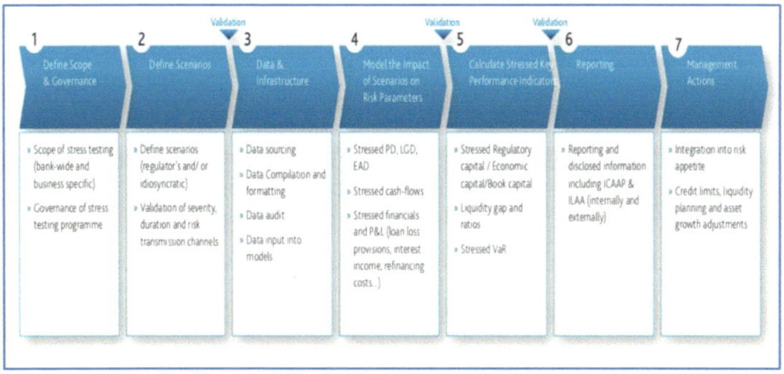

Source: Moody's Analytics - Common Pitfalls in Stress Testing (2013)

5.2.3. Bank Reverse Stress Testing framework

Reverse stress testing can be defined as "a stress test that requires assessment of scenarios and circumstances that would render a business unviable, thereby identifying potential business vulnerabilities" (Thun, Licari, and Zandi, 2010). Reverse stress testing starts from an outcome of business failure and identifies circumstances where this might occur (Licari and Suarez-Lledo, 2012). This approach is different from general stress and scenario testing, which tests for outcomes arising from changes in circumstances.

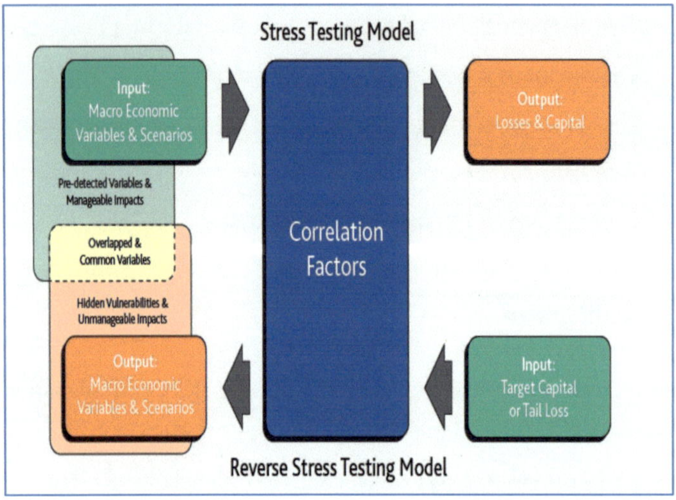

Source: Moody's Analytics - Understanding Extreme Risk: Reverse Stress Testing (2012)

The analysis of reverse stress testing provides a unique opportunity for banking organizations to comprehend their business activities better and draw management's attention on the areas where weakness could potentially become harmful to the entire banking organization. A reverse stress test explicitly pinpoints and measures the extreme risk scenarios most likely to turn banks as unviable and thus that can cause the organization to default and collapse. This is a core distinction when compared with classic stress testing approaches, where stress scenarios are selected based on expertise or historical evidence beforehand.

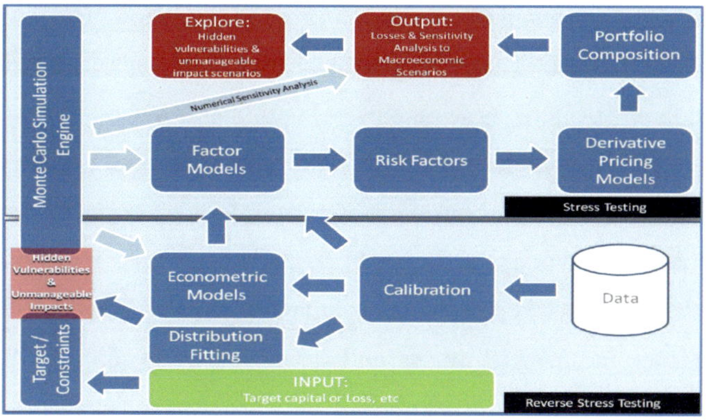

Source: Trading Intelligence - A Reverse Stress Testing Framework (2013)

Here is a case that would provide clarification about the distinction between a traditional stress test and a reverse stress test:

- A standard market risk stress test would utilize the worst-case market price shock accounted for in the history of financial markets over the last ten years. It would use this price shock and measure the size of the loss the banking organization would have to take on its balance sheet. That loss would be quoted as part of the stress test report. If the most adverse possible day in the history of the financial markets repeated itself, the value of the bank's investment book would collapse by 30% in a single day. The purpose is to assess how much damage a shock can cause and that is it.

- Usually, if a bank is heavily invested in stocks and equity markets collapse, bond prices rally as capital migrates from riskier equity securities to a relatively safer treasury and government fixed income securities. Moreover, if for some extreme reason the stock and bonds market both go belly up, the safer perceived to be currencies should rally. Depending on which market the bullish reaction is taking place that safe to be perceived currency could be the US dollar, the Swiss franc or the Japanese Yen. While a flight to safety test may already be in use at a banking organization, it would stop once the data set reaches its final threshold. A reverse stress test would use a range of flight to safety scenarios to pinpoint the specific one that would lead to a collapse of the bank and that no action on the part of senior management at the point of crisis would be able to mitigate.

- A reverse stress test would begin with a simple assumption. The entire stock of capital is wiped out on account of a market price event or a combination of such events. With the current book of positions, how much would the markets need to move by for such an event to happen? What would be the probability of such a move? Is there anything the bank could do to survive such a shock when it occurs? Is there anything one can do now to avoid that specific version of the future? Such a reverse stress test could be based on actual historical data, for instance, the collapse of market prices in October 1987 (Black Monday), the meltdown in financial stocks and debt markets in 2008-2009, or the Eurozone debt crisis (2010).

5.2.3.1. Bank Reverse Stress Testing And Regulators

It is key to acknowledge that regulatory authorities have not ignored the value of reverse stress testing; actually, they have been insisting that it is vital for banks to carry out these reverse stress tests (see, for instance, Basel Committee on Banking Supervision (2009), Committee of European Banking Supervisors (2010), or Financial Services Authority (2009)). In the United States, the Federal Reserve System (2012) states that "*a banking organization should employ several approaches and applications; these might include scenario analysis, sensitivity analysis, enterprise-wide stress testing, and reverse stress testing*".

5.2.3.2. Strengths And Weaknesses Of Bank Reverse Stress Testing

The main benefit of reverse stress testing is that the bank reverse engineers the dynamics of systemic contagion to come up with the scenario of smallest external shock that, should it occur, would result into a given systemic loss. This reverse stress test can be utilized to spot the potential triggers of systemic events, and it takes away the arbitrariness in the selection of adverse scenarios in stress testing.

Although an accurate modeling methodology that would have been able to characterize an institution's BM and portfolio compositions would be critical to identify and analyze hidden vulnerabilities within a reverse stress testing framework, the regulatory bodies have not yet provided methodological guidelines. Additionally, the findings of the reverse stress testing are not incorporated in the business planning of the banking organization. In other words, the reverse stress testing is seen as an operational instead of a strategic tool that could contribute to the strategic planning of the bank. Consequently, reverse stress testing receives relatively little top-management attention and buy-in (Mazingo et al., 2017). Top-management involvement would serve to highlight the importance of the exercise to both internal and external stakeholders.

5.2.4. BM Stress Testing framework

5.2.4.1. What Is BM Stress Testing?

According to a group of researchers that coin the term (Haaker, et al, 2017): "*BM stress testing is a systematic analysis of the robustness of BM components in different future environment using scenario planning in which future trends and uncertainties serve as stress factors*".

In other words, BM stress testing[8] is much broader all-encompassing stress test as it simulates the impact of stressors on the BM of an organization and looks at its capacity for resilience. As such, when applied to a banking organization, BM stress testing would not merely, for example, look on the impact in terms of credit risk or market risk exposures of the bank.

According to Bouwman et al. (2018) BM stress testing is a method "*used to evaluate the BM design against market scenarios, regulatory uncertainties, or technological uncertainties, and it leads to a changed BM that is more robust*". In this way the responsiveness and agility of the BM can be enhanced to the market situation.

The BM stress testing approach is especially adequate in a stage of business model experimentation, i.e., if a company has to choose between alternative business

---

[8] This BM stress testing approach is not very popular within the (mature) banking world as it is mostly used in a stage of business model experimentation, i.e. if a company has to choose between alternative business models or still has to implement the business model.

models or still has to implement the business model. Typically, that would be for technology driven companies, for example (Haaker et al., 2017).

5.2.4.2. Benefits And Weaknesses Of BM Stress Testing

BM stress testing would have a much stronger strategic and holistic footprint for the bank than regular bank stress tests. It would measure the resilience and robustness as a base for long-term viability and feasibility of a BM in a given future environment. Such an approach would not only take traditional risk metrics into account, but also legal, finance, technology, human resources or intellectual property as critical success factors for operationalizing the viability and feasibility of the BM. However, it does not look at testing the business model to destruction, meaning the approach is not attempting in trying to find which of the BM components (or interaction between BM components) could under stress lead to the collapse of the BM of the firm.

5.2.5. BM Reverse Stress Testing Framework

5.2.5.1. What Is BM Reverse Stress Testing?

The aim with BM reverse stress testing is to find out what will break the business model – that is, make it unviable. In an orthodox stress test, the scenario is defined and the firm calculates what the impact would be on the various BM components. In a BM reverse stress test, the firm identifies scenarios that could threaten the survival of the BM, and seeks to take precautions to ensure the BM can withstand them. BM reverse stress tests need to be event driven, focusing on events that cause the most damage. The Board has to try to think outside the box. Remember; as it develops the BM reverse stress test framework the Board will always lean towards its own preferences. Therefore, instead, the Board should start with the big picture and think about what are the external and emerging events that concern your Board from a BM perspective. Then once the Board starts to define those potential events, it needs to look at how these events impact the business model and then look at the implications for the various BM components.

5.2.5.2. BM Reverse Stress Testing

A bank reverse stress test looks at the worst events that could cause in terms of capital losses the collapse of the bank, while a BM reverse stress test will look for the worst emerging event and how it affects (the interaction of) the various BM components. The reverse stress testing of a BM heralds a new interest, namely the involvement of key internal stakeholders. Indeed, the latter play a pivotal role as they attempt to describe the BM of the organization, and thus the description of the BM requires the involvement of the business lines, strategic risk management, finance, operations, legal, etc. Also, this dialogue between these stakeholders in a context of BM reverse stress testing ultimately aims at discussing the resilience of the BM build upon the idea of strategic planning.

5.2.5.3. BM Reverse Stress Testing & Strategic Planning

In an ideal world, the outcomes of stress testing simulations should facilitate decision-making by the senior leadership. Stress testing findings should be utilized to inform the executive management about the alignment of the banking organization's risk profile with the board's opted risk appetite, as well as assist operating and strategic decisions. Stress testing results should be considered directly by the board and senior management for decisions relating to capital and liquidity adequacy, including capital contingency plans and contingency funding plans. Senior management, in consultation with the board, should ensure that the stress-testing framework includes a sufficient range of stress testing activities applied at the appropriate levels of the banking organization (i.e., not just one enterprise-wide stress test).

Sound governance also includes using stress testing to consider the effectiveness of a banking organization's risk mitigation techniques for various risk types over their respective time horizons, such as to explore what could occur if expected mitigation techniques break down during stressful periods. By delivering insight into a broader range of risk factors and their consequences, stress testing can become the bedrock of a broader, more proactive risk management strategy that spots potential threats to the current bank's

BM and throws up first warnings giving the banking organization more time to take necessary corrective decisions.

Stress testing has typically been driven mainly by prudential authorities, but also internally by risk management departments as they run dynamic as well as static simulations in response to both prudential and business requirements. The right management decisions could make sure these analyses are put to proper use in all layers of the banking organization. Having the capacity to run tailored stress tests or scenario analyses with not just market but also business scenarios as a base need to become the next development in stress testing. Being aware of the prevalent risks is one thing; responding on that knowledge is another. Assume a banking institution has been reporting an imminent high-probability market risk event -- for instance a sudden rise in interest rates as consequence of post-crisis economic recovery (not improbable at this moment looking at how interest rates evolve). This type of information should not only provide senior leadership with the conclusion that net interest margins might fall due to mismatches in maturity between long-term retail lending and short-term liability funding. It should also give senior leadership options to leverage the potentials of the business in such a way that it reaps the benefits from this risk.

5.2.5.4. Benefits And Weaknesses Of BM Reverse Stress Testing

The BM reverse stress test requires firms to identify one or more events that cause the failure of the firm's BM, and should, therefore, be linked to the overall business and strategic planning process. The findings of a BM reverse stress test would enable the organization to take precautions to ensure its BM can withstand these death threats.

While banks test their products before launching them through market studies and marketing analysis to make sure its fits customer expectations, they are not subjecting the future revenue and profit potentials to stress testing. Ultimately, integrating BM reverse stress testing into the strategic planning of the banks also allows the office of the Chief Risk Officer to become the "trusted business partner" with much higher visibility in shaping the strategic direction and Risk Appetite of the institution and working in much closer proximity with the CEO and CFO offices. Critical enablers in this convergence include (Klein, 2017) organizational alignment; risk appetite allocation granularity and dynamic recalibration capabilities; aligned decision processes, shared KPIs; as well as integrated metrics, analytics, and reporting.

Banks should welcome the ambition of the US Federal Reserve for banking organizations to turn stress testing exercises into an active part of their strategic risk management, rather than to look down at the exercise as a cumbersome yearly chore.

5.2.6. Conclusion

Stress testing plays a crucial role in shielding the financial system from systemic collapse. By demanding banks to conduct simulations of a range of macroeconomic scenarios, regulators have gained in transparency, namely into how bank organizations determine their capital levels and if they are adequately capitalized to survive systemic, severe adverse economic scenarios.

Stress testing commenced as a significant bank initiative – but prudential authorities did not stop there. With recent regulations such as, for example DFAST (Dodd-Frank Act Stress Test) in the US, a wide range of banks are expected to meet stress testing demands in accordance to their sizes, lines of business, geographic locations and more so they, too, can exhibit how their frameworks of setting capital levels are thorough and prudent. Concomitantly, regulators have modified their attention from merely understanding the impacts of stress scenarios on credit performance and revenue to enabling stress testing to become an integral part of a banking organization's capital plan. However, alas, traditional stress testing does not go far enough to test the resilience and viability of a bank's BM. There is therefore need for a change allowing board executives as well as prudential authorities to analyze the vulnerabilities of the BM of banking organization in much greater detail and from various perspectives. And, the answer is BM reverse stress testing as one of the qualitative approaches to evaluating the robustness of a bank when facing extreme risk events. The method builds upon concepts from both BM innovation and reverse stress testing. It is essential that organizations identify what could cause their business to fail and use this information to ensure that the relevant risks are sufficiently well understood and appropriately strategically managed to secure consumer protection and market confidence. In other words, the idea is to overcome human behavioral, cognitive biases, such as disaster myopia and optimism bias.

5.2.7. Afterthoughts:

Banking regulators around the globe will most likely insist with banks to further enhance their capabilities and incorporate stress testing in their business decision-making processes. Therefore, the banking organization needs to adopt and design such capabilities before they are compelled to do so. This is particularly true now as the US economy is gaining momentum: surfing on an economic wave, US banks have gained additional breathing room before the upcoming round. Bank organizations that have not yet done so should push hard to strengthen their quality of data, model performance, efficiency, not to mention scenario flexibility. The investment needed is only a small fraction of the structural advantages they can capture.

Banks that already have robust stress-testing capabilities should embed the critical insights heralded by a BM reverse stress test framework in their strategic and tactical decisions by widening the scenario coverage of their reverse stress test exercises and integrating these results into their existing decision-making processes, including operational and capital planning as well as risk management. The benefits, both strategic and tactical, are tangible.

However, concomitantly, BM reverse stress testing can make stress testing an even more complicated challenge, particularly as stress tests are increasingly multijurisdictional and data-intensive. They necessitate seamless, end-to-end execution of highly complex analytics at very high speeds. Moreover, finalizing all of this work is consuming even more of the banks' precious time and resources.

5.2.8. Appendix 1: Best Market Practice BM Reverse Stress Testing

The following rules should be applied when designing one (Gea-Carrasco and Nyberg, 2013):

- Granularity: Able to drill down to individual stress factors that may impact the BM, the products and services and the business lines as a whole.
- Consistency: Consistent with the banking organization's general stress testing framework.
- Integration: an integral part of the enterprise risk management architecture and function.
- Flexibility: Fully tailored to the BM of the banking organization.
- Scalability: Accommodate future needs concerning portfolios, regulatory guidelines, asset coverage, or, geographies.

From a data management and workflow perspective, as a best market practice, banking institutions should design centralized, enterprise-wide stress testing and BM reverse stress frameworks that endeavor to integrate the entire chain that consists of data, analytics, as well as reporting. All information pertinent to measuring, managing, reporting, and monitoring the BM reverse stress testing findings should be made easily accessible and cost-effective.

From a prudential compliance point of view, banks' enterprise risk management architecture should be capable of designing pre-configured BM reversing stress testing management information reports for the benefit of various prudential jurisdictions. The banking institutions should also preserve the analysis history for trend analysis purposes, auditing, not to mention benchmarking across several dimensions and for each legal entity of the banking organization.

From an operational perspective, management platform should allow banks to drill down into each scenario to see the detailed underlying factors' composition during the BM reverse stress testing calculation process. From a reporting perspective, the platform should perform side-by-side comparison analysis between the BM reverse stress testing results across jurisdictions, strategies, business lines, products, customer segments, portfolios, etc. To be effective, the BM reverse stress testing exercise should finalize an enterprise-wide contingency plan framework to address vulnerabilities before the changes hit and ensure the survival of the institution under those events.

Banking institutions should analyze the BM reverse stress testing findings using a bottom-up modelling method. The benefit of such a method is that it avoids solving inversion problems arising from maximization-based models and concomitantly accounts for all the risk dependencies during the simulation through the factors' correlation structure and migration dynamics. On the other hand, top-down approaches are usually not suitable for BM reverse stress testing analysis since the factors' realizations are aggregated and cannot be decomposed at an individual level.

Once the modelling flow and enterprise risk management architecture have been set at the institution, the BM reverse stress test analysis should start by specifying a target loss level, business line or sub-portfolio subject to the analysis. The analysis should then identify the macroeconomic shocks, scenarios, and extreme risk factors driving those losses. Subsequently, the connections with a portfolio's performance, strategic events (merger, acquisition, new portfolio composition, etc.), and BM weaknesses (insolvency, bankruptcy, etc.) should be analyzed as well. Therefore, the analysis would identify hidden vulnerabilities that may not have been detected during the stress testing analysis.

There are six main recommended stages when performing a bottom-up BM reverse stress testing analysis at the enterprise-wide level (Gea-Carrasco and Nyberg, 2013).

<u>Stage 1: Determine target metrics and survival values</u>

The first phase involves determining the proper loss level (e.g., confidence interval level) for the indicator of interest for the banking institution (e.g., solvency ratio, capital ratio, liquidity ratio, etc.). The horizon for the analysis should be in line with the requirements to complete the capital needs under the corresponding prudential jurisdiction and rules (e.g., one year under Basel III).

<u>Stage 2: Run extreme risk factor analysis</u>

The second phase is to map the factor draws and their combinations that had the most effect on the portfolio tail region through a quantitative discovery process. The metrics and the loss associated with the portfolio in the tail region, as well as which products, counterparties, countries, and industries that respond most to these states, are also known at this level. The correlation structure impacting the bank's balance sheet composition should equally be taken into consideration in the analysis.

Stage 3: Pinpoint macroeconomic variables

Once the most pertinent factors have been spotted from Stage 2, a sensitivity analysis is conducted to analyze the effect of all these factors on a banking institution's BM. This analysis is meant to uncover the severity of the scenarios required for the banking organization to default, or losses to exceed the given level of equity in Stage 1.

Stage 4: Spot unviable scenarios and hidden vulnerabilities

Factors from Stage 3 are ranked and mapped against macroeconomic variables and scenarios designed during the simulation. In detail, for each simulated trial and each analyzed area a unique vector (φ) determines the relevant macroeconomic variables (MV) and their weights (w) at counterparty level:

Stage 5: Conduct enterprise-wide sensitivity analysis

Macroeconomic variables from Stage 4 are mapped to macroeconomic variables from the stress testing analysis, thus identifying hidden vulnerabilities and overlapping effects.

Stage 6: Take corrective actions and establish business contingency plans

Finally, to be effective, the analysis should indicate how resilient a banking organization's BM is for a range of various capitalization and solvency ratios. An enterprise-wide risk management diagnostic matrix should disclose the information, sensitivity analysis, and facilitate analyzing the findings for regulatory reporting and decision-making initiatives. From a workflow and data management perspective, as a best market practice, banking institutions should develop centralized, bank-wide stress testing and reverse stress frameworks that endeavor to integrate data, analytics, and reporting. Having a bank-wide stress test framework that acknowledges both classic stress testing analysis and reverse stress test is a game changer for banking institutions.

BM reverse stress testing handles extreme risk analysis by beginning from a known stress test finding and then figuring what type of events could result into such an outcome for the banking institution, disclosing hidden vulnerabilities in the portfolio and in the bank's stress testing architecture that may not be detected during the stress testing analysis. Therefore, a robust and consistent portfolio bottom-up modelling approach is key to avoiding under or overestimation of risk for enabling flexible risk management policies and raising the return on equity for the shareholders. The introduced modelling framework allows banking institutions to comprehend and identify the bank-wide risks under adverse conditions that may have severe consequences for their solvency position. The architecture can be utilized to provide strategic guidance and perform analysis in order to uncover hidden vulnerabilities and extreme risks for various vital indicators.

5.2.9. Appendix 2: Practical Example BM Stress Testing On A Bank

The approach produces a heat map with the trends and uncertainties as columns and BM components as rows. For example, if based on the banking outlook for 2018 (EY, 2018) and the long-term trends that threaten the banking industry, the following uncertainties come to the forefront for the banking industry:

- The rise of FinTech,
- The adoption of cognitive systems,
- Compliance with never ending changing regulatory requirements (banking~, consumer~, and accounting), and
- Emerging risks from increasingly volatile and interconnected world scene (. f. ex. cyber risk, financial crime, reputational and culture risk).

Indeed, over the past years, the ability of banking organizations to maximize financial performance through optimization and growth has been restricted as a result of emerging risks, the entrance of new players and new technology, and constant regulatory change programs and compliance demands (look at how regulatory reporting is changing before and under U.S. President Trump) (Gordon, 2018).

While this exercise has great merits in better understanding in what way the BM components of a bank can become under threat and hence the viability and resilience of the bank's BM, it still shares similarities with the traditional bank stress tests, in the sense that it is based on a set of predetermined stress scenarios. However, in order to test the true resilience of BM, the organization should test the BM to its destruction. We do not want to run a BM stress test like it would be just a quick blip showing the organization where something is and gives it a rough shape for the level of risk that your organization take. Instead, one needs to run a stress test through which the organization identifies scenarios that could threaten the survival of its BM, and such a stress test would be BM reverse stress test.

5.2.10. Appendix 3: Example Of BM Reverse Stress Testing

BM reverse stress tests look for those scenarios that lead to a very unfavorable event for the BM of a bank. So, start with the big picture and think about what are the scenarios, what are the external and emerging events that concern the Board of the organization. Then once those potential scenarios are defined, look at how they impact the BM and then assess the capital implications.

One of the biggest challenges in developing effective BM reverse stress tests is defining what makes the BM unviable. And, this could happen well before the banking organization runs out of capital, such as, for instance, a reputational crisis involving a widespread scandal. Indeed, the point at which the capital and or liquidity of the bank are exhausted may not be the only point where the BM fails. Agreeing what makes the BM unviable is one of the most important parts of designing an effective reverse stress test.

Banking organizations must look at the whole picture (f. ex. the components described in the BM canvas) when considering what could make the BM unviable. The Board has to ask itself, what are the non-financial aspects that could cause the BM to fail. The Board needs to think about it in the context of bank's customers and other stakeholders. Reputational risk is absolutely crucial in this respect, and the challenge is how to quantify those risks. In other words, the Board must not stop at the financials; it is such a big mistake to do that. There is a bit of tendency to focus on capital requirements, liquidity, etc., but not on other important aspects, such as the relationship with the bank's customers and what they are thinking about, its reputation, or its capital quality. It is the total picture that the Board needs to be looking at.

Classic 'death sentence' scenarios can be, for example, an equity-exhausting loss, a non-fulfillment of the capital adequacy requirements, illiquidity, etc. But, it can also be the involvement of the bank in a money laundering scandal, embezzlement of clients' monies, a major reputational crisis as a result of a scandal, etc. More generally, scenarios shall be identified that lead to an outcome in which the bank's business plan becomes unviable and the bank collapses.

5.2.11. Appendix 4: Recent Survey About Stress Testing

Although the outcomes of internal and external stress testing frameworks have been utilized within the industry, the findings of these stress tests are usually not at a level of detail or run at a frequency that is interesting for banking decision-making beyond yearly high-level planning. Additionally, internal stress testing is not aligned with external stress testing making the whole process very cumbersome with the bank.

Internal stress testing is mostly aligned with the planning process of capital and the setting of capital cushions, and, to some degree, business recovery planning, notwithstanding the fact it was acknowledged that each mirrored a different level of severity of stress incident in the bank's action plan. Executives in business planning and product strategy utilize stress test outcomes to assist in informing high level risk appetite, but typically the stress testing process is not agile enough to be fully included in business decisions on a permanent basis. However, the timing of prudential stress testing does not match internal capital and strategic planning cycles within the bank. And, stress test exercises require significant resources, resulting in stress testing sometimes being utilized only as a final rubber stamp of strategy instead of proactively used throughout the entire planning process.

A recent survey by KMPG (Hinchliffe and Smith, 2016) has highlighted that participants typically flag insufficient time or 'business as usual' pressures as underlying reasons why there were very few alignments between business activities and stress tests. Last but not least, to decide what needs to be stressed, banking organizations many times align their efforts with prudential needs or market best practices, instead of deriving them from an internal business and risk analysis perspective (Thun, 2013).

KPMG survey highlights the following findings (Hinchliffe and Smith, 2016):

The imbalance between regulatory and internal stress testing is limiting its usage.

- Comprehending the actual cost of stress testing is paramount to the bank's investment policy into stress testing methods.
- More people on the ground are not necessary the best solution.
- Too much reliance on manual processes to complete stress testing.
- Data mining and reconciliation pinpointed as a significant hurdle and a primary concern for the bank's ability to address stress testing
- Must continue to reinforce the methods through the utilization of challenger models to benchmark model outcomes and make sure that model risk management rules are reinforced to embed all stress testing models.

However, the survey findings say nothing about the lack of reliability of these tests (cf. while the Franco-Belgian bank Dexia had passed in August 2011 the EBA stress test successfully, it required a bail-out three months later (Pignal and Jenkins, 2011); and a similar case affected the Irish banks that had received the green after passing the stress test August 2011 before falling into problems in November of that year (Jenkins, 2010) - both are compelling illustrations of how stress test findings can misrepresent a bank's situation). Already, the Federal Reserve is moving toward eliminating passing and failing grades for its stress tests of the nation's largest banks (Tracy, 2018), replacing them with a capital ratio that the lender must meet during the following year.

5.3. Solution #3: High Reliability Organization

5.3.1. Introduction

Could Global Systemically Important Banks (G-SIBs) act more like the airline or nuclear industry, meaning operate in a similar fashion as high-reliability organizations (HRO)? We strongly believe that the answer to this question is affirmative: the HRO theory can provide an added value for the G-SIBs, their clients, and other stakeholders alike.

Why are we interested in this concept? Naturally, because notwithstanding decades of research about how to prevent crises and manage them, it seems that financial catastrophes keep on happening. One reason is, of course, the fact that the nature of our economies has changed with the increased globalization, financialization, digitalization, and interconnectedness. The economic systems around the world have become more interdependent, and that makes them also more susceptible to volatility as a financial or economic incident in one part of the world can easily cause a domino effect and spread to other parts of the world.

However, another reason why we want to dig deeper into this concept of HRO theory is also that we feel that a lot of good best market practices on extreme (or tail) risk management prevail outside the sphere of the banking world. Alas, these practices remain out of reach of the banks, partly because the academic world tends to operate in a silo, but also because there are not enough bridges between the banking industry and the other industries of the economy. Additionally, regulators across industries typically do not share much information among themselves either. There is a vast collective knowledge about crisis avoidance and management. However, for reasons mentioned above, such knowledge has not yet fully permeated into the area of banking.

In this day and age of complexity, but also of easier access to information, it is crucial to have an interdisciplinary approach that fosters a change in how organizations can prevent financial crises, but foremost how their effects could be better mitigated.

There are many causes of financial failure: it is mostly as a result of human decision processes (Ciro, 2016), organizational policies, but also technological incidents and external events. However, a lack of imagination (US Federal 9/11 Commission Report, 2004) can also trigger a failure, in the sense that organizations are not sufficiently ready when facing a crisis. Many times, banking executives claimed that they did not see this global financial crisis in 2007 coming. Really, or is it because they were too complacent (Tucker, 2010) and lacked imagination?

Since the Global Financial Crisis of 2007-2008, there have been many articles written heralding the need for organizations to build more resilient business models. Resilience is the best remedy for an organization when facing turbulent times. However, in the world of financial markets, power rests with those who control the money, and they may seem reluctant to alter their current modus operandi. And, while culture and strategic planning are key factors that help promote trust (and thus stability) in the financial system, a recent study (Young, 2011) shows that the challenge in bringing about change should not be underestimated, especially in developed nations where plutonomies are predominant. Indeed, as a result of the increased financialization of the economy combined with the phenomenon of globalization and international financial markets, financial power is ever more concentrated around a few financial powerhouses (Azkunaga, 2013).

5.3.2. Why HROs?

Studies on the management of extreme (aka tail) risk in financial organizations have predominantly utilized quantitative and probabilistic approaches. Such approaches provide risk managers with a way to measure the probability of a failure occurring because of an extreme event; however, as the recent global financial crisis has highlighted, they do not provide sufficient insights about specific managerial actions that can be taken to avoid the occurrence and the effects of such failure.

Moreover, this is particularly important for the financial services industry as extreme risks affecting one banking entity might in turn quickly lead to a systemic risk that would propagate throughout the entire financial and economic system. Indeed, it is not just the too big to fail principle that can be a cause of systemic risk, but also the theory of the complex network that could be at play (Puliga, 2016). Looking at best practices regarding extreme risk management across other industries, one could intuitively value the implementation of an HRO theory as a qualitative risk tool for the banking industry as well, and particularly as it relates to G-SIBs.

In other words, HRO theories can make an essential contribution to the effective management of extreme risk for G-SIBs, and thus render them more resilient. It is possible to take steps to not only lower the likelihood that they will take place but also mitigate their effects thanks to a good comprehension of the underlying causal processes that contribute to failures rooted in extreme events.

5.3.3. What Are HROs?

One of the tools to achieve this goal of resilience is the use of the concept of "High-Reliability Organization (HRO)." HROs are an oddity, and they exist in the very complex, fast-evolving business environments where we would expect chaos to prevail, while instead customers perceive these business activities as being free of chaos. HROs, notwithstanding the fact that they are hazardous organizations, cope successfully with unexpected conditions as they enjoy high levels of safety for a long period of time, and that is what makes these unique organizations so attractive to scholars.

Knowledge about HROs is rooted in what is called intrepid organizations, that is where a thousand things must go right every moment, or someone dies. There are a couple of good examples of HROs, such as aircraft carriers, ER in hospitals, air traffic control systems, NASA, nuclear reactors, firefighters combating wildfires, the military, railroad freight companies, or prison logistics. We would like to broaden the application of this HRO concept to the banking industry, for example.

In essence, HROs are illustrations of mindful organizing, which entails sense-making (Weick, 2001), continuous coordination, and adaptive managing. The culture of organizational learning that characterizes HROs allows for a persistent drive toward improvement, as these organizations do not tolerate operations that are not running smoothly all the time.

Any significant deviation from planned courses of action is likely to evolve into a publicly visible human-made disaster that could lead to the destruction of the organization and harming the broader public. Also, they treat near misses with the same sense of urgency as a failure, being ever mindful that the circumstances that led to a near miss could reemerge as a disaster. Thanks to a structured system of gathering of feedback, not to mention the handling of operational and program reviews, HROs are able to continually focus on improvement. This principle forms a basis for a continuous drive for improvement that governs the way these organizations operate, and in particular, how they view failure. By continually monitoring performance, HROs promote an environment among their personnel of never being satisfied with the status quo. These organizations display a rather uncommon inclination to reward the uncovering and recording of errors in lieu of assigning blame. High-reliability organizations monitor organizational performance by maintaining thorough records about performance data.

As already mentioned, HROs are stable organizations with a low probability of failure and capable of continuing to operate efficiently in times of trouble. They are highly reliable evidenced by their ability to bouncing back quickly, but most importantly by being resilient. They pride themselves on focusing on excellent customer service (be it for internal or external stakeholders) with the ability to always deliver products and services of high quality notwithstanding the circumstances under which they have to operate. It is therefore that G-SIBs, in a context of ever more recurring black swans, would be well-advised to adapt their corporate culture as well as strategic planning in such a way that it embraces these principles of HRO. A big part of the reliability culture is the focus on the value proposition of the organization (Sullivan, 2014), and this core objective (mission statement) is then communicated to each member of the organization. Just like in a chain, the weakest link affects the stability of the entire chain. And, that is why for any incident that takes place at any level of the organization the appropriate remedial action is thorough, significant as well as swift. And, even more importantly, such remedial action is visible as it would be the result of a collective action. Operating under such conditions, HROs promote a culture of persistence that turns any company into an ideal working environment where learning from mistakes, continuously improving, and becoming more skillful are the daily leitmotivs.

5.3.4. Methods

In the past decades, researchers (i.e., C. Perrow, P.N Rasmussen, K.H. Roberts, and K.E. Weick & Sutcliffe) have found that agencies that operate according to certain principles, henceforth referred to as High-Reliability Organizations (HROs), both avoid mishaps as well as perform markedly better during system accidents compared to other organizations. The literature on the subject of HROs enumerates models that oscillate between enabling individuals to operate in an environment shaped by uncertainty and ongoing threats (van Stralen) to making organizations (Roberts)/ operations (Mercer)/ societies (Perrow) more robust. These organizations will be either operating as HROs (Roberts, and Weick), performing under uncertainty (van Stralen), or in an environment characterized by normal accidents (Perrow).

A model that caught our attention is the one from van Stralen, where starting from the micro-level, the model contemplates how an individual needs to operate in an environment conditioned by uncertainty and threat. It is indeed the individual that spurs the action whenever he/she perceives a lingering threat or potential incident. Subsequently, the individual will share and explain to other individuals the nature of the threat and the way to deal with it. As a result, through collaboration, the team will have a shared objective and action plan to deal with the threat

Generally speaking, two of the main contributors to the HRO theory have been Drs. Karl E Weick and Kathleen M. Sutcliffe who describe the five principles of high-reliability organizations in their book "Managing the Unexpected: Sustained Performance in a Complex World." Below are the five principles that they enumerate:

- Preoccupation with failure, meaning realize the importance of any job position in the organization (while concomitantly try not be paralyzed in anxiety). Absent-mindedness could lead to failure.

- Reluctance to simplify, meaning do not overgeneralize while at the same time conduct proper root-cause analyzes allowing to understand the complexity of the situation.
- Sensitivity to operations in trying to understand the reasoning behind policies and protocols and how they affect the larger picture.
- Commitment to resilience by looking at mistakes as opportunities for development and improvement.
- Deference to expertise, meaning be aware of weaknesses and strengths while at the same time recognizing the expertise that is vested with other colleagues.

With the aim to help G-SIBs becoming more resilient businesses when facing extreme risk events, one could reshape these five pillars fittingly for the banking industry into the following four pillars that will help transform banks into high-reliability organizations. However, we are talking here about a cultural change, and such a change cannot happen overnight. It cannot be the result of a one-time event, but instead of a movement. That is why when drafting these HRO principles for banks we also need to look at how the organization can implement the cultural change.

- Senior leadership needs to foster a culture of operational awareness within the entire organization. Ultimately decentralization and bottom-up feedback should be encouraged.
- An embodiment of resilience by changing the mindset of the employees of the organization. This embodiment should be achieved through constant learning in work groups to alter the thinking and reinforce the need for change. Such a learning organization should also value expertise and seniority.
- Reluctance to oversimplify while heralding redundancy. While concepts such as 'lean' are prevalent, they can also cause damage when a company needs extra resources as it faces a crisis.

- There should be a specific focus on safety in combination with performance, and this needs to be at the individual, team, and organizational level.

5.3.5. Principles Of HRO

So, how would these four principles apply to banks and impact their culture and strategic planning? Changing an entrenched culture is a challenging task, and to do so we need to conquer the hearts and minds of all the people that are part of the organization, not just the top leadership, but all banking employees. In other words, a mandate coming from the executive leadership (or regulators) does not suffice; to bring about a cultural change you need a movement.

5.3.5.1. Fostering A Culture Of Operational Awareness

So, firstly, given that the premise of HROs is about fostering a corporate culture of operational awareness about extreme risk, this means that not only banking executives, but, also, mostly banking staff need to be permanently aware of how systems and processes affect the bank. In other words, everyone needs to be aware of the bigger picture and how the contribution of each banking employee affects the banking strategy and activities. Banking employees in HROs are typically very attentive to details about ongoing activities, and are very much aware about what is going on and what is not working. There are no assumptions, and the approach should be integrated. This steady concentration on processes leads to observations that inform banking executives with decision-making powers as well as new operational initiatives aimed at improving the organization within the bank.

We could get the most out of this HRO concept by encouraging senior banking executives to become more transparent, which will in turn create an environment that nurtures awareness. The more banking employees know and are aware of the bank's strategy and how their job assignment fits within the big organization picture, the more likely they will pay attention. In other words, banking executives can steer employees into more organizational awareness through involvement and information sharing and, foremost, improved communication.

This need for transparent communicate should not only be geared towards internal stakeholders (i.e., senior management as well as other departments within the organization) but also external stakeholders (cf. clients, shareholders, vendors, suppliers, regulators, etc.). Banking executives that walk around the desks and the corridors of the bank develop a more textured understanding of the existing business processes.

Leaders should go down their hierarchical ladder and on a weekly basis take a couple of hours to attentively watch operations and talk directly with employees and their supervisors. Connecting with staff and having an open-door policy promotes direct and constructive communication. Going around on the field will help senior executives understand which processes are failing as well as those that are creating a lousy customer experience (be it towards either internal or external stakeholders).

However, it is crucial that those rounds should be deliberately driven by an enthusiasm to identify operational problems and find solutions that add value by asking questions, such as 'Have you noticed anything that worries you?'; 'Is there anything we are doing that is causing harm to our stakeholders?' Banking staff needs to know that the door of any senior executive is always open to direct communication and that no matter is unimportant. In order to hear out employees' concerns, business leaders should hold regular discussions with them that are proactive.

5.3.5.2. HRO Needs To Be A Learning Organization.

As leaders and senior executives take ownership of the need for a culture shape in embracing the HRO theory, they can only turn this into a lasting change if it occurs through the personal insights of all employees. People within the organization who have the most knowledge and expertise of the tasks at hand need to be able to communicate easily with senior leadership. Moreover, even if those individuals might still be somewhat junior, they must still be incited to make their concerns and ideas known to other staff members — regardless of hierarchy.

There has to be two-way communication between on the one hand leaders & supervisors and the other hand their teams & employees. If a banking executive does not pay attention or listens to employees about processes and operations within the banking organization, it will be very difficult to promote an awareness culture that fosters high-reliability. One thing that would demotivate employees is when a leader responds to someone's concern or idea as 'I already know that.' From that moment onwards staff will stop telling things to senior executives.

In essence, the best place for conversations between leaders and staff is casually within the work area (f. ex. during a coffee or lunch break or while doing your rounds on the field) — and not formally in conference rooms or meetings. In other words, those rounds that senior executives should be doing will help them obtain feedback from employees, supervisors and other staff members alike. In return, whatever important information the senior manager has gathered should be shared with the rest of the staff so that they could all learn from it.

By observing firsthand on the field, the existing business processes and meeting with employees in their actual workspace, managers and supervisors can more easily defer to employees' customs and expertise. Another way to turn this principle of learning organization into something substantiate is asking staff about their prior experiences. Most people who work in banking have previous experience with another banking organization. Banking executives should treasure this vast source of expertise, and the best place to get a fresh perspective on existing processes is from the new hiring. In the financial services industry (like in many other sectors), organizations hire consultants and pay them thousands of dollars to tell them what team could say to them for free. In practice, senior managers should hold monthly or quarterly reviews with new employees during which senior managers would ask them whether based on their previous work experience, what would be some of the ideas they might have to improve existing operations here.

5.3.5.3. Reluctance To Oversimplify While Promoting Redundancy.

HROs are extremely resistant to solving complex problems with seemingly effortless explanations. Simplistic solutions can put the organization at risk by not digging deep enough to find the actual source of a specific problem. There is no such thing as a general solution to a specific problem. Simplifying business processes can be a good thing, but oversimplifying things can also be not good. It is tempting for an organization when facing a crisis to point to a simple reason for failures such as poor communication or a lack of resources. If the organization's probes were so much more in-depth, they might then find an explanation underlying the cause of the event.

High-reliability organizations will keep on drilling down into the cause of a problem until finding the specific source of the problem. Another critical theme with HROs is the need for having excess capacity and backup systems, which enables an organization facing a failure. In other words, there needs to be some degree of overlapping of policies, strategies, and systems to provide services to stakeholders. A certain degree of redundancy of assets and resources allows for the banking organization to maintain its core function during a time of crisis. Additionally, if the bank promotes flexible policies and strategies, these might be helping the bank better cope and adapt to a changing environment as a result of a crisis.

The best way to embrace this concept of resisting to oversimplification is to be willing to challenge long-held beliefs and be imaginative. When they walk around on the field meeting staff, leaders should continuously look at data, benchmarks and other performance metrics, and see how things could be further improved. Also, a good way to avoid oversimplification is when banking executives continually seek data that challenges their current train of thoughts as to why difficulties may occur and are more imaginative in how the existing business processes could potentially derail.

Businesses need to take a deep dive into their metrics, compare data sets and question simple explanations that may seem at first sight reasonable, because the very opposite may be very much true. As it relates to redundancy, its basic form used by all organizations is safety stock. In the banking industry, this means having sufficient back-ups regarding resources (IT and staff). However, one needs to keep in mind that severe excess can also be the culprit in hidden business processes. Indeed, with extra capacity, it is very tempting to managers to tap into extra resources rather than investigate the cause of a problem: When resources are lean, any defect requires immediate management attention. So, there has to be a balance when talking about extra slack: it does not necessarily entail a large number of additional assets but rather the existence of robust procedures and backup plans (be it for IT or staffing).

5.3.5.4. HRO Always Focus On The Avoidance Of Failure.

All banking employees need to be entirely on top of their daily duties, and, therefore, need to think proactively outside of the box about ways how their work process could be improved or how their work might one day fail. Moreover, all members of staff should share this ongoing preoccupation about failure avoidance. Even seemingly trivial incidents need to be brought to the attention of the leadership as domino effects can quickly turn an incident into a catastrophe for the entire organization.

Again, every organization should encourage all banking employees to voice their concerns for potential incidents, because such an attitude could help the organization in building a collective experience about these incidents and as a result, establishing a best practice. When employees make mistakes, HRO call them 'near-misses' as a way for not blaming an employee for a mistake while on the contrary encouraging staff to come forward when a mistake has been made. This allows the HRO to respond more quickly so that the stakeholder would end up not being harmed. These near-misses or perceived minor incidents are in reality an opportunity for the organization to learn from these failures, and thus move forward with better and improved banking processes.

We harness best this value by identify what is working and what is not working correctly. Innovation in an organization is the result of a set of learning processes that are iterative, thereby encouraging critical debates and experiments as well as accepting failures as a necessary part of the banking processes. From failure comes learning and adaptation that are both key to help banking organizations become more resilient. Also, when in an HRO a business process is incorrectly implemented one should endeavor to try to find a best practice in, for instance, another department where a similar process there works smoothly. An excellent way to approach working processes is by asking 'How come we cannot do it in our department, while it is possible in theirs?' In other words, learn about best practices from other successful operations, be it from within the organization or outside.

5.3.6. Findings

Notwithstanding widespread and serious regulatory and corporate efforts to improve the quality of the banking industry, many banks still suffer preventable harm every day, such as excessive risk taking, overleveraging, strained liquidity, asset quality problems, etc. But, alas, banks suffer from 'change management torpor' as they seem overwhelmed by a myriad of issues and can no longer cope with it simultaneously. And, alas, no banks or banking systems have achieved consistent excellence throughout their institutions.

As pointed out in a study from the Milbank Quarterly (Chassin, 2013) the science of high-reliability is in essence the study of organizations active in hazardous industries, such as airlines and nuclear power utilities, for instance, that need to run at all times error-free operations. Adapting and applying the lessons of this science to banks offer the promise of enabling banking institutions to achieve levels of error free operations and quality that would be similar to those of the best HROs.

But, as banks will make more progress toward high reliability, they will need to include safety (aka zero harm) culture metrics as part of their strategic planning programs, set goals for reinforcing those metrics, and monitor the compliance with those metrics to their executive boards, similar to the metrics they already monitor on financial performance or client satisfaction.

The concept of HRO has already been tested for the banking industry, namely through the works of Weber, Medeiros & Pinto, but also Young, as well as Leaver & Reader. According to a study (Weber, 2015) the Basel III supervisory reform agenda has heralded resilience and containment through additional and more robust capital adequacy rules, not to mention the creation of an orderly liquidation authority allowing for liquidations of nearly defaulting large complex financial organizations to be more predictable and efficient. Weber contends that better-capitalized institutions are deemed to be more resilient and better able to preserve solvency covering a range of future scenarios. Moreover, no matter how interconnected or large the financial institution is, supervisors would be able to contain the effect of an unexpected failure of an institution thanks to this new resolution mechanism that would cover all G-SIBs.

However, the whole rationale of this Ph.D. thesis is to claim that the compliance with quantitative measures alone does not make banks more resilient. What is needed is a set of qualitative risk tools that would affect not only the strategic planning of the bank but foremost the corporate culture, namely the way how the organization runs its hazardous business activities on a daily basis. That is why the study by Young (2011) carries more weight as it emphasizes the need for a cultural change to bring about the concepts of HROs in the banking industry. He too believes that solely probabilistic quantitative measures used as tools for risk management do not suffice to make banks resilient.

To that respect, the writing by Medeiros & Pinto (2009) is equally compelling as both researchers looked at how the (Brazilian) banking industry could apply the HRO principles. Finally, there is also the research conducted by Leaver & Reader (2017). However, we feel that the latter is too oriented towards operational risks intended to cover mostly fraud and conduct - although we agree these events can also be a cause of extreme risk; our concept of extreme risk goes further and is, therefore, broader in its scope (Hodgson, 2013).

Now, quite clearly, the ways that HROs today generate and maintain high levels of safety cannot be directly applied in overnight to today's banks. The progress toward this goal of high reliability will have to be gradual given the broad changes that banks would need to undertake. Indeed, for those changes to take place, the leadership will have to commit to achieving a goal of zero stakeholder harm, infuse a new corporate culture revolving around safety and avoidance of failure, and deploy a range of tools to improve the business processes.

There is an interesting study (Chassin and Loeb, 2013) that has been written about how HRO's could be applicable to hospitals, and what incremental steps would need to be taken to reach that goal of HRO excellence. We recommend digging deeper into this study and see how its findings might be of interest for the Ph. D. thesis as it relates to G-SIBs.

5.3.7. Conclusion

The combination of these principles and actions will allow for banks to gradually become high-reliability organizations, and thus more resilient and adaptable, and able to bounce back quicker. Leaders at high-reliability organizations foster an environment where employees are encouraged to constantly seek to add value. When organizations become highly reliable they are able to better respond to incidents while coming up with new answers to tackle the effects of these emerging risks. Thanks to their resilience and adaptability, not to mention their capacity to bounce back quickly, HROs are uniquely positioned to respond to extreme risks.

Similar to what takes place in the airline industry, G-SIBs do complex, high-stakes work where mistakes can result in significant harm. That is why so many G-SIBs should likewise be embracing the values of high-reliability organizations that are characteristic for air traffic control towers, nuclear power plants, wildlife firefighters, and astronauts, to name but a few.

The paradigm should operate well in the promotion of trust among clients and the delivery of efficient financial services as it relates to G-SIBs. The processes and systems that HROs are putting in place enable them to be resolute in pursuing their objectives for the sake of their stakeholders while concomitantly preventing potentially catastrophic mistakes from happening. High-reliability organizations can only be as successful as the level to which corporate culture and strategic planning of the organization ingrains specific behaviors, processes, tools, systems and techniques.

5.4. Solution #4: Self-Disruption/ Complexity/ IoT/ Chaos/ God

5.4.1. Self-Disruption

Since the financial crisis in 2008, banks have been focusing on the disruption of the status quo, not only due to increased interconnectedness, globalization, and financialization of corporate organizations, but also because of the rise of Fintech. In the face of successful digital disruptors, the question became whether banks would be replaced or even exist in the future. Sure, there are multiple data points that support this view – 2018 saw record highs of venture capitalist-backed Fintech deals[9], and PwC[10] reported that 88% of financial services companies fear losing revenue to innovators. With funding, the Fintech industry matured rapidly, and it's evident that banks that refuse to participate in today's "banking industry sandbox" are setting themselves up for self-destruction (Haering, 2019).

However, is it enough to just participate? Banks have come to realize that the value of their brands lies in how quickly they are able to meet consumer demands for a more seamless, transparent and secure financial lifecycle. Consumers today are often vocal about their demands, and it's up to the banks to listen and be proactive. They cannot sit back and wait to react. Simply put, banks should decide to self-disrupt. Those who wish to stay ahead in the decades to come need to shape the future business model for banking, rather than wait to conform to the future status quo. And at Finastra, we believe an open platform approach can fast track innovation and encourage agile collaboration.

That said, there are key factors every bank should consider when looking to shape the future status quo. The problem of lack of resilience has gotten worse (Denning, 2018). Since 2003, enormous amounts of wealth have been lost as the pace of disruption

---

[9] See KPMG report: https://home.kpmg/content/dam/kpmg/us/pdf/2018/07/pof-1H-18-report.pdf
[10] See PwC report: https://www.pwc.com/jg/en/publications/pwc-global-fintech-report-17.3.17-final.pdf

accelerates. The marketplace has become faster paced and increasingly complex to such an extent that traditionally managed bureaucratic firms simply can't keep up. As a result, the life expectancy of public firms –once 75 years–continues to decline and is now less than 15 years.

Disruption is increasingly coming from unexpected directions outside the industry, not from known competitors. The picture of once-stable intra-industry competition is no more. Now disruption can come from anywhere. The legendary search for sustainable competitive advantage is proving increasingly futile: competitive advantage is mostly temporary. Firms must go on innovating merely to survive. To add to management's woes, activist investors have joined forces with institutional investors to extract value from existing firms, often forcing a management preoccupation with short-run returns over long-term investment and sustainability. Similar challenges are also occurring in the public sector. For example, an intelligence agency may be tasked, every year, to implement a set of activities. Yet every year their capabilities degrade (as new, unplanned threats emerge, trade-craft and tools become obsolete, and security breaches occur), even if they brilliantly execute their current mission. Moreover, leaders don't always realize that they not only have to execute their current mission: they also have to create new capabilities for security threats over the horizon.

While "platformification" in the U.S. banking landscape is still in its infancy, banks have the opportunity to set the industry benchmark by embracing a platform-centric business model and investing in smart technologies such as cloud infrastructure, machine learning or artificial intelligence (AI). The nature of open banking brings banks and Fintech firms together to move the industry forward. But with existing infrastructure, the sheer breadth of data and a historically large customer base, banks have the upper hand in shaping the future of open banking with platformification (Haering, 2019).

A 2018 study by Celent[11], in partnership with Finastra, Platformification: How Banks Can Transform Their Innovation Efforts, reported that flexibility plays a major role in platformification, as it gives banks the vital tools they need to innovate. Banks

---

[11] See Finastra report: https://www.finastra.com/viewpoints/market-insights/platformification-how-banks-can-transform-their-innovation-efforts

collaborating with Fintechs can move more rapidly and effectively than they could on their own to introduce new products, accelerate growth, streamline processes and enhance customer relationships.

A smooth transition toward open banking requires the following:

- A bank-wide unified data strategy and AI/business intelligence tools that enable banks to provide truly personalized offerings to customers.
- An agile collaboration mindset to break functional silos.
- A company culture that stimulates and fosters innovation.

First, movers should be aware that being an "open bank" will put pressure on them to step up business transformation efforts, both externally to meet consumer demands and internally to transform culture. Traditional C-suites simply will not be able to shape the future of banking unless they look to augment their domain knowledge by cultivating a more innovative and agile company culture. Open banking initiatives should be discussed internally, and the benefits should be clearly accessible to key members of staff. Of course, it's not easy to bring down the walls of history and tradition. After all, it took banks decades to gain two of their most valuable assets: trust and reputation. However, open banking will require a change in company culture – an environment in which to embrace innovation executed by top management.

According to a 2018 report by MIT Technology Review[12], "Open banking: The race to deliver banking as a service," the key to success is uniting business and technology and, with the rapid integration of both, "staff education and culture change is a top priority for banks looking to accelerate innovation". Culture change must begin at the top and facilitate buy-in across the whole organization. Encouraging employees to embrace new opportunities and showing them the benefits of the change are also musts. As technology has given consumers more control over how they choose to bank, banks have the choice to self-disrupt or self-destruct. With open banking on the horizon, banks should grasp the opportunity to be movers in shaping the future of the banking system. After all, banks

[12] See MIT report: https://www.technologyreview.com/2018/09/28/139995/open-banking-the-race-to-deliver-banking-as-a-service/

and Fintechs share one of the same end goals: to deliver on the changing expectations of a digital-savvy consumer. As banks drive partnerships with Fintechs by embracing platformification, customer focus becomes clearer and opens endless possibilities.

The management revolution now under way is about working smarter, not harder, and achieving more value from less work, with much greater adaptability. It began emerging many decades ago but took off in a major way in the software development industry in the last 15 years. Sparking dramatic improvements in quality, innovation, and speed to delivering value, the Agile movement is now spreading quickly, throughout all parts and all kinds of organizations. It enables a team, a unit, and an entire organization to nimbly adapt and upgrade products and services to meet rapidly changing technology and end-user needs and create new businesses. The new way of managing includes three "laws": the Law of the Customer, the Law of the Small Team and the Law of the Network. Fundamental to everything is a recognition that the new way of managing is not a process but a mindset; in which the entire organization embraces the new principles. This is about "being Agile," not just "doing Agile."

Yet while the capability to improve existing products and services ("Operational Agility") is important, and indeed vital to survive, it's not enough for a firm to thrive. Major financial gains are more likely to come from "Strategic Agility", i.e. generating innovations that create entirely new markets and that turn non-customers into customers. Instead of being slightly better than everybody else in a crowded and established field, a firm practicing Strategic Agility creates new markets and dominates them. The profit margins are bigger, and the value to society is often larger. Achieving Strategic Agility, involves mastering a playbook for systematically generating market-creating innovations and the necessary shift in culture that is required.

5.4.2. Complexity

Banking institutions, and the financial markets into which they navigate, reveal aspects of a complex adaptive system that is not suitable to statistical analytics. Banking organizations may fail or can be notably impacted by numerous events that take place during their regular business activities. In this context, scholars and risk professionals alike have been looking at ways to the strengthen the risk management of the banks' activities by relying on forecasting events, measuring their impacts and designing risk mitigation techniques. However, banking environments are getting more complex and volatile, and thus prone to the occurrence of rare and extreme events. Subsequently, stakeholders come to realize that even with more elaborate risk forecasting models, banks cannot fully project themselves fully into their future and unexpected events will continue to impact the banks activities. Their prevalence is driven by two types of complexity:

- The complexity of the bank itself. Similar to projects, a bank's activities is determined by its components and the vast number and nonlinearity of relations between these components.
- The other type of complexity stems from the banking environment and its relations with the bank. For instance, a condensed network of connections within the broader environment generates unstable dynamics that can affect the bank unexpectedly.

Irrespective whether detrimental or beneficial, the impact of extreme and rare events poses a challenge to those organizations that have to through them, namely one of comprehending these experiences. There are two ways how organizations, including banks, view extreme and rare events:

- they describe extreme and rare events as measures of probability based on the calculation of the frequency of an event.
- they define these events as a unique opportunity for the organization to learn from them

A key pillar in the Behavioral Theory of Firms is revolving around the notions that organizations assiduously steer away from uncertainty,. and they also tend to address conjectures in a boundedly rational way. There are two approaches through which organizations achieve these objectives:

- by avoiding forays that would last too long (Dew et al., 2008). Organizations deal first and foremost with immediate concerns from their environment, staying clear from the complications in making long term projections of an uncertain prospect

- by settling for stability with their environment and stakeholders. Organizations will negotiate with the stakeholders to stabilize as much as possible the environment

Other mainstream schools of management state that organizations have a choice between either trying harder to predict better, or moving faster to adapt better. The stronger the ability of the organization to adapt to changes in its business environment, the less confident the latter will be to rely on prediction.

Decision-making in organizations is about a rational choice involving two guesses: "… a guess about uncertain future consequences, and a guess about uncertain future preferences..". The Behavioral Theory of Firms asserts that: "… three basic rules appear to govern at the general level: avoid uncertainty, maintain the rules, and use simple rules…". And "… Rather than treat the environment as exogenous and to be predicted, firms seek ways to make it controllable..." .

And in a context of entrepreneurship and decision-making it can prove beneficial to have control. The meaning of control suggests to work things out that are within the control of the organization itself and not trying to achieve ascendency over things that are beyond the power of the organization. Alas, notwithstanding well documented observations, decision-making theories tend unfailingly to stimulate the adoption of augmented prediction analytics. It seems that as organizations will tend to drive action mostly by leaning on causal analyses that in turn rely in predictive methods, they might forego existing control mechanisms that do not necessitate to forecast events in the future.

The analytics of predictions are based on the hypothesis that what can be projected, can be controlled. While this premise might hold true in an attempt to control natural events, for the study of organizational behavior in a context of threats and hazards, one needs to remember the meaning of uncertainty: there is a distinction between the probabilistic risk (for which there are known or unknown distributions) and non-probabilistic uncertainty for which there are no distributions. Some scholars have been advocating an interdisciplinary approach that would transpose the findings of modern theoretical physics and chemistry, as they relate to the behavior of nonlinear systems, to the fields of economics and business management. However, the development in predictive analytics do not provide the key to unlock Knight's uncertainty. Therefore, the concept of logic of control deserves to play an important role in organizational behavior as what can be controlled, does not need necessarily need to be predicted

Indeed, Knight notably asserted that the methods of probability cannot assist in forecasting the economic ramifications of decisions made in an uncertain setting. Organizations will tend to identify which parts in their environment are controllable and non-controllable, and focus on the ones that they can control through transformation, by relying on available resources and adopting a holistic view. Thus, the organization will attempt to control its environment by manufacturing new opportunities and work its way through problems by designing solutions. In other words, organizations can achieve control of their environment and the future by promoting non-predictive strategies.

When applying this notion of non-predictive control to the realm of risk management in the banking world, the theory of effectuation comes to mind. It promotes the idea that uncertainty can be addressed through non-predictive control. The effectual logic rests on the premise that if an organization can control the risks, it does not need to predict them. Risk management needs to focus on controlling risks that stem from the controllable aspects of an unpredictable future. Or in other words, risk managers need to make a distinction between prediction and control.

5.4.3. The Internet of Things/ Financial Risk Management/ Resiliency

Tomorrow's world will be defined by more than just shared (big) data and cloud technology; it will be determined by connected technology that can create, analyze, process, transfer, and communicate data without the need of human inputs. In other words, thanks to the connectedness of devices brought about by the Internet of Things (IoT), executives have much more information in real-time at their disposal for assessing risk than before.

Notwithstanding the fact this new "industrial revolution" automatically brings to mind dramatic effects for the manufacturing, retail, transportation, and energy industries, financial services do not always come to mind. And, still, applying this concept to the world of financial markets makes sense as well. For example, by using IoT from sensor devices installed at the borrower's warehouse, banks and investors can track raw materials and inventory stocks. And, other financial institutions such as insurance companies and auto loan firms can leverage the IoT via sensors installed in cars and trucks for which they have disbursed loans.

5.4.3.1. IoT And Resiliency

For financial risk managers, IoT boils down to introducing a layer of technology on top of the business. Unfortunately, the downside of the IoT is the higher risk to data security given that sensitive data is being created and put in storage on networks. Given this, a new risk management approach is needed to protect an enterprise's critical information.

With lower costs of computing and storage and greater capabilities to analyze large sets of data, the rise in Big Data in combination with the Internet of Things technologies being used across a variety of sectors will have striking implications for development and building more resilient financial institutions. Indeed, the more accurate the information, the better informed the company, and hence the agiler it is to face adverse situations.

IDC Financial Insights predicts that financial institutions worldwide will spend by 2019 more than $310 billion, of which $20 billion by the branch channel and this spending will continue to increase. In fact, according to PWC's 6th annual Digital IQ survey, financial services is one of the top 10 industries that has been investing in sensors for potential IoT innovations (Forbes):

- The consulting firm Bain forecasts that within three years from annual revenues could be higher than $470B for the IoT vendors offering the hardware, software and comprehensive solutions.
- McKinsey predicts the total IoT market size in 2015 was up to $900M, increasing to $3.7B in 2020 reaching a 32.6% CAGR.

- General Electric forecasts investment in the 'Industrial' Internet of Things (IIoT) is to total $60 trillion by the next fifteen years.

Key lessons from the sampling of IoT forecasts and market estimates include the following:

- IHS predicts that the Internet of Things market will increase from a base of 15.4 billion devices (already fully installed) in 2015 to 30.7 billion devices five years later and 75.4 billion in ten years later.
- Forrester predicts (i) fleet management in security, transportation, (ii) surveillance applications in government, (iii) inventory and warehouse management applications in retail, and (iv) industrial asset management in primary manufacturing will be the hottest areas for IoT growth. The firm Forrester also found corporates are more likely than smaller enterprises to use the IoT. Twenty-three percent of global enterprise respondents make use of the IoT, while only about 14% of small and medium-size business (SMB) respondents do. For example, the German airline company Lufthansa Airlines is making use of real-time planes, airport, and weather sensor data to strengthen on-time performance and optimize operations.
- McKinsey estimates the Internet of Things (IoT) has a potential economic impact of $2.7 to $6.2T until 2025.

Which companies are the most prominent global players providing IoT services?

Zillion of connected devices means significant opportunities for IoT companies. Here is a non-exhaustive list of these biggest players (Source: NetworkWorld):

- Amazon Web Services, with tools such as Kinesis (a real-time streaming service), S3 (the Simple Storage Service), and DynamoDB (the massively scalable NoSQL Database)
- AT&T, with M2X being a cloud-based data storage service of data flow
- Bosch, a German company that has built an IoT cloud to process data

- Cisco, providing IoT services from network connectivity, fog computing facilities, to data analytics, security, management, and automation.
- Dell, with its IoT lab in Silicon Valley in partnership with Intel
- GE, with its Asset Performance Platform as well as Predix, a cloud-based analytics and data service
- Google, with its combination of fiber optics back-end network and massive public cloud
- Hitachi Data Systems, with HDS rolling its cloud-based platform to collect and analyze IoT data.
- Huawei, join the Open Foundry cloud community with LiteOS a micro-operating for IoT devices
- IBM, pushing its Watson smart products IoT platform.
- Intel, with its Quark line providing low power computing for small form factor devices to Atom processors that are perfect for vibrant graphics rendering.
- Microsoft, rolling out an IoT Suite for its Azure public cloud.
- Oracle, building connections for its SQL, NoSQL, and Hadoop databases to ingest IoT data
- PTC that bought ThingWorx, Coldlight, and Axeda.
- Samsung, promising to make all its devices IoT ready by 2020.
- Siemens, partnering with SAP building a Web of Systems
- Qualcomm, with its AllJoyn Initiative to create an open-source protocol for IoT devices

5.4.3.2. What Will The IoT Bring To Financial Risk Management?

Emerging technologies and new sources of information to compute vast volumes of data are allowing asset management firms, banks, insurance companies, financial analysts and others to derive a more meaningful comprehension of past and future financial performance and risks. Whether data is being used to process simulations of how unexpected global crises could affect asset holdings, defining the likelihood a borrower will fall into default on his/her loan or assessing potential negative impacts on leverage ratios, financial institutions will rely on IoT more than ever. Here are a couple of areas within the financial risk management scope that could be affected (non-exhaustive list):

- Real-time market surveillance: The future of the financial services industry lies in real-time market surveillance changing, for example, the debt capital markets as well as the equity capital markets. Comprehensive real-time data flow firms could develop analytics that might better evaluate suspected market bubbles. This theory has real-life examples as seen by hedge funds now working towards running entirely on AI without human interaction.
- More robust underwriting: By using IoT solutions, risk managers within the capital markets activities will gain real-time data on the bank's counterparties activities and assets, which leads to effective risk management. In commercial real estate finance, smart sensors could help underwriters and portfolio managers have a better control on the monitoring of operating expenses whereby properties would be managed based on the actual foot traffic and room occupancy data (and not projected data). In consumer banking, by analyzing biometrics and sensor data, retail banks could reinforce the process of credit underwriting and target clients with no credit history.
- Fine-tuned enterprise risk management: By pushing processing, computing, and analytic capacity ever farther out the companies' networks, the IoT facilitates unprecedented levels of insight into processes that otherwise would be inscrutable to management. And, the same goes for financial services firms as the IoT enables timelier, more granular assessment of processes to deliver ever more distant early warning of threats as well as opportunities. Most banks' KRIs (Key Risk Indicators) are the result of an exigent compromise between what's affordable and what's knowable about its mission-critical processes. With IoT, those operations can be surveyed at ever-finer levels by connected sensors that provide live feedback reporting, not just of machines and their controls, but of people, events, externalities like share prices - the list is very long. And thanks to fog and cloud computing, responses and alerts can be triggered not just by binary alarms (like a traditional smoke detector), but by the output of sophisticated algorithms and even predictive analytics.

- Enhanced transparency of risk reporting: Standard, static reports are not suitable for the ever-changing requirements of today's business departments. Banks need access to all relevant data in Real-Fast-Time (RFT) (through IoT), such as counterparty and deal data, for reports to shed light on specific situations, such as exposure estimates. They should also use applicable statistical methods and visualizations of relationships allowing even non-IT people and non-statisticians quickly understand the relationships between underlying data and what they reveal about risk.
- Real-time stress testing economic capital consumption: to account for the uncertainty of future fluctuations of economic capital and predict cash flow changes, a bank must be able to run through possible scenarios quickly. For that reason, scenario analyses, using IoT, as well as stress tests, concern the evaluation of underlying transactions into which the banks are involved, and their risks are given unknown general conditions. Scenario assumptions must be defined in a brief and focused way for groups of underlying transactions with shared characteristics. Both future activities, changing evaluations, and cash flows must be tested by flexible, clear rules – and ideally be available in real time.
- Real-time decisions for credit committees: Industrialized knowledge generation processes – when powered by high-performance technologies – enable banks to validate the correctness of credit decisions before they are carried out. Simulations thanks to IoT can assist them forecast and visualize the probable effects of a choice (for instance, how the completion of a hedging transaction, immediately after the deal is settled, impacts the overall portfolio as well as the risk profile). Simulation results should be readily available early in the decision-making process so they can affect final decisions. When financial institutions can do this faster than their competitors, they have a clear competitive advantage: their choices are more objective, informed and timely.
- Regulatory compliance: In the wake of the Global Financial Crisis of 2008-09, policymakers in the global financial centers cast a wave of new regulations to shield consumers and investors by enforcing best practices about capital, liquidity, credit quality, and transparency. Those provisions include Basel II, the Dodd-Frank Act, the Volcker rule, Solvency II, as well as other regulations coming from the US, the EU and elsewhere in the world. Complying with these regulations often requires

running millions of simulations across incredibly large data sets. IoT and real-time data can help crunch massive data volumes and delivers near real-time insights to assisting financial institutions to keep pace with the enormous size of data required to comply with these financial regulations.

- Fraud Detection: Identifying deceiving activity – whether in a telecommunications network, the banking system, or an online retailer – is vital given the growing sophistication of deceptive methods and the requirement for businesses to preserve consumer confidence in their products and services. As perpetrators become more sophisticated, so too are the internal units tasked with identifying fraud. The IoT can help insurance companies, banks, and online retailers identify deceptive activity using advanced baselining and profiling of user-behaviors, near real-time transaction analytics, and anomaly detection, all with the proven performance to scale over the most extensive data sets.

Financial institutions now need to continually run many simulations and scenarios to determine risk and other regulator-ready metrics and benchmarks. It's not only risk analysis that financial firms and other corporates must worry. Identifying and detecting and deceptive activity – with deposits, credit cards, insurance, and more – has turned out to have become an area of increased importance to organizations across the financial value chain. IoT enables the financial services ecosystem to analyze and make informed decisions in near real time with, for example SQL-based Monte Carlo techniques, integration with statistical modeling tools, built-in machine learning algorithms, and unparalleled efficiency, performance, and scalability.

Despite the benefits, companies need to be mindful of how to protect against IoT risks, such as getting access to information being fed from devices back to the head office. Security, similar to any new technology, has to be part of utilizing IoT in the firm. Scanning for vulnerabilities now goes beyond the devices and network such as tablets, smartphones, and laptops. Information technology (IT) departments need to ensure the security of machine-to-machine units, RFID tags, and so on. Fortunately, none of this is insurmountable. Taking due diligence and evaluating the cybersecurity strategy permanently should be an essential matter in a digital world. Again, the IoT is delivering the impetus to do so. Relying on the IoT as an optimal technology means risk managers are engaging themselves in the digital age. The reward is that technology can provide organizations more flexibility regarding efficiency, cost savings, and risk mitigation than in former years.

5.4.4. The Chaos Theory And Tail risk Management

Most contemporary business models have been designed to avoid complications and thereby aim at operating in stable environments. Think about it: for the past decades, companies have thrived and survived by building mighty fortresses to defend their positions. To ward off competitor incursions, organizations identified competitive advantages, put entry barriers that were as high as possible, and built powerful organizations to realize the entity's aims. These nearly as perceived impenetrable walls were a potent dissuasion when change was usually predictable and manageable.

A quick look around, however, is all it takes to realize that the world and business are evolving at a faster pace than ever before (due to globalization, digitalization, widespread information sharing, etc.), and that stability and predictability do not exist (but actually they never ever existed, but the pace of change is faster than before). Fueled by technological advancements, emerging markets, empowered consumers, and evolving regulations, the pace of change has left many forts (= businesses) struggling to protect themselves. The harsh reality is that stability is becoming increasingly rare in today's marketplaces and instability makes fortress building a poor choice for sustainable advantage. The businesses that will prosper in tomorrow's world will have to build ships that are able to maneuver nimbly through ever-changing business environments. Ships and their crews are keenly aware of their surroundings and are able to adapt quickly. Building ships is a strategic imperative. Companies cannot dig moats deep enough to make them immune from the external forces that change markets and customer demands (Kuder et al., n.d.) .

Most global companies have their business models allocating resources and assets based on their current revenues in their existing markets, in other words they built forecasts by relying on data and an environment that is deemed manageable. Current business strategies assume homogeneity of markets and customer needs, but that is no longer valid (and actually has never been valid): as they say one size does not fit all. Or, to put it differently, there is an implicit assumption that objective measurement of risk is possible (and that risks would be falling under a normal distribution). Theoretically speaking in a quantitative methodology there is no such thing as qualitative differences between types of risks (= whereby risk is being defined as "probability of negative outcome X the severity of the outcome").

So, to draw a parallel with history: if you are a firm that wants to conquer new markets: yes of course Place, People, Promotion, Price and Product are important features (the famous 5 Ps from marketing) but foremost act like a smart Power (= an empire) that is seeking to expand itself. How? By building a resilient business model that defines a strategy that embraces volatility and disorder, and not one that shuns it. The British empire did not become great by remaining cloistered onto the British isles, or Alexander the Great did not build his vast empire by remaining in Greece. The essence of being a ship lies in the company's operating model—a flexible configuration of capabilities organized in business units, shared functions, and throughout the organization's ecosystem. The right operating model stems from a clear business strategy that defines a company's core customers and what the business will offer them. With a clear tail risk strategy, an organization can systematically evaluate its capabilities and determine what the company needs to do today and what investments it will need to make in the future.

That is why tail risk management is a necessity. However, as I have explained in a multitude of articles tail risk management is not something to be exploited for application. It doesn't represent some mathematical or scientific discovery that can be used in novel ways. Instead, it represents a set of techniques and processes for analyzing what could lead to volatility, how you could identify tail events, and foremost mitigate their effects.

In essence, we are talking about something very similar to the chaos theory. Indeed, the chaos theory is an array of approaches aimed at understanding and assessing dynamical systems that are deterministic (i.e., they follow apparently simple rules that lead to behaviors which depend only upon their initial conditions) and yet very sensitive to perturbations of input (i.e. remember the Butterfly Effect). Consequently, advances in understanding certain classes of these systems lead to advances in either understanding the physical/ socio-economic world or designing technology/ processes that interfaces with such systems.

Just like Black Swans (although many of these Black Swans could actually rather be attributed to bad strategic decisions or human behavioral mistakes) chaotic systems are perceived as unpredictable due to "sensitive dependence on initial conditions"—"The Butterfly Effect". Telling examples of chaotic systems in nature: the weather, waves, and heartbeats. But when you think about it chaos is actually not "pure" randomness; it only seems random. Indeed, the apparent randomness is due to our finitude - our human inability to measure initial conditions in chaotic systems with enough accuracy to predict long-term results.

But there is order in chaos: "chaos describes a complex, unpredictable, and orderly disorder in which patterns of behavior unfold in irregular but similar forms" (Tetenbaum, 1998, p. 24) (Example: snowflakes).

Again, I repeat: there is order out of chaos. Other examples of such systems that produce novelty are biological evolution and the "world economy" as well as Silicon Valley. Now, although we cannot predict the long-term future, we can anticipate it and have a general idea of the paths it might take - similar to long-term weather forecasts. And, yes, with this many variables that businesses and organizations are facing, the old paradigm of predictability is unrealistic - but there are still ways the company can manage risks better in a chaotic world, by means of:

- flexibility/ adaptability (resilience)
- gaining adequate information (through risk mapping and early warning)
- openness to knowledge sharing and emphasis on creativity and innovation
- building high tolerance for conflict (through supply chain risk management, scenario planning, and reverse stress testing = cause intentional turbulence in a company to stimulate innovation)
- anticipating risks and managing contingencies (through financial contingency planning)

So, if you're a risk manager, you would be careful to constrain your parameters to stress factors with manageable equilibria. So chaos theory gives us a way to reason about complicated systems. We can use the reasoning to keep us out of trouble, or we can use the reasoning to evaluate whether theoretic models of nature make sense. And, this how tail risk management is embracing chaos theory.

5.4.5. In God We Trust, All Other Risks We Monitor

I often compare the art of risk management with the profession of intelligence gathering. As such, I have always felt the motto of the U.S. Office of Naval Intelligence is the perfect summary for what the mission statement of a risk management department should be: "In God We Trust, All Others We Monitor."

Indeed, similar to an intelligence agency, a risk management department should be responsible for the collection, analysis, and exploitation of risk data in support of the business model and the objectives of the organization. Risk management should be much more than merely monitoring and managing risks (which is already a very demanding task); its mission should add value to the business model of any organization. In other words, the goal of risk management should also be to gain and hold a decisive information advantage over an organization's potential adversaries (i.e., it could do that by relying, for structured finance assets, for instance, on internal rating methodologies instead of external rating agencies).

To that effect, similarly as an intelligence agency, the risk management department within an organization should collect, analyze and produce relevant risk intelligence and disseminate that knowledge rapidly to critical strategic, operational, and tactical stakeholders to meet the organization's requirements. Therefore, risk management should be all about integration: integration of all risk information, integration of all risks, and integration of (cooperation between) all stakeholders within the company. This integrated approach enables the support of business operations as well as the provision of vital information for planning the company's resilience against threats at home and around the world.

To help achieve these objectives, risk management should rely, just like an intelligence agency, on several sources of information:

- SIGINT - use of technology to collect and analyze data through the use of predictive data analytics, algorithms, and mathematical models.
- HUMINT - gathered from the people on the field: this entails regular (weekly) meetings of risk management with account managers, front office, business development managers, and portfolio managers.
- GEOINT - Geospatial intelligence gathered from the analysis of country and geopolitical risks, or the environment into which the organization is operating.
- OSINT - gathered from open sources, such as press articles, industry research, meetings with customers and peers, conferences, etc.
- MASINT - measurement of risks through robust data analytics and reporting (in close cooperation with the Finance Department)

Over the last decades, risk management has developed enormous usability and popularity by scholars but also by organizations and practitioners. Although the risk management function has always been part of humankind and their organizations, it had to pass some decades before the integrated approach was finally understood and the benefits of its method came to the view for managers and decision makers.

The best practice for risk management is the comprehensive approach of the discipline which is often colloquially labeled as Enterprise Risk Management (ERM), Organizational Risk Management (ORM) or Corporate Risk Management among other distinctions. Under this perspective, organizations are supposed to proactively manage risk, monitoring in a continue and conscious way the risks associated with their strategic objectives. Similar to an intelligence agency the latter would indicate then, permanent measurement of the severity and evolution of threats within the organization, with the aim of maintaining an overall risk profile aligned with the strategic objectives of the organizations.

The management of risk is therefore in this sense, an integral part of the organization and its processes, in the understanding that potential upside and downside factors can affect the organization. In other words, it is holistic, meaning it is not fractured into departments and functions, but instead is organized with the intention of optimizing risk management performance. Accordingly, under this approach risk management would contribute to increasing the possibility of success and reducing both, the likelihood of failure and the uncertainty of achieving the organizations' overall objectives.

The comprehensive perspective of risk management is oriented to consider all types of risk that an organization might face. This means as well leaving a purely "defensive" approach in favor of a proactive approach designed to increase organizational performance. Enterprise risk management is a structured approach that aligns strategy, processes, people, technology, and knowledge with the objective to assess and manage threats and opportunities that companies face in trying to create value. Under this perspective, the risk management function within the organization is responsible for the direct management of the risk management policy of the entity.

The latter considers the coordination with the all the operational and business areas of the organization, which is ultimately responsible for the implementation of risk management, as well as the performance a permanent monitoring procedure. Therefore, this perspective of risk management assumes that whether at the planning stage of a new project or as a part of day to day strategic and operational management, risks need to be managed in an integrated fashion, encompassing potential threats in each level of the entire organization.

A holistic view of risk tries to grasp the big helicopter view picture by identifying the critical risks that matter through an enterprise-level, portfolio view of risk. This is where management considers risk from an entity-wide perspective and assesses whether the entity's residual risk profile is at par with its overall risk appetite. Each manager responsible for a business unit, function or process must determine, from an enterprise perspective, the risks triggered by the activities for which he/she is responsible. With a composite view at each level of the organization, senior executives, and the board then determine whether the entity's overall risk portfolio is commensurate with its desired risk profile.

A keynote to add to the observance of a holistic approach when managing risks is that it remains a better option to focus on the resilience of the system (organization) instead of attempting to predict the likelihood of an event striking the system (organization). Indeed, although quantitative methods are used most often in risk assessment, their usefulness wanes in the realm of tail risk management. To effectively mitigate extreme risks and preserve a firm's survivability, the focus must genuinely be on building a resilient business model.

Robust tools that help create resistant and agile business models are, for example, supply chain risk management, risk mapping, reverse stress testing, highly reliable organizations, and financial continuity planning. Over the last ten years, significant and well-respected financial institutions have experienced failure in the face of tail risks, revealing the inadequate protection provided by the current quantitative practices. More than just capital management, tail risk management takes a qualitative approach that involves business strategy.

A final word is about the added value that risk management should uphold, and what is currently too much missing: helping to discern the intentions of current or potential clients as well as rival companies.

It can do that by adding a simulation aspect when conducting, for instance, the underwriting of an investment/ business proposal. For example, if the company invests in a particular business what would be the severity to the firm if suddenly that business goes bankrupt? How many proceeds could the company recover from the liquidation of the assets of the business?

Or, as it relates to portfolio management, what are the intentions of the rival banks concerning, for instance, Greek, Italian or Venezuelan risk exposures held in the portfolio? Will our competitors decide to keep those positions on their books, will they apply a risk provision or a haircut, or will they try to sell those assets on the markets, etc.?

Another important aspect about adding value through risk management is that to be genuinely effective in adding value risk management should be closely involved with the organizational strategy linking strategy and critical success factors. Connecting risk management to the company's strategy in this way puts it into context and within the understanding of all areas and staff. This approach also lends itself to looking at missed opportunities and not just downside risk.

Chapter 6. Recommendations

One of the most effective ways to manage extreme risk in a global enterprise is to transform the culture into one of risk awareness, identification, analysis, and mitigation. Tail risk hedging strategies can be a temporary solution, but do not provide a structural shield for protecting portfolios and business models from downside risks. Since 2008, the desire to avoid significant losses has, more than ever, been at the front of senior executives' minds. The approach to managing downside risk or extreme risk has been restricted in a primeval way to extreme risk hedging strategies. However, as I already mentioned, these strategies are costly and not necessarily efficient. In any case, while extreme risk hedging strategies necessarily differ for every firm, a sustained TRM can be applied across all types of firms.

Since the GFC in 2008, "the demand for strategies that protect against significant negative returns has increased substantially. It is partly the fear that we are in a market environment unfamiliar to most market participants with limited central bank policy options and with uncertain outcomes that have led to this interest."[13] Meanwhile, yields on "safe-haven" government bonds have fallen so low that there is no obvious diversifying asset. Traditional balanced portfolios have better diversified over time through the addition of new asset classes, but increased globalization and the consequent interdependence of asset classes have led to an increase in their correlation in times of crisis.

Institutional investors and other stakeholders look for new ways to "limit risks as they face greater pressure from stakeholders to be better protected in the event of a repeat of the 2008 crisis. This is evidenced by an exponential increase in the demand for volatility-based instruments, such as options and volatility futures,"[14] but as already mentioned, hedging instruments are merely a temporary solution to long-term problems.

---

[13] A. Forest, "Effective Downside Risk Management," Schroders Global, 2016, http://www.schroders.com/en/sysglobalassets/digital/expert-magazine/pdfs/sro_expert-19_3_2016_en.pdf.
[14] Ibid.

As an alternative to resorting to (quantitative) hedging instruments, I propose a three-pronged approach to extreme risk management:

- Be cognizant of the environment in which you are operating (through risk mapping and early-warning systems).
- Have a clear understanding of where your most vulnerable link in your company is (through scenario analysis, reverse stress testing, risk strategy and appetite, and supply chain risk management).
- Know what actions can be taken to prevent your company from falling to its knees (through FCP, supply chain resilience, and building a sustainable business model).

In other words, there is a need for a crucial shift in regulatory philosophy that looks at extreme risks and the sustainability of business models rather than assuming that all risk can be identified and managed at the level of the individual firm. Flawed business models and processes have led firms to large-scale disasters.

One strategy to achieve this goal is by having managers conducting an analysis of the business' comfort zones. The concept of comfort zone stems from understanding that each firm has an area business line that is a comfort zone. The comfort zone can be defined as an area of business, product, or service in which the firm has a competitive advantage, core competencies, deep knowledge of risks, and decent control over key risk factors, where all of the above are proved by long, successful business experience in both benign and downturn periods. A comfort zone is an area where a firm is less exposed to risks, including extreme risks. The longer the history of its successful business within the comfort zone, the stronger the ability to moderate its business in different circumstances.

Also, contrary to popular belief, the GFC was caused by ineffective management of extreme risks by financial institutions—and not by model risks, greed, or globalization. Consequently, the new changes "championed by regulators may not prevent future meltdowns in the financial system unless the fundamental reasons for the crisis are properly addressed."[15] The secret to preventing future financial crises lies in effectively identifying and managing low-probability, high-severity events. Companies must, therefore, inculcate techniques, such as extreme risk crisis identification, contingency planning, and extreme risk crisis communication, into their regular risk management routines. Obviously, there is no one-size-fits-all solution, but just as firms have business continuity plans from an operational risk perspective, the financial risk aspect should likewise be the object of BCP. A lot could be learned from the existing operational business continuity plan that firms have put in place, and nearly the same disciplined approach should be heralded for financial BCP, namely:

- building an early-warning system that identifies extreme risk, allowing the firm to switch to extreme risk alerts;
- developing and implementing a financial continuity plan that should be multileveled;
- ensuring that a solid crisis management framework has been put in place in terms of governance and resources;
- ensuring that data mining and reporting are fast, flexible, arch-encompassing, and detailed enough to allow decision makers to immediately map the risks and take appropriate actions (to that effect, IT will play a key role); and
- communicating with both internal and external stakeholders.

As a risk manager, it is not enough to use enterprise risk management to identify, prioritize, treat, and monitor risks. A risk manager is also required to consider the black swans after this process and analyze whether more needs to be done. It is a matter of behaving professionally and being keen to create an added value that will protect, and even help grow, the business. The recent recession, which was caused in part by an erroneous belief that the status quo would continue and the housing market would never decline, is one case in point. Nor is there anything new about the disastrous consequences

[15] Risk Management Events, "Effective Tail Risk Management versus Excessive Protection," https://prmiadc.wordpress.com/themes/governance/effective-tail-risk-management-v.

of complacency; consider the overconfidence of the engineers who built the *Hindenburg* or the misplaced confidence of Spain's King Phillip II "in the ability of his Armada to defeat Queen Elizabeth's British navy. Complacency, after all, is a human characteristic." (Zavatsky, 2017)

This shows that extreme events can afflict any culture, not just that of an energy giant or a too-big-to-fail banking institution. It also highlights the importance of organizational culture and a consistent commitment to safety by industry (whether operational or financial safety), from the highest management levels down to the employee. Feeding this inertia is a combination of risk management fatigue toward ever-complex banking regulations with a sense that, as a result of these massive prudential rulings (several thousand pages), all risks ought to be covered.

Senior risk executives seem so overwhelmed by the sheer size of the demands from various stakeholders that they have become confused, perplexed, and even lost on how to improve things from a risk management perspective, given that all their energy has been drained. Risk management (under the instruction of the management board) is inundated with regulations, thereby erasing the desire needed to change, leaving it with no time to look creatively at new risk-management solutions and techniques.

Financial services businesses are likely to be so busy complying with prudential rulings, carrying out internal audit action plans, or conducting regular risk management work that they no longer find time to review the risk management strategies and set up a framework to deal with the risk management of black swans. Alternatively, perhaps the financial activity already turns a profit; therefore, businesses do not see the point in reviewing existing risk management plans. Even in the latter case, it is important to realize that, eventually, a TRM strategy will be needed, resulting in a requirement to adapt the ERM framework of the financial institution.

It is important for businesses to fight the urge to remain complacent toward extreme events. They must find the time to reassess their risk management strategies, even if only in a cursory way once a year. Keeping an eye on the marketplace, building an early-warning system, setting up unbiased risk mapping, defining reverse stress testing scenarios, and so on will help businesses know when a revamp of their risk management plans is necessary. But if businesses never conduct an introspective risk management audit, they may be blindsided by the competition or by an extreme risk event carrying such an immense severity in the event of a full-blown exposure that the firm's business model will be wiped out.

Most alternatives are not feasible. Risk avoidance for complacency is impossible unless one replaces every human in the "organization with a robot. To my knowledge, robots do not become complacent. Accepting and monitoring the risk is also not much of a solution. This treatment requires a practitioner to set a baseline monitoring condition," (Zavatsky, 2017) which, if met, means the risk will be reviewed again for treatment. At best, it means putting off a decision on how to deal with complacency until a later day. At worst, it means the deadly risk event will happen before deciding what to do about it. This was probably one of Lehman Brothers' errors.

"Risk transfer is unlikely to be cost effective; a company that would contract to operate my organization would still need to address complacency risk." (Zavatsky, 2017) Risk hedging does not address the core of the problem in the event of a black swan. Reducing the impact is unfortunately not always an option, because complacency risk often encompasses substantial risks that are game changers outside the control of the organization (such as Lehman Brothers and the global economy or BP and the highly pressurized oil a mile underwater). Reducing the likelihood is the only real solution. The likelihood of complacency will decrease if a firm establishes a culture that embraces TRM. At a minimum, such an organization is much more responsive to risks and treatments. It is very unlikely to hear a TRM-savvy CEO say, "I don't care about these risks, as I cannot measure them." Treat complacency risk by creating a high-requirement functioning TRM culture built into the ERM framework. Senior leadership typically does not get it, as financial firms, despite recent regulatory rules (Dodd-Frank, EMIR, and Basel III), largely continue to operate only in the context of known risks that can be priced. Uncertainty management needs to focus beyond the pricing of known risk, as actual results are also determined by how unknown events and market conditions can unfold. In extreme scenarios, unexpected losses can exceed the capital and thus threaten the survival of the institution. Therefore, the objective of TRM must be to leverage resources to mitigate and absorb unexpected losses in such a way that the capital (firm) is always protected and preserved.

Enthralled by new revenue opportunities, over the last twenty-five years, the industry has been focusing on what quantitative analysis and models could do at the expense of realizing what they could not do (there has always been a tendency since the 1980s to attempt to transform economics into an exact science, while it will always remain a social science). In the frenzy to drive revenue models, the downside was so eclipsed by the upside that institutions, rating agencies, and regulators neglected to focus on or even ask about the downside. The so-called sophistication of these quantitative models has distracted people from remembering what models can and cannot do. In many cases, people could not even comprehend these limitations. Models often are meant to convey one thing through resemblance, but due to the lack of an understanding of the full picture, their meaning can become something else.

Interestingly, the answer to sophistication and complexity is de facto simplicity. Risk management is based on the theory of probability and thus has an implied assumption that events can be predicted. Therefore, effective decision making that relies on data mining, such as today in risk management, requires turning complexities into simpler inputs. Even with modern quantitative models that pretend to have an ability to predict all events with up to 99 percent or higher probabilities, they always rely on assumptions. While unknown uncertainty cannot be quantified, it can be effectively managed through an a priori contrarian approach; applying complex decision rules in a complex environment is a recipe for disaster. Lending has been around for many centuries, and unfortunately, there have been financial failures regularly. However, except for cases of financial misconduct or fraud, these failures have typically been caused by problems with extreme risks. In today's world, large financial firms derive a much larger proportion of their revenues from market risk instead of from credit activities, thereby changing the magnitude and severity of extreme risks particularly. On one hand, today, risks can be transferred through securitization and CDS, for instance. On the other hand, the world has become much more interconnected and global. Market risk policies also require the robustness and objectivity of credit policies to shield the firm from extreme financial market risks.

Chapter 7. Epilogue

It is now clear that quantitative finance methodologies and internal risk modelling techniques based on normality assumption and historical statistical relationships have failed to adequately capture the extreme events which occur in periods of systemic stress.

This research considers the risk management of extreme events in U.S. globally systemically important banks, using a combination of the findings of a survey of these banks with a multi-case study analysis involving three U.S. banks that collapsed in the aftermath of the Global Financial Crisis. U.S. government and academic studies into the failures of these U.S. GSIBs have evidenced that these banks are highly exposed to extreme events. Alas, these public and private inquiries reveal that notwithstanding the breadth of current banking regulations, both the GSIBs as well as banking authorities remain very concerned about the fallout of an extreme event hitting the banking industry. While risk managers and regulators pay a lot of attention to the use of quantitative models to calibrate the required economic capital in the event of an extreme stress, they appear not to pay enough attention to concept of extreme risk management. Risk management embodies much more than merely the adoption of quantitative models to assess the likelihood a bank would survive an extreme event. It also encompasses culture, organization, and processes. The same can be said about extreme risk management.

The research maps a couple of deficiencies in the risk governance of banks relating to the risk management of extreme events illustrated by assertions claiming that banks consider the probability of occurrence of a hypothetical stress scenario that would result in the non-viability of the bank as extremely low. Such a statement highlights that banks invest a lot of time in measuring the probability of occurrence of an extreme event, while focusing insufficiently on engineering a stronger operational resilience and organizational agility of the banks.

By calibrating organizational agility banks can boost operational resilience to adapt to changing environments and lessen the detrimental effects of these changing environments. One way to achieve resilience is for banks to modify their organizational strategy for managing uncertainty. Given that the management of uncertainty is paramount to the business model of any bank, such an institution could examine how other risk-prone industries handle change and potential disruptions. In particular, banks could investigate ways of changing the underlying organizational processes that influence decision processes when banks face disruption.

Instead of designing a risk governance that would help banks not only mitigate the effects of an extreme events, but also bounce back and grow stronger out of it, the lion share of banks seems to operate on -auto-pilot'. The entire banking industry seems sticked to replicate yesterday's risk governance, merely contenting themselves to view risk management as an exercise of compliance, in the sense of abiding with the various provisions of the banking regulations, betting on the perception of 'too big to fail to' for obtaining bailouts from the taxpayers. Most of the banks behave like a herd betting on the same risk governance tools.

Considering the systemic failures that most of these banks had to endure and the fact that nearly all of them were bailed out through taxpayers money, both risk managers and regulators should consider resilience engineering as a complementary tool to help achieve overall stability of the financial system. Banks need to have a better understanding on the ways how to make themselves operationally more

References

- Aboura, S. (2012) *Disentangling Crashes from Tail Events.* Paris: Universite de Paris Dauphine.
- Acharya, V and Richardson, M (2009): "Causes of the financial crisis", Critical Review, Vol. 21, pp. 195–210.
- Adhikari, U., 2020, Basel III Accord: A Risk Management Framework.
- Agyris, C. (1973). Some Limits of Rational Man Organizational Theory. Public Administration Review. 33, 253-267.
- Akgiray, V. & Booth, G. G. (1988) "The Stable-law Model of Stock Returns", *Journal of Business & Economic Statistics*, 6(1), pp. 51–57.
- Akoundi, K. (2010) *Tail Risk Hedging: A Roadmap for Asset Owners.* New York: Deutsche Bank.
- Alchian, A.A., & Demsetz, H. (1972). Production, information costs and economic organization. American Economic Review. 62, 772-795
- AMF (2017) " The use of stress tests as part of risk management, Guide for asset management companies", Autorités des Marchés Financiers. Available at: amf-france.org (Accessed: 20 August 2018).
- Appel, F. (2012) "New Models for Addressing Supply Chain and Transport Risk", *World Economic Forum.* Available at https://www.weforum.org/reports/new-models-addressing-supply-chain-and-transport-risk (Accessed: 3 August 2018).
- Atik, J. (2009) Basel II and Extreme Risk Analysis, Loyola Law School, Legal Studies Paper No. 2010-40, 16pp.
- Aven, T. (2012) "The risk concept—historical and recent development trends", *Reliability Engineering and System Safety,* 99(1), pp. 33–44.
- Azkunaga, J., Leire, S-J. and Urionabarrenetxea, S. (2013) 'The Impact of Financial Globalization and Financialization on the Economy in the Current Crisis through Banking Corporate Governance', *Contemporary Economics,* 7(3), pp. 79-94. Available at https://ssrn.com/abstract=2362276. (Accessed: 20 May 2018).

- Bachelier, L. (1900) Theorie de la speculation. Annales Scientifiques de l'Ecole Normale Superieure 17, 21–86. VIII, 37, 80
- Banks, E. (2009) Risk and Financial Catastrophe, London: Palgrave MacMillan Finance and Capital Markets Series.
- Bardin, J. (2007) "Risk as a Service", *CSO*, November 23.
- Barquet, A. et al. (2011) *Business model elements for product-service system." Functional Thinking for Value Creation.* Heidelberg: Springer.
- Basel Committee on Baking Supervision (2016) "Standardised Measurement Approach for operational risk", *Consultative Document*, https://www.bis.org/bcbs/publ/d355.pdf
- Basel Committee on Banking Supervision (2001) "Pillar 2 (Supervisory Review Process)", *Consultative Document*, https://www.bis.org/publ/bcbsca08.pdf
- Basel Committee on Banking Supervision (2011) Basel Committee on Banking Supervision (2017) High-level summary of Basel III reforms, Bank for International Settlements.
- Basel Committee on Banking Supervision (2017) High-level summary of Basel III reforms, Bank for International Settlements.
- Basel Committee on Banking Supervision (2019) Overview of Pillar 2 supervisory review practices and approaches.
- Behm, M., and powell, D., 2014, Are Higher Order Controls Ignored?, Professional Safety, 59(2), February.
- Bhamra, H.S. and Uppal, R. (2016) Do Individual Behavioral Biases Affect Financial Markets and the Macroeconomy? (November 18, 2016). Available at SSRN: https://ssrn.com/abstract=2893013 or http://dx.doi.org/10.2139/ssrn.2893013
- Bhansali, V. (2008) "Tail Risk Management: Why Investors Should Be Chasing Their Tails", *Pimco.*
- Bhimani, A. (2008). Making Corporate Governance Count: The Fusion of Ethics and Economic Rationality. Journal of Management and Governance. 12(2), 135-147

- Bier, V. M., Haimes, Y. Y., Lambert, J. H., Matalas, N. C., and Zimmerman, R. (1999) "Assessing and managing the risk of extremes", *Risk Analysis* 19:83–94.
- BIS (2001) "Pillar 2 (Supervisory Review Process)", *Basel Committee on Banking Supervision Consultative Document.* Available at https://www.bis.org/publ/bcbsca08.pdf
- BIS (2009) "Principles for sound stress testing practices and supervision", *Basel Committee on Banking Supervision Consultative Document.* Available at: https://www.bis.org/publ/bcbs147.pdf
- BIS (2009) "Principles for sound stress testing practices and supervision", *Basel Committee on Banking Supervision Consultative Document.* Available at: https://www.bis.org/publ/bcbs147.pdf (Accessed: 17 August 2018).
- BIS (2017) "Summary Table Basel Committee on Banking Supervision reforms – Basel III", *Bank for International Settlements.* Available at: https://www.bis.org/bcbs/basel3/b3_bank_sup_reforms.pdf (Accessed: 20 August 2018).
- BIS (2017) "Supervisory and bank stress testing: range of practices", *Bank for International Settlements.* Available at: https://www.bis.org/bcbs/publ/d427.pdf (Accessed: 20 August 2017).
- Black, F. and M. Scholes (1973) The pricing of options and corporate liabilities, The Journal of Political Economy, Vol. 81, No. 3 (May - Jun., 1973), pp. 637-654
- Blattberg, R.C. & Gonedes, N.J. (1974) "A Comparison of the Stable and Student Distributions as Statistical Models for Stock Prices", *The Journal of Business*, 47(2), pp. 244–280.
- Blos, M. F., Wee, H. M., and Yang, W-H. (2012) "Supply Chain Risk Management: Resilience and Business Continuity", *Intelligent Systems Reference Library.* Available at https://link.springer.com/chapter/10.1007/978-3-642-25755-1_12 (Accessed: 6 August 2018).

- Board of Governors of the Federal Reserve System (2018) "Comprehensive Capital and Analysis Review and Dodd-Frank Act Stress Tests, Questions and Answers", *Federal Reserve.* Available at https://www.federalreserve.gov/publications/files/CCAR-QAs.pdf (Accessed: 19 August 2018).
- Boholm, Å. (1996) "Risk perception and social anthropology: Critique of cultural theory", *Ethnos*, 61(1), pp. 64–84.
- Bonish, P., 2013, Excuse me. How Many Lines Of Defense? The New Maginot Lines, Paradigm Risk, March 18.
- Bonti, G. et al. (2005) "Credit Risk Concentrations under Stress", *Bank for International Settlements.* Available at: https://www.bis.org/bcbs/events/crcp05bonti.pdf (Accessed: 15 August 2018).
- Borghesi, A. and Gaudenzi, B. (2012) "Operational Risk and Supply Chain Risk Management" *Risk Management. Perspectives in Business Culture.* Available at https://link.springer.com/chapter/10.1007/978-88-470-2531-8_8#citeas (Accessed: 10 August 2018).
- Borio, C and H Zhu (2014), "Capital regulation, risk-taking and monetary policy: A missing link in the transmission mechanism?", Journal of Financial Stability, vol 8, no 4, pp 236–251.
- Bouwman, H. et al. (2018) "Achieving agility using business model stress testing", Electronics Markets 28: 149, Berlin: Springer. Available at: https://link.springer.com/article/10.1007/s12525-016-0243-0 (Accessed: 21 August 2018).
- Bradley, R. (2011) *Edison to Enron: Energy Markets and Political Strategies.* Beverly: Wiley-Scrivener Publishing.
- Breuer, T. (2006) "Providing against the worst: Risk capital for worst case scenarios", *PPE Research Centre, Vorarlberg University of Applied Sciences.* Available at: https://homepages.fhv.at/tb/cms/?Publications (Accessed: 17 August 2018).
- Brindley, Cl. (2004) *Supply Chain Risk.* England: Ashgate Publishing Ltd

- British Standard Institutions (2007) "Occupational health and safety management systems (OHSAS) – Requirements", *BS OHSAS 1800.*
- Buchholz, W., Schymura,M., 2012. Expected utility theory and the tyranny of catastrophic risks. Ecol. Econ. 77, 234–239.
- Caddick, M. and Buchanan, T. (2011) "Business continuity and supply chain risk", *PwC.* Available at https://www.pwc.co.uk/assets/pdf/business-continuity-and-supply-chain-risk-April-2011.pdf (Accessed: 3 August 2018).
- Camerinelli, E. (2017) "Supply Chain Collaboration: Why Banks Should Care", *Finextra.* Avalaible at https://www.finextra.com/blogposting/14219/supply-chain-collaboration-why-banks-should-care (Accessed: 10 August 2018).
- Caplain, J., Fry, F., and Topping, S., 2017, Navigating The Impact Of Geopolitical Change On Banking Regulation, KPMG Frontiers in Finance.
- Chassin, M. and Loeb J. (2013) 'High-Reliability Health Care: Getting There from Here', *The Milbank Quarterly*, 91(3), pp. 459-490. Available at https://www.ncbi.nlm.nih.gov/pmc/articles/PMC3790522/. (Accessed: 19 May 2018).
- Chockalingam, A., Dabadghao, S. and Soetekouw, R., 2018. Strategic risk, banks, and Basel III: estimating economic capital requirements. The Journal of Risk Finance.
- Christopher, M. and Peck, H. (2004) "Building the Resilient Supply Chain - The Five Principles of Supply Chain Resilience," *Logistics Europe*, Vol. 12 No. 1, pp.16-21. Available at https://theicor.org/art/present/art/ARSC00038.pdf (Accessed: 7 August 2018).
- Ciancanelli, P., & Gonzalez, J.A.R (2000). Corporate Governance in Banking: A Conceptual Framework. European Financial Management Association Conference, Athens, 2000.
- Ciro, T. (2012) *The Global Financial Crisis: Triggers, Responses and Aftermath.* Farnham, UK: Ashgate.

- Clark, T. (2004). Theories of Corporate Governance: The Philosophical Foundations of Corporate Governance. London and New York: Routledge.
- Clarkson, M.B.E. (1995). A Stakeholder Framework for Analyzing and Evaluating Corporate Social Performance. Academy of Management Review. 20(1), 92-117.
- Committee of European Banking Supervisors, (2010) "CEBS Guidelines on Stress Testing (GL32)", *European Banking Authority*. Available at: https://www.eba.europa.eu/documents/10180/16094/ST_Guidelines.pdf (Accessed: 14 August 2018).
- Conerly, B. (2013) "Uncertainty and Risk Management: What to Do About Black Swans?", *Forbes Magazine*, February 20.
- Covaleski, M.A., & Dirsmith, M.W. (1988). An institutional perspective on the rise, social transformation, and fall of a university budget category. Administrative Science Quarterly. 33, 562-87.
- Cox, J.L.A., 2012. Community resilience and decision theory challenges for catastrophic events. Risk Anal. 32, 1919–1934.
- Crotty, J. (2011) "The Realism of Assumptions Does Matter: Why Keynes-Minsky Theory Must Replace Efficient Market Theory as the Guide to Financial Regulation Policy," *Working Papers wp255*, Political Economy Research Institute, University of Massachusetts at Amherst.
- Davis, J.H., Schoorman, F.D., & Donaldson, L. (1997). Toward a Stewardship Theory of Management. Academy of Management Review. 22, 20-47.
- Davis, L. (2017) "Mortgage Supply Chain Failure and Innovation", *Boston College Journal of Law & Social Justice* , Vol. 37, No. 6. Available at https://lawdigitalcommons.bc.edu/cgi/viewcontent.cgi?referer=https://www.google.com/&httpsredir=1&article=1116&context=jlsj (Accessed: 10 August 2018).
- Denning, S., 2018, Understanding Disruption, Forbes, February 12.

- Diebold, F. (2010) *The Known, the Unknown, and the Unknowable in Financial Risk Management.* Princeton: Princeton University Press.
- DiMaggio, P.J., & Powell, W.W. (1983). The iron cage revisited: institutional isomorphism and collective rationality in organizational fields. American Sociological Review. 48, 147-60.
- Donaldson, L., & Davis, J. (1991). Stewardship Theory or Agency Theory: CEO Governance and Shareholder Returns. Academy Of Management Review. 20(1), 65.
- Dowd, K. (2011) "Capital Inadequacies: The Dismal Failure of the Basel Regime of Bank Capital Regulation", *Cato Institute Policy Analysis*, NO. 681.
- Dvorak, B. (2005) *Uses and Misuses of Required Economic Capital.* New York: Moody's KMV Company.
- Eisenhardt, K..M. (1989). Agency Theory: An Assessment and Review. Academy of Management Review. 14, 57-74.
- Eisenhardt, K. M. (1989). Building theories from case study research. The Academy of Management Review, 14(4), 532-550.
- Empiricus, S., trans., Loeb, R. & Bury, G. (eds.) (1933) *Outlines of Pyrrhonism.* London: W. Heinemann.
- Ernst & Young, n.d., Is it time to shift your perspective of third-party risk?", *EY.* Available at https://www.ey.com/Publication/vwLUAssets/ey-global-financial-services-third-party-risk-management-survey/%24File/ey-global-financial-services-third-party-risk-management-survey.pdf (Accessed: 10 August 2018).
- Fama, E. (1963) "Mandelbrot and the Stable Paretian Hypothesis", *Journal of Business*, 36(4), pp. 420–429.
- Fama, E. (1970) Efficient Capital Markets: A Review of Theory and Empirical Work *The Journal of Finance* Vol. 25, No. 2, Papers and Proceedings of the Twenty-Eighth Annual Meeting of the American Finance Association New York, N.Y. December, 28-30, 1969 (May, 1970), pp. 383-417

- Fama, E.F. (1980). Agency Problems and the Theory of the Firm. Journal of Political Economy. 88, 288-307.
- FDIC (2018), "RMS Manual of Examination Policies Federal Deposit Insurance Corporation", *Federal Deposit Insurance Corporation*, Section 3-2. Available at https://www.fdic.gov/regulations/safety/manual/ (Accessed: 3 August 2018).
- Federal Reserve (2012) "Guidance on Stress Testing for Banking Organizations with Total Consolidated Assets of More Than $10 Billion", *Board of Governors of the Federal Reserve System*. Available at: https://www.federalreserve.gov/supervisionreg/srletters/sr1207a1.pdf (Accessed: 18 August 2018).
- Felea, M. and Albăstroiu, I. (2013) "Defining the concept of supply chain management and its relevance to Romanian academics and practitioners", *Academy of Economic Studies, Supply Chain Management*, Vol. XV, No. 33. Available at http://www.amfiteatrueconomic.ro/temp/Article_1176.pdf (Accessed: 5 August 2018).
- Fiksel, J. (2015) "From Risk to Resilience: Learning to Deal with Disruption," MIT Sloan Management Review & Report. http://tribunecontentagency.com/article/from-risk-to-resilience-learning-to-deal
- Financial Times Lexicon (2017) "Fat Tails", *Financial Times*. http://lexicon.ft.com/Term?term=fat-tails
- Flyvbjerg, B. (2006). Five misunderstandings about case-study research. Qualitative Inquiry, 12(2), 219-245.
- Foster, J.B. (2008) The Financialization of Capital and the Crisis, Monthly Review. https://monthlyreview.org/2008/04/01/the-financialization-of-capital-and-the-crisis/
- Forest, A. (2016) "Effective Downside Risk Management," Schroders Global, http://www.schroders.com/en/sysglobalassets/digital/expert-magazine/pdfs/sro_expert-19_3_2016_en.pdf

- Franklin, J., 2008, Operational Risk Under Basel II: A Model for Extreme Risk Evaluation, Banking & Financial Services Policy Report, 27(10), October.
- Franklin, J., Sisson, S.A., Burgman, M.A., Martin, J.K., 2008. Evaluating extreme risks in invasion ecology: learning from banking compliance. Divers. Distrib. 14, 581–591
- Freeman, R. E. (1984). Strategic Management: A Stakeholder Approach, Pitman, London
- Freeman, R.E. (1999). Response: Divergent Stakeholder Theory. Academy of Management Review. 24(2), 233-236.
- Friedman, Milton (1953). Essays in Positive Economics. Chicago: University of Chicago Press.
- FSA (2009) "Stress and Scenario Testing, Feedback on CP08/24 and final rules, *Financial Services Authority*. Available at: http://www.fsa.gov.uk/pubs/policy/ps09_20.pdf (Accessed: 18 August 2018).
- Gea-Carrasco, C. and Nyberg, M. (2012) "Understanding Tail Risk: Reverse Stress Testing", *Moody's Analytics*. Available at: https://www.moodysanalytics.com/-/media/whitepaper/2012/2012-30-10-understanding-tail-risk-white-paper.pdf (Accessed: 16 August 2018).
- Gordon, M. (2018) "Trump signs law rolling back post-financial crisis banking rules", *Chicago Tribune*. Available at: http://www.chicagotribune.com/business/ct-biz-trump-dodd-frank-rollbank-20180524-story.html (Accessed: 16 August 2018).
- Gorton, D. (2015) "Aspects of Modeling Fraud Prevention of Online Financial Services", *Doctoral thesis*, KTH Royal Institute of Technology, Stockholm, Sweden.
- Gray, A. and Jopson, B. (2018) "US banks clear first round of Fed stress tests", *The Financial Times*. Available at https://www.ft.com/content/59d77520-758e-11e8-a8c4-408cfba4327c (Accessed: 10 August 2018).

- Haaker, T., Bouwman, H., Janssen, W., and De Reuver, M., 2017, Business model stress testing: A practical approach to test the robustness of a business model, Futures, 89, May.
- Haering, M., 2019, To Infinity And Beyond, Finastra, 12 March.
- Hamel, G. & Välikangas, L. (2003), 'The Quest for Resilience', Harvard Business Review, September. Available at https://hbr.org/2003/09/the-quest-for-resilience
- Hamel, G. and Valikangas, L., 2003. 'Zero Trauma'-the Essence of Resilience. The Wall Street Journal, pp.2-2.
- Hinchliffe, M. and Smith, R. (2016) "Stress testing: A benchmarking analysis of systemically important banks", *KPMG International*,. Available at: https://home.kpmg.com/xx/en/home/insights/2016/11/stress-testing-a-benchmarking-analysis-of-systemically-important-banks.html (Accessed: 19 August 2018).
- Hnateck, E. (1998) "Testing During Product Development and Manufacturing", *Evaluation Engineers (EE)*. Available at: https://www.evaluationengineering.com/testing-during-product-development-and-manufacturing (Accessed: 21 August 2018).
- Hodgson, T and Yin, L (2013). *Extreme Risks - 2013*. Towers Watson. Available at https://www.towerswatson.com/en-US/Insights/IC-Types/Survey-Research-Results/2013/10/Extreme-risks-2013. (Accessed: 20 May 2018).
- Holmstrom, B., & Milgrom, P. (1994). The firm as an incentive system. The American Economic Review. 84(4), 972-991.
- Hols, M.C.A.B. & De Vries, C.G. (1991) "The Limiting Distribution of Extremal Exchange Rate Returns", *Journal of Applied Econometrics*, 6(3), pp. 287–302.
- Hume, D. (1777) *Enquiries concerning Human Understanding and concerning the Principles of Morals*. Oxford: Clarendon Press.
- Ingber, L. (1984) Statistical Mechanics Of Nonlinear Nonequilibrium Financial Markets, Mathematical Modelling. Vol. 5. pp. 343-361

- Ingves, S (2014): "Banking on leverage", keynote address to the 10th Asia-Pacific High-Level Meeting on Banking Supervision, Auckland, New Zealand, 25–27 February.
- International Organization for Standardization (2002) "Risk management Vocabulary: Guidelines for use in standards", *ISO/IEC Guide,* 73:2002.
- Ivantsov, E. (2013) *Heads or Tails.* Farnham: Gower Publishing
- Jackson P., and Davis, P. O. (2015) "Rethinking risk management, risk management survey of major financial institutions, Banks focus on non-financial risks and accountability", *EY.* Available at https://webforms.ey.com/Publication/vwLUAssets/EY-rethinking-risk-management/$FILE/EY-rethinking-risk-management.pdf (Accessed: 3 August 2018).
- Jackson, P. and Schlich, B. (2013) "Remaking financial services, risk management five years after the crisis, a survey of major financial institutions", *EY and IIF.* Available at https://www.ey.com/Publication/vwLUAssets/Remaking_financial_services_-_risk_management_five_years_after_the_crisis_-_Complete/$FILE/EY-Remaking_financial_services_risk_management_five_years_after_the_crisis.pdf (Accessed: 4 August 2018).
- Jansen, D.W. & De Vries C.G. (1991) "On the Frequency of Large Stock Returns: Putting Booms and Busts into Perspective", *The Review of Economics and Statistics*, pp. 18–24.
- Jenkins, P. (2010) "Seven banks fail EU stress tests", *FT.* Available at: https://www.ft.com/content/c14b9464-9678-11df-9caa-00144feab49a (Accessed: 11 August 2018).
- Jensen, M.C. & Meckling, W. H. (1976) Theory of the firm: Managerial behavior, agency costs and ownership structure, Journal of Financial Economics, Volume 3, Issue 4, October 1976, Pages 305-360

- Johnson, A., 2011, The Relationship Between Corporate Governance and Insolvency Risk Among Commercial Banks in Liberia, University of Nairobi.
- Jones, C., 2010, Predicting Financial Crisis: The Interesting Case of Nassim Taleb, Business Forecasting Blog. January 9. https://businessforecastblog.com/predicting-financial-crisis-the-interesting-case-of-nassim-taleb/.
- Jones, H. (2012) BoE's Haldane says Basel bank rules may need rethink, Reuters, https://www.reuters.com/article/uk-banks-regulation-boe-idUKBRE87U0UT20120831
- Kapinos, P., Mitnik, O., and Martin, C. (2015) "Stress Testing Banks: Whence and Whither?, *Journal of Financial Perspectives*. Available at: https://www.fdic.gov/bank/analytical/cfr/2015/wp2015/2015-07.pdf
- Kapinos, P., Mitnik, O., and Martin, C. (2015) "Stress Testing Banks: Whence and Whither?, *Journal of Financial Perspectives*. Available at: https://www.fdic.gov/bank/analytical/cfr/2015/wp2015/2015-07.pdf (Accessed: 16 August 2018).
- Karamjeet, P. (2014a) "Boards Must Make Extreme Risk A Priority", *Agenda, A Financial Times Service*, February 10.
- Karamjeet, P. (2014b) *Managing Extreme Financial Risk: Strategies and Tactics for Going Concerns*. Amsterdam: Elsevier.
- Keynes, J. M. (1973). The General Theory of Employment, Interest and Money. London: Macmillan
- Khusboo, n.d. Ethical Theories for Corporate Governance, Delhi University. Available at: https://www.cakart.in/blog/ethical-theories-corporate-governance-ethics-social-responsibility-business-mcom-sem-4-delhi-university/ (Accessed on 15 May 2018).
- Kim, M., Raghuvanshi, K., Bucciarelli, R., and Sodhi, V. (2016) "Optimizing the retail bank supply chain: How retail banks can lower costs, reduce inventory and boost productivity: Lessons from consumer business", *Deloitte Canada*. Available at

https://www2.deloitte.com/content/dam/Deloitte/global/Documents/Financial-Services/gx-fsi-ca-optimizing-the-retail-bank-supply-chain-2013-10.pdf (Accessed: 5 August 2018).

- Klein, L. et al. (2017) "The Future of Stress Testing", *Accenture Consulting.* Available at: https://www.accenture.com/t20170630T023851Z__w__/us-en/_acnmedia/PDF-57/Accenture-Future-of-Stress-Testing.pdf (Accessed: 20 August 2018).
- Knight, F. H. (1921) *Risk, Uncertainty and Profit.* Boston: Houghton Mifflin.
- Krusenvik, L. (2016) 'Using Case Studies as a Scientific Method: Advantages and Disadvantages', Halmstad University. Available at http://www.diva-portal.se/smash/get/diva2:1054643/FULLTEXT01.pdf
- Kuder, D., Locker, M., Schreibels, M., and Wittenberg, A., n.d., Operating Models That Navigate Business Volatility, Deloitte, https://www2.deloitte.com/us/en/pages/operations/articles/operating-models-that-navigate-business-volatility.html
- Larry S. (2015) *The Four Principles of Culture Change.* Heidrick & Struggles. Available at http://www.heidrick.com/Knowledge-Center/Article/four-principles-of-culture-change (Accessed: 20 May 2018).
- Leaver, M. and Reader, T. (2017) 'Safety culture in financial trading: an analysis of trading misconduct investigations', *Journal of Business Ethics.* Available at http://doi.org/10.1007/s10551-017-3463-0 Google Scholar. (Accessed: 20 May 2018).
- Leitch, M, 2016, Powerful and Recjkess, Finance & Management, October. Available at" https://www.icaew.com/-/media/corporate/archive/files/technical/business-and-financial-management/financial-management-faculty/ffm-updates/ffm-october-2016-articles/p28-30-powerful-and-reckless.ashx?la=en (Accessed: 15 May 2018)

- Licari, J., and Suárez-Lledó, J. (2012) "Reverse Stress Testing from a Macroecomic Viewpoint: Quantitative Challenges & Solutions for its Practical Implementation", *Moodys Analytics.* Available at: https://www.economy.com/home/products/samples/whitepapers/2012-10-10-Reverse-Stress-Testing-From-Macroeconomic-View-Point.pdf (Accessed: 17 August 2018).
- Lindvall, J. (2007). Fallstudiestrategier. Statsvetenskaplig Tidsskrift, 109(3), 270-278
- Luhmann, N. (1995) "Soziologische Aufklärung 5 Konstruktivistische Perspektiven, Gleichzeitigkeit und Synchronisation", *Verlag für Sozialwissenschaften*, Auflage 3.
- Lyon, B, and G. Popov, 2020, The Role of Risk Management with Covid19, Professional Safety, American Society of Safety Engineers, 65(12), December.
- Macey, J., & O 'Hara, M. (2003). The Corporate Governance of Banks. FRBNY Economic Policy Review. 9(1), 91-107.
- Malevergne, Y. & Sornette, D. (2005), *Extreme Financial Risks: From Dependence to Risk Management,* New York: Springer Finance, 312pp.
- Mandelbrot, B. (1963) "The variation of certain speculative prices", *Journal of Business*, 36(4).
- Markovitz, H. (1959) Portfolio Selection: Efficient Diversification of Investments.
- *Marx, Karl (1959), 1818-1883. (1959). Das Kapital, a critique of political economy. Chicago :H. Regnery*
- Mazingo, C. et al. (2014) "Introducing a holistic approach to stress testing", *McKinsey Working Papers on Risk*, Number 55, Available at: https://www.mckinsey.com/~/media/mckinsey/dotcom/client_service/risk/working%20papers/55_introducing_holistic_stress%20testing.ashx (Accessed: 20 August 2018).
- McKinsey, 2017, Bringing Basel IV Into Focus. https://www.mckinsey.com/business-functions/risk/our-insights/bringing-basel-iv-into-focus

- Medeiros J. J. and Pinto W. (2009) 'High-Reliability Organizations and Operational Risk Management', *Brazilia Business Review*, 6(2). Available at https://www.researchgate.net/publication/287381356_High_Reliability_Organizations_and_Operational_Risk_Management. (Accessed on 20 May 2018).
- Merriam, S. B., & Nilsson, B. (1994). Fallstudien som forskningsmetod. Lund: Studentlitteratur
- Meyer, J.W., & Rowan, B. (1977). Institutional organizations: formal structure as myth and ceremony. American Journal of Sociology. 80, 340-63.
- Meyer, J.W., Scott, W.R., & Deal, T.E. (1983). Institutional and technical sources of organizational structure: explaining the structure of educational organizations. In Meyer, J.W. and Scott, W.R. (Eds), Organizational Environments: Ritual and Rationality (pp. 45-67.). Sage, Beverly Hills, CA.
- Michel-Kerjan, E. and P. Slovic, 2010, Misunderstanding Risk, Newsweek, February 18. Available at: https://www.newsweek.com/misunderstanding-risk-michel-kerjan-and-slovic-75103 (Accessed: 15 August 2018).
- Milligan, A. (2013) "A Reverse Stress Testing Framework", *Trading Intelligence Cambridge Churchill Risk20:20 Toolkit.* Available at: https://www.filepicker.io/api/file/OpAC8MuSSuq7rbgKpPMG?dl=true (Accessed: 16 August 2018).
- Minsky, H.P. (1980), Money, financial markets and the coherence of market economy, Journal of Post Keynesian Economics, v. 3, 21-31
- Misra C. Subhas, Vinod, K., & Uma, K. (2006) *Different Techniques for Risk Management in Software Engineering: A Review*. Banff: ASAC.
- Mizuno, Y. (2015) Improving Risk Governance Frameworks to Adapt to the New Banking Environment, Moody's Analytics Risk Perspective, Volume VI.

- Moog, M. et al (2018) "Global financial services third-party risk management survey:
- Moosa, I., 2011, Why Basel III Won't Protect Banks From Another Global Crisis, The Conversation, June 26.
- Murphy, M. (2014). What are the benefits and drawbacks of case study research? [Website]. Retrieved from http://socialtheoryapplied.com/2014/05/24/benefits-drawbacks-casestudy-research/ [2016-12-02]
- Narvaez, K., n.d., Enterprise Risk Management: Application & Case Studies.
- National Commission on Terrorist Attacks upon the United States (2004) *The 9/11 Commission report.* Washington, DC: National Commission on Terrorist Attacks upon the United States. p. 339.
- Newhouse, J. (1982) "A Reporter at Large: A Sporty Game: 1-Betting the Company", *The New Yorker*, June 14, pp. 48–105.
- Noll, R., 1996. The complex politics of catastrophe economics. J. Risk Uncertain. 12, 141–146.
- Nordhaus, W. (2011) "Elementary Statistics of Tail Events", *Review of Environmental and Economic Policy.*
- Noyes, C. (2015a) "Beware the most extreme risks in your supply chain", *Computerworld*, November 1.
- Noyes, C. (2015b) "Beware the 'black swans' in your supply chain", *CIO*, October 30.
- Oliver, C. (1991). Strategic responses to institutional processes. Academy of Management Review. 16, 145-79.
- Ong, L. and Pazarbasioglu, C. (2014) "Credibility and Crisis Stress Testing", Available at: www.mdpi.com/2227-7072/2/1/15/pdf (Accessed: 17 August 2018).
- Padilla, A. (2002). Can Agency Theory Justify The Regulation Of Insider Trading. The Quarterly Journal of Austrian Economics. 5(1), 3-38.

- Palley, T. I. (2007) "Financialization: What It Is and Why It Matters," Working Papers wp153, Political Economy Research Institute, University of Massachusetts at Amherst.
- Park, K., Sen, S., and Griffiths D. (2015) Third Party Governance & Risk Management: *Deloitte*, Available at https://www2.deloitte.com/content/dam/Deloitte/uk/Documents/audit/deloitte-uk-third-party-governance-risk-management-report.pdf (Accessed: 10 August 2018).
- Patel, B. (2017) "Stress Testing in Banks", *Finextra.* Available at: https://www.finextra.com/blogposting/14742/stress-testing-in-banks
- Patel, B. (2017) "Stress Testing in Banks", *Finextra.* Available at: https://www.finextra.com/blogposting/14742/stress-testing-in-banks (Accessed: 16 August 2018).
- Patel, B. (2017) "Stress Testing in Banks", *Finextra.* Available at: https://www.finextra.com/blogposting/14742/stress-testing-in-banks (Accessed: 16 August 2018).
- Peck, H. (2006) "Reconciling supply chain vulnerability, risk and supply chain management", *International Journal of Logistics: Research and Applications*, Vol. 9 No. 2, pp.127-142. Available at https://www.tandfonline.com/doi/abs/10.1080/13675560600673578?journalCode=cjol20 (Accessed: 6 August 2018).
- Peristiani, S., Morgan, D., and Savino, V. (2010) "The Information Value of the Stress Test and Bank Opacity", *Federal Reserve Bank of New York Staff Reports*, no. 460. Available at: https://www.newyorkfed.org/medialibrary/media/research/staff_reports/sr460.pdf (Accessed: 14 August 2018).
- Perrow, C. (1999) *Normal accidents: Living with high-risk technologies.* 2nd edn. Princeton, NJ: Princeton University Press.
- Peters, E. & Miranda, B. (2014) "How 'Tail Risk' Changes Over the Market Cycle ", *First Quadrant*, July.

- Pignal, S. and Jenkins, P. (2011) "Dexia poses setback for EBA stress tests", *FT*. Available at: https://www.ft.com/content/0f638a80-ef6a-11e0-bc88-00144feab49a (Accessed: 20 August 2018).
- Ponomarov, S.Y. and Holcomb, M. C. (2009) "Understanding the concept of supply chain resilience". *International Journal of Logistics Management.* **20**(1): 124-143. Available at doi:10.1108/09574090910954873 (Accessed: 5 August 2018).
- Popper, K. (1959) *The Logic of Scientific Discovery.* London: Hutchinson & Co
- Prescott, Edward S. Regulating Bank Capital Structure to Control Risk, 87(3) Fed. Reserve Bank Of Richmond Econ. Q. 35 (2001).
- Prpić, J. (2016) "Project Risk Management Incorporating", *IEEE Computer Society Press*, last revised 11 April 2016.
- Puliga, M, Flori, A, Pappalardo, G, Chessa, A, Pammolli, F. (2016) 'The Accounting Network: How Financial Institutions React to Systemic Crisis', *PLoS ONE,* 11(10). Available at https://doi.org/10.1371/journal.pone.0162855 (Accessed: 20 May 2018.)
- Rabobank (2018) Position Paper, Basel 3.5 Capital Requirements.
- Rabobank (2017), Basel 3.5 Capital Requirements: are the proposals feasible, Position Paper, https://www.rabobank.com/en/images/position-paper-basel-3-5-capital-requirements-14-9-2017.pdf
- Radford, P., 2020, The missing middle?, World economics Review blog, August 11.
- Risk & Compliance, 2018, Basel Committee on Banking Supervision: Basel III reforms, 05 January.
- Roberts, K., Yu, K. and van Stralen, D. (2013) *Patient Safety is an Organizational Systems Issue: Lessons from a Variety of Industries.* 2nd edn. Burlington, MA: Jones & Bartlett Learning, pp. 143-155
- Rösch, D. and Scheule. H. (2007) "Stress-testing credit risk parameters: an application to retail loan portfolios", *The Journal of Risk Model*

Validation, 1(1): 55–75. Available at https://papers.ssrn.com/sol3/papers.cfm?abstract_id=1951850 (Accessed: 19 August 2018).

- Ross, S.A. (1973). The Economic Theory of Agency: The Principal's Problem. The American Economic Review. 63(2), 134-139
- Rossi, C., 2013, How to Treat Side Effects of Strong Risk Management, American Banker, July 11.
- Sarkisyan, A. and Casu, B. (2013) "Retained interest in securitizations and implications for bank solvency", ECB Working Papers, No. 1538. Available at https://www.ecb.europa.eu/pub/pdf/scpwps/ecbwp1538.pdf (Accessed: 10 August 2018).
- Schlich, B. et al. (2018) "Global banking outlook 2018, Pivoting toward an innovation-led strategy", *EY.* Available at https://www.ey.com/Publication/vwLUAssets/ey-global-banking-outlook-2018/$File/ey-global-banking-outlook-2018.pdf (Accessed: 10 August 2018).
- Schmidt-Bies, S. (2004) 'Remarks by Governor Susan Schmidt Bies At the International Center for Business Information's Risk Management 2004 Conference', Federal Reserve Board, 7 December. Available at https://www.federalreserve.gov/boarddocs/speeches/2004/20041207/default.htm
- Schoeman, D. (2016) "Concert interrupted - an agenda for the chief supply chain officer to develop countermeasures for supply chain risks and disruptions", *SAPICS.* Available at https://www.slideshare.net/TristanWiggill/concert-interrupted-an-agenda-for-the-chief-supply-chain-officer-to-develop-countermeasures-for-supply-chain-risks-and-disruptions (Accessed: 10 August 2018).
- Schroeck, G. (2002) *Risk Management and Value Creation in Financial Institutions.* Hoboken: John Wiley & Sons.

- Scott, K.E., 1996. Social treatment of catastrophic risk — introduction. J. Risk Uncertain. 12, 99–100.
- Scott, W.R. (1987). The adolescence of institutional theory. Administrative Science Quarterly. 32, 493-511
- SCRL (2011) "Supply chain risk management: a compilation of best practices", *Supply Chain Risk Leadership Council.* Available at http://www.scrlc.com/articles/Supply_Chain_Risk_Management_A_Compilation_of_Best_Practices_final[1].pdf (Accessed: 5 August 2018).
- Securities and Exchange Commission, 2009, SEC Release NOS. 33-9052 Proxy Disclosure and Solicitation Enhancements, August 13.
- Securities and Exchange Commission, 2019, https://www.sec.gov/Archives/edgar/data/1039765/000119312519237796/0001193125-19-237796.txt
- Shah, K., 2018, Integrated Risk Management in Banks, Slideshare. February 13.
- Shleifer, A., & Vishny, R.W. (1997). A survey of corporate governance. Journal of Finance. 52(2), 737-83.
- Simchi-Levi, D. (2013) *Operations Rules: Delivering Customer Value through Flexible Operations*, Cambridge: the MIT Press.
- Simchi-Levi, D. (2015) "Find the Weak Link in Your Supply Chain", *Harvard Business Review.* Available at https://hbr.org/2015/06/find-the-weak-link-in-your-supply-chain (Accessed: 10 August 2018).
- Simchi-Levi, D., Schmidt, W, and Wei, Y. (2014) "From Superstorms to Factory Fires: Managing Unpredictable Supply Chain Disruptions", *Harvard Business Review.* Available at https://hbr.org/2014/01/from-superstorms-to-factory-fires-managing-unpredictable-supply-chain-disruptions (Accessed: 9 August 2018).
- Small, C., 2013, The Procyclical Effects of Bank Capital Regulation, HLS Forum on Corporate Governance and Financial Regulation, on Monday, January 14.

- Smith, A. (1776) *The Wealth of Nations*, London: W. Strahan and T. Cadell.
- Sonnier, E.B. (2014) "Understanding your risk exposure index", *Dupre Logistics.* Available at https://www.duprelogistics.com/understanding-your-risk-exposure-index/ (Accessed: 10 August 2018).
- Soy, S (1997) 'The case study as a research method'. Unpublished paper, *University of Texas at Austin*
- Springboard Home loans (2018), "Loan products", *Springboard CDFI.* Available at http://www.springboard.org/loan-products/ (Accessed: 10 August 2018).
- Steven L. Schwarcz, Systemic Risk, 97 GEO. L.J. 193 (2008).
- Stulz, R.M. (2014) "Governance, risk management, and risk-taking in banks", *Technical Report*, National Bureau of Economic Research.
- Sullivan, J. J. (2014) 'Modeling Operational Reliability: The Discovery of the Organizational Learning Loop', *Journal of Business and Economics*, 5(9), pp. 1536-1550. Available at http://scholarcommons.usf.edu/si_facpub/317/. (Accessed: 20 May 2018)
- Sundaram, A.K., & Inkpcn, A.C. (2004). The Corporate Objective Revisited. Organization Science. 15(3), 350-363.
- Taleb, N. N. (2008) *The Black Swan: The Impact of the Highly Improbable.* New York: Pantheon Books.
- Taskinsoy, J., 2013, Rigorous Capital Requirements Under Basel III: Possible Impact On Turkey's Financial Sector, Journal of WEI Business and Economics, 2(1), April.
- Thoma, M., 2008, Soros: The Theory of Market Equilibrium is Wrong, Economist' View, December 21.
- Thun, C, Licari, J., and Zandi, M. (2010) "Reverse Stress Testing: Challenges & Benefits", *Moody's Analytics.* Available at: https://www.moodysanalytics.com/-/media/presentation/before-2011/10-23-11-reverse-stress-testing.pdf (Accessed: 12 August 2018).

- Thun, C. (2013) "Common Pitfalls in Stress Testing", *Moody's Analytics*. Available at: https://www.moodysanalytics.com/-/media/article/2012/2012-10-12-common-pitfalls-and-challenges-in-stress-testing-of-banks.pdf
- Thun, C. (2013) "Common Pitfalls in Stress Testing", *Moody's Analytics*. Available at: https://www.moodysanalytics.com/-/media/article/2012/2012-10-12-common-pitfalls-and-challenges-in-stress-testing-of-banks.pdf (Accessed: 19 August 2018).
- Tracy, R. (2018) "Banks Failing Stress Tests? Not for Much Longer", *WSJ*. Available at: https://www.wsj.com/articles/banks-failing-stress-tests-not-for-much-longer-1530005400 (Accessed: 13 August 2018).
- Trowbridge, M. (2017) "Five Techniques to Manage Supply Chain Risk", *Supply Chain Management Review*. Available at http://www.scmr.com/article/five_techniques_to_manage_supply_chain_risk (Accessed: 10 August 2018).
- Tucker, J. (2010) 'Financial crises: A culture of complacency', *Journal of Organizational Transformation and Social Change*, 7(1). pp. 7- 23. Available at http://eprints.uwe.ac.uk/11326. (Accessed: 20 May 2018).
- Turner, A. (2009), 'The Turner Review A regulatory response to the global banking crisis', *Financial Services Authority*, March, 126p. Available at http://www.fsa.gov.uk/pubs/other/turner_review.pdf
- Turner, M.D. (2011) "Be prepared to bounce back: Building a resilient supply chain", *strategy&*, Booz & Company (PwC) Available at https://www.strategyand.pwc.com/media/file/Strategyand_Be-prepared-to-bounce-back.pdf (Accessed: 9 August 2018).
- Vallascas, F and J Hagendorff (2013): "The risk sensitivity of capital requirements: Evidence from an international sample of large banks", Review of Finance, vol 17, pp 1947–1988.
- Van Deventer, R. & Bar-Adam, E. (2010) Basel III and the Problem with Risk Management by Excel, Harvard Business Review. https://hbr.org/2010/09/basel-iii-and-the-problem-

with?gclid=EAIaIQobChMI6fyK8ZvD3wIVDrXACh34UwYnEAMYAiAAEgJHXvD_BwE

- Van Stralen, D. (2006) *Dynamic Resilience: High Reliability Organizing from the Ground Up*. High-Reliability.org. Available at http://www.high-reliability.org/Resilience_and_Reliability.pdf. (Accessed: 20 May 2018).
- vander Straeten, P. (2016) "How To Apply Supply Chain Management To The Financial Services Industry", *LinkedIn*, Available at https://www.linkedin.com/pulse/how-apply-supply-chain-management-financial-services-pascal/ (Accessed on 9 August 2018).
- Vander Straeten, P. (2017) *Tail Risk Management: Building a Resilient Financial Business in a Volatile World*. Dallas: Value4Risk.
- Vander Straeten, P. (2018) *An Overture to Geofinance: Global Finance, Geopolitics, and the Wielding of Power: Theory and Praxis*. Dallas: Value4Risk.
- Venkatesh, S. S. (2012) *The Theory of Probability: Explorations and Applications*. Cambridge: Cambridge University Press.
- Weber, R. F. (2015) 'Post-Crisis Reform of the Supervisory System and High-Reliability Theory', *Georgia Law Review*, 50(25). pp. 249-292. Available at https://papers.ssrn.com/sol3/papers.cfm?abstract_id=2644631. (Accessed: 18 May 2018)
- Weick, K. (2001) *Making sense of the organization*. Malden, MA: Blackwell Publishers, Inc.
- Weick, K. and Sutcliffe K. (2001) *Managing the Unexpected-Assuring High Performance in an Age of Complexity*. San Francisco: Jossey-Bass.
- Wheeler, D., Colbert, B., & Freeman, R.E. (2003). Focusing on value: reconciling corporate social responsibility, sustainability and a stakeholder approach in a network world. Journal of General Management. 28, 1-28.
- Wieland, A. and Wallenburg, C.M. (2012) "Dealing with supply chain risks: Linking risk management practices and strategies to performance", *International Journal of Physical Distribution & Logistics*

Management, 42(10) pp. 887-905. Available at DOI: 10.1108/09600031211281411 (Accessed: 5 August 2018).

- Wiley, New York. VIII, 1, 2, 13, 31, 38
- Wong, K. and Fong, T. (2006) "A framework for macro stress testing the credit risk of banks in Hong Kong", *HKMA Research Department.* Available at: https://www.hkma.gov.hk/media/eng/publication-and-research/quarterly-bulletin/qb200612/E_25_38.pdf
- Wong, K. and Fong, T. (2006) "A framework for macro stress testing the credit risk of banks in Hong Kong", *HKMA Research Department.* Available at: https://www.hkma.gov.hk/media/eng/publication-and-research/quarterly-bulletin/qb200612/E_25_38.pdf (Accessed: 13 August 2018).
- Wu, T. and Blackhurst, J. (2009) *Managing Supply chain risk and vulnerability*, New York: Springer.
- Young, B. (2011) 'Leadership and high-reliability organizations: Why banks fail', *Journal of Operational Risk* 6(4). pp. 67-87. Available at https://www.researchgate.net/publication/265799305_Leadership_and_high-reliability_organizations_Why_banks_fail. (Accessed: 18 May 2018).
- Zaher, F., 2012, Using Economic Capital To Determine Risk, Yahoo News, January 27. Available at: https://news.yahoo.com/news/using-economic-capital-determine-risk-175214645.html (Accessed: 20 April 2018)
- Zavatsky, "Complacency: The Greatest Risk of All," Food Safety News, accessed on April 2, 2017 http://www.foodsafetynews.com/2013/02/complacency-the-greatest-risk-of-all/.
- Zibel, A. (2012) New Capital Rules Elicit Squawks, The Wall Street Journal, https://www.wsj.com/articles/SB10001424052970203400604578072971165861356

- Zsidisin G.A., Ellram L.M., Carter J.R. and Cavinato X. (2004) "An analysis of supply risk assessment techniques" *Int J Phys Distrib Logist Mngt* , Vol. 34 No. 5, pp.397-413. Available at https://www.researchgate.net/publication/235264645_An_Analysis_of_Supply_Risk_Assessment_Techniques
- Zucker, L.G. (1987). Institutional theories of organization. Annual Review of Sociology. 13, 443-64

Made in the USA
Las Vegas, NV
04 November 2026

57423060R00145